The Machines Inside Our Brain

COGNITIVE MECHANISMS OF INFORMATION PROCESSING

The Machines Inside Our Brain

COGNITIVE MECHANISMS OF INFORMATION PROCESSING

EDITED BY

Geoffrey Woodman

Vanderbilt University

Ashleigh Maxcey

The Ohio State University

cognella® | ACADEMIC PUBLISHING

Bassim Hamadeh, CEO and Publisher
Jennifer Codner, Senior Field Acquisitions Editor
Michelle Piehl, Senior Project Editor
Laureen Gleason, Production Editor
Emely Villavicencio, Senior Graphic Designer
Stephanie Kohl, Licensing Associate
Natalie Piccotti, Senior Marketing Manager
Kassie Graves, Vice President of Editorial
Jamie Giganti, Director of Academic Publishing

Front Cover: Copyright © by Aseel Brodd. Reprinted with permission.
Back Cover: Copyright © by Aseel Brodd. Reprinted with permission; copyright © by Jessie Holloway Photography. Reprinted with permission.

Printed in the United States of America

ISBN: 978-1-5165-2087-9 (pbk) / 978-1-5165-2088-6 (br)
978-1-5165-9449-8 (pf) / 978-1-5165-9414-6 (ap)

Contents

Introduction

How to Read a Journal Article

Ashleigh Maxcey

There are several things to consider when reading the research and results presented in a journal article. These include understanding the basic sections of the article in order to anticipate where information can be found and what information will be encountered next, having a goal (or goals) in mind while you are reading, recognizing the process by which the article was published, knowing how to physically mark the text in order to fully engage with the material and enhance memory, and deepening comprehension by applying the work to the real world, putting yourself in the author's shoes to plan the next logical experiment in a research program, and critiquing the article like a peer reviewer. Here you will learn about each of these unique steps to mastering the skill of reading journal articles.

WHY READ JOURNAL ARTICLES

I have been working with undergraduate students for over ten years and I am very passionate about providing useful tools in my classes that will propel students forward into their chosen future goals. I have come to realize that the ability to read journal articles is imperative for any concerned citizen in our society, but is even more important for students who are geared toward graduate school. Here I discuss some reasons why you should want to hone this generalizable skill, the ability to read journal articles, under a variety of circumstances.

If you have little experience reading and analyzing journal articles, this task can be daunting. However, if you put aside some time and devote your energy to reading an article, you start to realize you are a lot smarter than you give yourself credit for. Some things that work for me are putting aside a couple hours, grabbing a colorful pen, and sitting at a desk—not my bed.

Sarah Burens, Behavioral Neuroscience Major, The Ohio State University, Class of 2019

Evaluate the Research

The textbooks commonly used for undergraduate courses very briefly summarize the research you are learning about, leaving out most of the details that allow you to evaluate the research. In order to really evaluate the research you are learning about in class, you want to be able to examine the actual research that was conducted like a peer reviewer. A peer reviewer is someone selected by the journal considering publishing an original manuscript. Peer reviewers ask questions such as (1) Can the authors conclude what they claim to be concluding? (2) Did the authors run the appropriate statistical analyses? (3) Does similar work already exist in the field? (4) What are the real-world applications of this work? If you think back to the most recent chapter you read in your textbook for any course, you will realize that you can't answer most or any of these questions because the textbook only briefly summarized the study, leaving out most if not all of the details relevant to answering them. As a budding scientist yourself, it's time to start examining research like a peer reviewer.

Understand the Scientific Process

In order to either pursue a research career, work with patients in a clinical setting, or fully grasp the topics of the course, you need to understand the scientific process in a more complete way than is presented in textbooks. Indeed, much of what undergraduates learn about the research process is unfortunately different from how research is actually conducted. For example, completing a hands-on project within a semester for an advanced research methods course presents a very unreasonable timeline, in which everything is rushed and not well thought through. Reading articles gives a much better picture of everything that truly goes into the scientific process and the research you read about in your texts.

> It is easy to blow through an assignment or do it just to get it done for the class. You're a busy person, you have other things to do. However, when it comes to your science classes, it is very important that you take your time and actually understand everything. What you're doing today is preparing you for tomorrow. If you don't have a firm grasp on the scientific process, the steps, and how to read/write articles, you will have a hard time in the future. Spend the time today in order to spend your time more wisely in the future.
>
> Sarah Burens, Behavioral Neuroscience Major, The Ohio State University, Class of 2019

Learn to Go to the Source

In real life, you need the skills to go to the original source. This empowers you to have the experience and ability to comprehend and evaluate research. Even if you don't want to pursue a career in academia, there will be plenty of instances in which you need to understand the research behind a product you are thinking about buying, a medical treatment you are considering for a loved one, or the policies proposed by a particular political candidate. Reading journal articles practices a generalizable skill that will serve you well later in life, regardless of your major, future plans, or career path.

Scientific Writing

Although we know it's much easier to criticize writing than do it ourselves, you have full permission to critique these articles as you learn about scientific writing. Very few students realize how much of being a good scientist involves being a good writer. In order to communicate their findings, scientists need to write well. There is a movement afoot among scientists to make research more approachable to the general public by undertaking relatively simple tasks like rewriting Wikipedia pages to remove any field-specific jargon. Although many of us may be tempted to use big words and jargon to sound smart, research actually shows that writing simply leads folks to attribute higher degrees of intelligence to the writer. You are likely to experience something similar in this book. That is, those articles that you understand more clearly, you will likely find to be more interesting and therefore more important.

If you do come across an article that uses those big words, don't get frustrated. Just look up the words you don't know and push your way through.

It's also beneficial to meet up with peers and discuss the paper. You can discuss what you liked about it, but also ask questions about things you didn't understand fully. They may understand something really well that you don't, and vice versa. Also, being able to discuss a paper with others is important because you will be doing this often as a scientist. You may be discussing something with your team, presenting at a forum, or simply having a stimulating conversation with a colleague. It's imperative to feel comfortable discussing research.

Sarah Burens, Behavioral Neuroscience Major, The Ohio State University, Class of 2019

Transferable Skill

The exercises in this book will help you learn how to read a journal article, which is a transferable skill. You are not simply supposed to learn the information in the articles; in fact, I see that as secondary. I mention this above when discussing going to the original source, but I think it's worth repeating that this book differs from most other books in that I do not think there is anything particularly special about the articles I've selected here. The articles are ones that are relevant to a course on cognitive psychology, and are mostly ones my co-author Geoff Woodman has used with undergraduates in the past and that received positive feedback from the students after their reading. However, what we really want you to gain from this book is the ability to read articles, much more than the knowledge about these specific articles.

Being able to read a journal article will really transfer over to many aspects of your life and career. I read articles in my neuroscience classes but I've had to use the same skills in my biology and chemistry classes. It's important to build these skills today because you never know when you'll be expected to use them. Most of the time you'll be reading articles for their content. However, sometimes it's important to read articles for enjoyment and to get used to reading them.

Sarah Burens, Behavioral Neuroscience Major, The Ohio State University, Class of 2019

UNDERSTAND THE BASICS OF AN ARTICLE

There are two main organizational clues that experienced readers know to look for when they read a journal article to enhance and accelerate their reading of the material. The first involves understanding what journal the article was published in, in order to calibrate their expectations of aspects of the work, such as the impact of the work, the length of the article, and the type of research reported. The second can be found in the typical sections of an article, which give information about the background literature, the methods used, and the results. Advanced knowledge about this organization allows the reader to rapidly skim portions of the paper and focus on the relevant sections as a function of the reader's goal. Here you will learn about each of these aspects and why they are important for reading successfully.

Abstract

The abstract is a short paragraph at the beginning of the article, offset from the rest of the article, briefly describing what the authors did and what they found. Depending on the journal in which the article was published, the abstract may be shorter or longer because journals have rules about the word count for an abstract. In the annotated article that demonstrates my suggestions on how to annotate your article, you'll notice that I did not underline the abstract. This is because the entire abstract is informative, as it is a very condensed summary of the paper. I strongly recommend you start with the abstract so you have a roadmap of where the paper is going to go.

If you don't understand something (anywhere in the paper), reread the sentence(s) once or twice then move on. Don't think you missed something, because most of the time they are about to explain it. Avoid the mistake I made several times by encountering a section I didn't understand and giving up, moving on to the next section feeling defeated, then realizing the next paragraph had the answer to all my questions. This is a good way to waste your time (speaking from experience). Dr. Maxcey gave us this advice in class. She also said that if you really don't understand something, it's okay, a lot of other students probably don't either—go discuss it with others and ask questions. Engaging yourself is the best way to learn and grow.

Sarah Burens, Behavioral Neuroscience Major, The Ohio State University, Class of 2019

Introduction

The Introduction section of the paper tells you the background of the issue at hand. It's essentially the author's opportunity to explain to you what has been done and why their work is special and needed. The Introduction section is usually the hardest to write when you are first learning how to write papers because you need to both give a sense of what has already been done in the field as well as describe what lacuna exists that you intend to fill with your work. This means the author is striking a delicate balance of starting really generally, surveying the state of the field, and then getting to the heart of why their paper is necessary. Because so much is accomplished throughout the Introduction, it can also be hard to read and parse. I suggest reading each paragraph and then describing in the margin the larger purpose the paragraph served next to each individual paragraph. That will help organize the Introduction into chunks, which will both aid your comprehension and increase your ability to search the Introduction later when you are trying to answer questions about the article.

> When I figured out how amazing it was to take note of what each individual paragraph did for the larger purpose of the paper, reading the articles became so much easier. I was spending less time reading because I learned how to break them down. I could very easily go through and remember exactly what was being said and why. I also found that putting a one-sentence Post-it note on the first page of every article summarizing the entire paper was extremely helpful. It drove the point home for me and was one final push to make sure I comprehended everything I needed to get from the paper.
>
> Hannah Glenn, Cognitive Neuroscience Major, Manchester University, Class of 2016; PhD student, University of Wisconsin, Madison

Methods

This section tells you what it was like to be a subject in the study being discussed. As you get better at reading articles, you should be able to just check the figure (provided the article includes a Methods figure) to get a good idea of what it was like to be a subject and only skim this section if you are just doing a quick read of a paper. Another purpose of the Methods section is to allow for replication. An important part of science is detailing exactly what the researchers did so that other researchers can try to replicate and build upon the work. Since you are not currently replicating the study, you should read this section to make sure you understand exactly what it was like to be a subject; you can then feel confident that you gleaned the critical information and move on.

It's actually very important to understand what they did in the methods. They reference their methods throughout the whole paper and you need to know what they're talking about. Most of the time you don't need to know it well enough to replicate it, but you should know the key words, the different trials, and the controls versus manipulations. It's also important to recognize any confounding variables. If they don't mention them, think about it for a couple minutes yourself. This is a valuable skill that forces you to think outside of the box, and one that you can transfer to your own experiments.

Sarah Burens, Behavioral Neuroscience Major, The Ohio State University, Class of 2019

Results

The Results section reports the descriptive data (i.e., a general picture of the data) and inferential data (i.e., statistical analyses that allow you to draw conclusions) for a paper. If you are extremely overwhelmed by a paper and unfamiliar with statistics, you may be able to skip this section and go straight to the Discussion, because the Discussion section should report the findings in layman's terms. But when you go back over the journal article a second time, or as you get better at reading articles later on in the semester, you should try to understand what happened in each condition (e.g., whether the results are statistically significant). Statistical significance means that there is a high probability that a difference between the conditions truly exists. Despite the term, significance does not mean *substantial*, so many journals also now require significant results be accompanied by measures of effect size. This is a great place to see your statistical knowledge in action as you parse the Results sections. As a side note, if any of the articles refer to supplemental materials, they are not included in this anthology. You will be able to understand the main points of the article without consulting the supplemental materials.

I hate to admit this, but when I started reading articles and got to the results section, I would just see a bunch of numbers I didn't understand and skip right over it. It's easy to skip over it and it may be okay to do this on some papers, but you also need to build up the skill of reading and understanding this section. As stated by Dr. Maxcey, this section will show whether the results are statistically significant. When trying to analyze a paper or write one of your own, you will need to understand these numbers. If you are having trouble understanding this section after trying a couple times, don't hold back from going to your professor to ask questions; they would love to help you.

Sarah Burens, Behavioral Neuroscience Major, The Ohio State University, Class of 2019

Discussion

This section reports the findings in layman's terms. You should not need an advanced understanding of statistics to understand this section, but you will likely need to know the conditions and variable names that were introduced in the Methods section or the Methods figure. If there are multiple experiments in the paper, each experiment will likely have its own short Discussion section, and then the group of experiments will be tied together in a General Discussion.

I spend time in the Results section trying to see how much I can understand, but then I move to the Discussion. I really use this section to understand exactly what the results were; they are laid out in words rather than numbers this time. This is also where I make a lot of marks. If they are presenting multiple things, I will number each one. If they reference a table or figure, I put a box around it so I know to go check out that table/figure. I will also write the findings in my own words in the margins. Doing this allows me to test my knowledge of the paper. If I can put the findings into my own words and describe it to someone else, I have a good grasp on it.

Sarah Burens, Behavioral Neuroscience Major, The Ohio State University, Class of 2019

General Discussion

The General Discussion will draw together the findings from multiple experiments in a multi-experiment paper. This is the section of the paper where the author makes the grandest statements regarding conclusions they can draw, emphasizing the theoretical implications as well as the real-world applications of the work. If you only read the General Discussion, you will have a loose understanding of what the authors found and how they think it relates to the larger issues in the field, such as theoretical implications or real-world applications. However, you will not have a good grasp on what other work has been done in the field that necessitated the present paper (that information came from the Introduction), nor will you have a good idea what it was like to be a subject (from the Methods section and figures).

> This is where everything is pulled together and explained in a broad manner. The reasons, findings, conclusions, and sometimes the next steps of the experiment(s) are discussed here. This is another section you should be able to explain to your friend in your own words.
>
> Sarah Burens, Behavioral Neuroscience Major, The Ohio State University, Class of 2019

HAVE A GOAL IN MIND WHEN YOU ARE READING AN ARTICLE

Your goal for reading a journal article will vary as a function of the reason you are reading the article in the first place. You might read for a variety of reasons, including for a course, for your own research you are conducting, or because the article is somehow relevant to your personal life.

Course

You might be reading a journal article for a course, like the one you are enrolled in now. Under this circumstance, gaining a general understanding of the work so that you can answer a variety of potential test questions is likely your initial goal. To this end, I have created a general guide for each article that you read in the form of worksheet questions, which should serve to help you consider the big picture issues that generally apply to most articles and then to ask some more specific questions to ensure that you understand more details in each particular article.

> Pay attention in class if this is the case. The professor may point out things that are important and things you should look for. Also, use the resources your professor gives you. Worksheets, example questions, and the professor themselves!
>
> Sarah Burens, Behavioral Neuroscience Major, The Ohio State University, Class of 2019

Research

You might be reading a journal article for your own research project. For example, you may be aiming to examine the boundary condition of a previously published paradigm. Under these circumstances, the methodological details and statistical analyses will be more relevant when you are thinking of replicating the work or trying to relate their findings to your own.

Media

You might be reading because you heard something on the news and want to delve deeper into a topic because it relates to you in some way. Perhaps you are reading an article about improving memory, avoiding laptop use in the classroom, improving sleep habits, why we dream, or a new treatment for Alzheimer's. The Introduction will give you an overview of what has been done in the field prior to the study, and the Discussion will describe their findings, ideally relating it to the real world.

> Knowing and recognizing your goal for reading is important for the type of analytic process you will be using. When I dive into a paper, I find it useful to identify the goal of reading it; this helps me decide what to focus on. For example, in class, I focus on abstracting main ideas from the paper. However, for my own research I focus on the methods and results. And, if I'm reading for enjoyment because something interests me, I can relax and just enjoy reading the paper, because now I know how to.
>
> Sarah Burens, Behavioral Neuroscience Major, The Ohio State University, Class of 2019

WHAT DOES IT MEAN TO BE PEER-REVIEWED?

All the journal articles included in this book are peer-reviewed publications. This means that each article was submitted to a journal that uses the peer-review process to determine what will be published. Here I briefly describe the peer-review process to enlighten you about what the manuscript has been through in becoming the published work that eventually made its way into your hands.

- Authors select a relevant journal and submit their manuscript to that journal. Occasionally authors actually select a journal that might be too good for their paper (as measured by the impact factor[1] of the journal and how impactful the manuscript is) and try it there first, with the mentality that the reviewers might like their paper and they will get a more prominent publication. Then, if the paper is rejected, they do what's called *falling down the ladder* by submitting the paper to progressively lower-tier journals (again, as measured by impact factor) until they find one that accepts the manuscript.

- The editor of a journal is the head person on the editorial board and is employed by the journal but also has another job, typically a faculty appointment at an academic institution. The editor selects an associate editor (aka action editor) to handle the paper.

- The associate editor is one of several experts in the field, also usually faculty members at academic institutions, who are employed by the journal in either half-time or full-time appointments. These appointments usually mean they handle roughly 15-50 (half-time) or 40-100 (full-time) papers per year. (These are just rough estimates, but you get the idea.)

- The associate editor then sends the manuscript out to roughly three reviewers who are experts in the field examined in the paper. Oftentimes these experts are selected from a list of folks called consulting editors, who are unpaid members of the editorial board for the journal. The authors of the manuscript can also suggest certain preferred reviewers (experts in the field who the authors believe will be helpful in reviewing the manuscript or otherwise have credibility in the area) as well as request that any non-preferred reviewers not be invited to review the manuscript (typically for strong differences in theoretical opinion).

---

1 A metric for a given journal measuring the yearly average number of citations for recently published papers.

- The three experts are given about three weeks to respond with comments and a decision regarding the viability of publishing the paper. There are ethical reasons that a reviewer would decline the review, including if they have published with any of the authors in the past three years, as well as if they have any personal relationship with the authors that may potentially interfere with their ability to objectively evaluate the work. The reviewers then make recommendations about the work according to the following categories: accept, minor revisions, major revisions, and reject. The reviewers are also asked whether they want to remain anonymous or whether the associate editor may reveal their identity to the authors, known as signing the review. In our field, it's fair to say that the majority of reviewers elect to remain anonymous.

- The associate editor also reads the paper and, weighting the feedback from the reviewers, *acts on* or makes a decision about the paper. This is why the associate editor is also referred to as the action editor. Once the associate editor composes the response to the authors and includes the feedback from the reviewers, the editor of the journal then approves the decision before it is passed along to the authors.

- If the paper is accepted or invited for resubmission with either minor or major revisions, the authors will likely incorporate those comments, detailing the changes they made in a cover letter with point-by-point responses to the reviewers, while also highlighting changes in the body of the manuscript, and resubmit to the same journal. If the paper is rejected, the author likely incorporates the comments and criticisms of the reviewers and then selects another journal to which they submit the paper.

Understanding everything that goes into getting a paper published and each step of the peer-review process creates an appreciation for the article.

Hannah Glenn, Cognitive Neuroscience Major, Manchester University, Class of 2016; PhD student, University of Wisconsin, Madison

Before I was in a lab, I did not understand the extent of everything that went in to a single experiment. Many things have to be reviewed and approved before you can even start conducting the experiment. Then, after you finally write the paper, it has to be reviewed. This is a long process and really shows you the careful and precise method used by scientists in order to deliver the best work.

Sarah Burens, Behavioral Neuroscience Major, The Ohio State University, Class of 2019

HOW TO ANNOTATE YOUR ARTICLES

Here I summarize the main tricks that I use when I'm annotating a journal article. These apply to most articles you will read. I have also included an example of an article that has been annotated following these suggestions.

Present Study

I always get excited when I see the words *in the present study* or *here we* because they indicate that I have located a place in the text where the authors are going to be straightforward and concisely tell me either what their paper is about or exactly what the authors did and why they did it in one sentence. I try to make sure to emphasize such locations in the text by underlining or putting a box around these important phrases.

Define Unknown Vocabulary

There are two broad reasons why you need to look up the words you don't know when you encounter them in an article. First, you can't move forward if you get stuck on vocabulary. In many academic contexts, it is recommended that you pre-read an article looking for vocabulary that you do not know, with the suggestion that you learn those words or terms before you begin reading. I think that might be too burdensome for the purpose of an undergraduate course, but you do need to recognize that the more words you don't know and skip over, rather than look them up, the greater the likelihood that you will be unable to answer comprehension questions about the article. A good friend of mine who is an English professor really likes the website www.onelook.com as a dictionary and thesaurus during both reading and writing.

I do want to caution you against feeling compelled to look up absolutely every word you do not know, particularly if it's likely to be terminology that will become clear by reading the paper. One of my children had a well-intentioned teacher who advised them to look up every word they did not know and it paralyzed my child and caused them to regress in their reading. A better tactic when suggesting you look up the definition of words while reading is to try and figure out what a word means from the context, particularly if the term is specific to the field and can't be easily found in an online dictionary. While scientific terms will likely be defined in the paper, advanced non-scientific vocabulary will not be defined when it is used. I'm specifically encouraging you to look up words that will serve the dual purpose of increasing your vocabulary and enhancing your comprehension of the reading.

Second, you should use reading journal articles as an opportunity to increase your vocabulary. Underline and look up words you don't know. There is a place on the Reading Comprehension Questions worksheet to list the words that are unfamiliar to you. In my example article, I've assumed that many students might not know or at least need a reminder of the definition for the words *seminal*, *latent*, and *overt*. In order to serve multiple purposes, I suggest using this opportunity to study for the vocabulary portion of the GRE by creating digital flashcards using an app or challenging yourself to use the words the same day you read them in the article. I have been surprised by the words students have asked me to define for them during multiple-choice tests because I would have assumed they were common terms the students should have known, so please embrace this opportunity to increase your vocabulary.

Don't always rely on context clues! When I first started reading articles, pulling out a dictionary (or phone) wasn't something I was accustomed to. Eventually, I realized I used some of the context clues incorrectly and taught myself a wrong definition for a word. After I got over the idea of using a dictionary, I realized those words came back in other articles and I started creating course glossaries. Words like latent, overt, and seminal were added to my glossary so I could easily review them when they came up again. This also helped to keep me on track with doing the reading. ... Dictionary.com didn't turn into Facebook, Reddit, Instagram, and Twitter when my glossary was right there for me to reference.

Hannah Glenn, Cognitive Neuroscience Major, Manchester University, Class of 2016; PhD student, University of Wisconsin, Madison

I actually make a list of words that I didn't know on a separate page, along with their definitions. First, you can use this list as a good review of vocab right before a test. Second, it's a great way to build your vocab for the future. When you're studying for the GRE or similar tests, you can just gather up all these papers and study them.

Sarah Burens, Behavioral Neuroscience Major, The Ohio State University, Class of 2019

Figures and Tables

The figures (and maybe the tables) are your friends! By the time you are an advanced reader of journal articles, you should be able to get a relatively solid gist of an article by just looking at the pictures. However, at this stage I suggest that when a figure or table is referenced in the text, emphasize it with a box. Remember that the purpose of a figure is to present the method or figures in a manner that will be easy to understand. The purpose of a table is often to present a large amount of information in a straightforward format. Although I'm biased toward a preference for figures, I would argue that figures are usually helpful in understanding the main take-home points of a paper, whereas tables can oftentimes be skipped because they usually contain considerably more information than a figure (and therefore they may be unhelpful for a first-time reader), unless you are trying to replicate a study or glean more than just a general understanding of the work.

I'm almost embarrassed to admit that I still catch myself focusing solely on the text and not the figures. Somewhere early on, I was taught to not look at the pictures. I remember one class during my freshman year of college when a professor was absolutely bewildered as everyone in my class told him that we never look at the pictures. The tables and figures are your friend! There's information there that can help the rest of the paper make sense. But, even just looking at them isn't enough either. You HAVE to read the captions, too. They're there for a reason!

Hannah Glenn, Cognitive Neuroscience Major, Manchester University, Class of 2016; PhD student, University of Wisconsin, Madison

Don't skip over tables and figures. Like Hannah, I hate to admit I also used to glance over them. But now I know all they can offer me. It is easy to get confused or overwhelmed when reading the methods or discussions. However, the tables allow you to look at things side by side and compare trial to trial to see their manipulations.

Sarah Burens, Behavioral Neuroscience Major, The Ohio State University, Class of 2019

Levels of Processing

The concept of levels of processing refers to the extent to which you might process information—in a shallow manner (e.g., rereading your textbook) or at a deeper level (e.g., discussing how it relates to another course with your roommate). Studies show that we are more likely to remember information when we process it deeply, so be mindful of your levels of processing as you read journal articles. In order to deeply process information and increase the likelihood of remembering it, follow the simple suggestions below.

- Ditch the highlighter—all that highlighting communicates is that the text is important. Of course it is important, it's in the article. What you need to do is interpret, process, and remember the information—in your own words, related to what you already know; hence the next steps below. Only use a pen or pencil when you are reading an article, never a highlighter.

My world collapsed when I took cognitive psychology and I was told to ditch the highlighters. It was some sort of existential crisis because I relied so heavily on them. When just underlining in pen wasn't enough and I felt like I NEEDED to highlight something, I began to draw shapes. I created this system where something would be marked with squares, hearts, or triangles. A square was put by/around something that I would've highlighted, a heart by one sentence that I felt was key to my ability to understand and grasp the point, and a triangle by something that was confusing because it was similar to a road sign telling you to use caution.

Hannah Glenn, Cognitive Neuroscience Major, Manchester University, Class of 2016; PhD student, University of Wisconsin, Madison

The first time I heard this in class, I was confused and scared. I've been through years and years of schooling and being told to use highlighters. But this advice to "ditch the highlighter" couldn't be more useful. You see yourself eventually using symbols, lines, and circles that help you identify several things in a paper rather than just highlighting whole paragraphs.

Sarah Burens, Behavioral Neuroscience Major, The Ohio State University, Class of 2019

- Make a connection with other information in your memory by noting any information you come across that is related to your other courses, previous readings, or your own interests. This allows you to more deeply process the information in the article, increasing the likelihood that you will understand and remember the material.

- Rewrite the information using your own words. Summarize many of the paragraphs in the margin. When I'm writing an article I try to make sure that each paragraph has a purpose and could be summarized in a few words in the margin. For example, if the authors are describing their previous work because they are going to use a similar paradigm or method, I emphasize that in the margin. If they are describing a potential alternative explanation that they rule out in Experiment 2, I make a brief note in the margin that it is an alternative explanation and they are running Experiment 2 (or E2 for short) with the intention of ruling it out.

- Do NOT use your computer to read the articles. For one, you need to be annotating them up with a pen or pencil. Further, there is plenty of empirical evidence that using laptops in classrooms decreases test scores. One reason we created this anthology was because we wanted our students to have paper copies of all these articles and the cost of printing became greater than a book.

Recognition Practice Results in a Generalizable Skill in Older Adults

Decreased Intrusion Errors to Novel Objects Belonging to Practiced Categories

Applied Cognitive Psychology, Appl. Cognit. Psychol. 30: 643–649 (2016) Published online 12 May 2016 in Wiley Online Library (wileyonlinelibrary.com) DOI: 10.1002/acp.3236

This journal specializes in relating work in cognitive psychology to the real-world contexts in which they occur.

abstract

Summary: Accessing memories is often accompanied by both positive and negative consequences. For example, practice recognizing some visual images held in memory can improve memory for the practiced images and hurt memory for related images (i.e., recognition-induced forgetting). However, visual stimuli have been shown to improve memory for older adults by decreasing false memories. This suggests that older adults may be immune to recognition-induced forgetting and that recognition practice may decrease susceptibility to intrusion errors. We first tested the hypothesis that older adults are immune to recognition-induced forgetting. We found older adults exhibit recognition-induced forgetting. Next, we tested the hypothesis that recognition practice decreases older adult's rates of intrusion errors. We found lower intrusion errors for novel objects from practiced categories. This represents a generalizable learning effect; practice recognizing a target object (e.g., your pill bottle) improves the rejection of new lures (e.g., identifying the pill bottle that is not yours). Copyright © 2016 John Wiley & Sons, Ltd.

"intrusion error"

The potential severity of classifying a novel item as familiar is clear under many real-world circumstances. This is particularly true as people age. For example, it is dangerous if someone mistakes a housemate's pill bottle as one's own or incorrectly thinks a stranger at the door is a familiar face. Incorrectly reporting a novel item as having been encountered before is called an *intrusion error* (Jacobs, Salmon, Troster, & Butters, 1990). The gravity of these errors increases when committed by more vulnerable populations, like older adults. Indeed, older adults commit intrusion errors at higher rates than younger adults (Borella, Carretti, Cornoldi, & De Beni, 2007; Borella, Carretti, & De Beni, 2008; De Beni & Palladino, 2004; Lustig, May, & Hasher, 2001), especially for objects that belong to highly familiar categories, such as a faces (Bartlett & Fulton, 1991; Bartlett, Leslie, Tubbs, & Fulton, 1989; Fulton & Bartlett, 1991; Lamont, Stewart-Williams, & Podd, 2005; Searcy, Bartlett, & Memon, 1999). While relatively few studies on long-term memory and aging have used visual (i.e., picture) stimuli (Park & Gutchess, 2005), recent evidence has demonstrated that visual stimuli reduce older adults' false memories (Gallo, Cotel, Moore, & Schacter, 2007; Schacter, Israel, & Racine, 1999; Smith, Hunt, & Dunlap, 2015), consistent with a large body of work that memory for visual stimuli is superior to memory for verbal stimuli (e.g., Hockley, 2008; Paivio, Rogers, & Smythe, 1968). This begs the question whether experience (or practice) recognizing a visual object can boost older adults' immunity to intrusion errors. Our goal in the present study is to determine whether recognition practice can effectively improve memory for aging individuals by reducing the rates of memory intrusions.

It is particularly plausible that practice recognizing an object may affect rates of intrusion errors given strong evidence that accessing memory representations does not simply involve retrieving a memory and putting it away unaltered.

Specifically, research on retrieval-induced forgetting (Anderson, Bjork, & Bjork, 1994) has shown that accessing a memory can change other memory representations. This memory phenomenon illustrates that the act of remembering an item actually alters its representation, typically by

---

Margin annotations:

pulation studied

rusion error

real world examples

population studied

older adults show more intrusion errors

most work done without pictures

memory for pictures is good

Research question: GOAL

why they might expert this to be the case

this access-based forgetting shows that accessing memory has consequences and exists in older adults

strengthening that object's representation. However, these changes do not only affect the memory representation of the remembered item. Memory representations of items that are semantically related to the retrieved memory, but are not themselves retrieved, are also altered. This memory-modifying effect occurs in the opposite direction, by weakening the memory representations of related objects that are not retrieved in the course of practice. Retrieval-induced forgetting has been shown with older adults who are normally aging (Aslan, Bäuml, & Pastotter, 2007; Hogge, Adam, & Collette, 2008) and patients with Alzheimer's disease (Moulin et al., 2002).

define seminal: original, influenced later work

Since the seminal study of Anderson, Bjork and Bjork (1994), the literature has grown rife with applications of retrieval-induced forgetting (for a great review, see Storm et al., 2015). Studies have examined retrieval-induced forgetting across applications such as education (e.g., Carroll, Campbell-Ratcliffe, Murnane, & Perfect, 2007; Little, Storm, & Bjork, 2011), eyewitness memory (e.g., Camp, Wesstein, & Bruin, 2012; Garcia-Bajos, Migueles, & Anderson, 2009; MacLeod, 2002; Migueles & García-Bajos, 2007; Shaw, Bjork, & Handal, 1995), social cognition (e.g., Coman & Hirst, 2012; Coman, Manier, & Hirst, 2009; Storm, Bjork, & Bjork, 2005), autobiographical memory (e.g., Harris, Sharman, Barnier, & Moulds, 2010; Hauer & Wessel, 2006), and creative cognition (e.g., Storm & Angello, 2010; Storm, Angello, & Bjork, 2011). Interestingly, some studies have also shown better memory for typically forgotten information in these paradigms (e.g., Little, Bjork, Bjork, & Angello, 2012; Little et al., 2011; Storm, Bjork, & Bjork, 2008). Evidence that memory for semantically related items is improved under some conditions suggests that despite being vulnerable to retrieval-induced forgetting, older adults may show some benefit of practice.

many real world applications of remembering & forgetting

this would be the benefit of practice from the previous page

Specifically, older adults may be able to overcome intrusion errors (such as those discussed previously) with practice. The potential importance of such an applied finding would be wide reaching. If recognition practice can improve intrusion error rates, then the present data would serve as empirical evidence that recognition practice provides a generalizable benefit to

consistent with the journal the authors tie this study back to its real-world application

data indicating the practice benefit also decreases intrusion error

novel stimuli, improving individuals' ability to reject new items that they have never seen before.

We next review a novel paradigm that allowed us to address whether practice recognizing objects affected rates of intrusion errors in the present paper. Recently, Maxcey and Woodman (2014) found a memory impairment, similar to retrieval-induced forgetting, in visual long-term memory of college-age adults that they called recognition-induced forgetting (see also Maxcey, 2016; Maxcey & Bostic, 2015). Evidence of this impairment is found using a recognition task to assess memory for visual stimuli. In this recognition-induced forgetting paradigm (Figure 2), participants are shown objects from a variety of categories (see Figure S1 for an example of complete categories) in a study phase. Participants are instructed to remember the objects for a later memory test. In the recognition practice phase, participants practice recognizing half of the objects from half of the categories in a two-alternative forced-choice recognition judgment task. This recognition practice phase creates three classes of objects: those that the participant has had practice recognizing (known as *practiced objects*[2]), those that belong to a category that was practiced, but they themselves were not practiced (known as *related objects*), and those drawn from categories that the participant has only been exposed to in the initial study phase but does not have practice recognizing (known as *baseline objects*). At test, participants are sequentially presented with objects, half of which are new (i.e., novel) and half of which are old (i.e., from the study phase in the experiment). Participants are instructed to report whether they have ever seen the exact object previously in the experiment with a button press response. Importantly for the present study, half of the novel objects are from practiced categories, and half are from non-practiced categories. The typical finding that results from recognition practice in this paradigm is significantly worse memory for related objects relative to baseline objects, hence the term *recognition-induced forgetting*.

describe this paradigm because they use it

online supplemental material

① ②

(2 AFC)

label in Figure 2

③

✱

relevant for this paper

worse memory for related vs. baseline

---

[1]In order to be more accessible to the reader, Maxcey and Bostic (2015) revised the nomenclature for these objects from the previous terms used by Maxcey and Woodman (2014). Here, we continue to use the revised nomenclature.

Using this recognition-induced forgetting paradigm with older adult participants allowed us to answer two questions in the present study. First, does recognition-induced forgetting exist in visual long-term memory of older adults? Given the evidence reviewed previously for the role of pictures in improving memory in older adults, it is possible that older adults will be immune to such forgetting. Second, does practice recognizing a category of objects (e.g., gloves) decrease rates of intrusion errors for novel gloves relative to novel objects from non-practiced categories (e.g., fans)? In other words, does repeated experience (or practice) with a category (e.g., pill bottles) make an older adult less likely to incorrectly identify a novel pill bottle as familiar and subsequently take the wrong medicine?

① two research questions

② real-world application

Two patterns of results for rates of intrusion errors can be motivated by the literature. The first potential outcome stems from research suggesting that the mechanism of induced forgetting effects is inhibition (Anderson, 2003). Consistent with this view, recognition practice decreases susceptibility to intrusion errors in children (Maxcey & Bostic, 2015). Given that older adults are believed to have inhibitory deficits (Hasher & Zacks, 1988) as do children (Bjorklund & Harnishfeger, 1990; Friedman & Leslie, 2004), it may be that recognition practice also decreases susceptibility to intrusion errors in older adults. This possibility would result in higher rates of correct rejections for novel objects from practiced categories versus non-practiced categories.

explain why two alternatives are possible

performance or novel objects in the test phase

Alternatively, because it has not been conclusively shown that this task involves inhibition (Maxcey, 2016; Maxcey & Bostic, 2015; Maxcey & Woodman, 2014), older adults may instead show no effect on intrusion errors between practiced and non-practiced categories. This possibility would result in no reliable difference in correct rejections between practiced and non-practiced categories. The goal of the present study is to distinguish between these two alternatives, using a recognition-induced forgetting paradigm with older adult participants.

what they did to address/answer this issue/question

METHOD

Participants

Our participants were 30 older adults (16 members of the Manchester University community and 14 members of the Montana State University community), with a mean age of 79.5 years (standard deviation = 7.36, age range: 65–91 years). Participants passed the Ishihara color blindness test and reported normal or corrected-to-normal vision. Participants reported no history of cognitive deficit diagnoses. Participants scored above the recommended cutoff on the Mini Mental Status Exam (Folstein, Folstein, & McHugh, 1975) of 24/30, with an average score of 28.2. Informed consent was obtained prior to the beginning of the experiment. All procedures were approved by the appropriate Institutional Review Board.

ages of older adults

used MMSE to check cognitive ability

Stimuli and procedure

Stimuli were presented using E-prime 2.0 software (Schneider, Eschman, & Zuccolotto, 2012). Participants were comfortably seated at a viewing distance of approximately 80 cm. Stimuli were drawn from public domain images downloaded from Google Images (http://images. google.com), viewed on a white background, with each subtending 4.85° × 4.85° degrees of visual angle. An example of a subset of stimuli for one participant is shown in Figure 1 (please see Figure S1 for a complete set of stimuli). The stimuli consisted of 12 categories of real-world objects with 15 exemplars in each category. Two additional categories (tables and goggles) with three exemplars in each served as filler items for the first and final three trials of the study phase.

relevant info only if replicating or comparing

be sure to understand the stimuli

12 categories (e.g. apples, lamps) with 15 objects in each

recognition-induced forgetting paradigm described previously

We used the methods of Maxcey and Woodman (2014) as described below. An example of the stimuli and procedure is shown in Figure 2. The experimental session consisted of a study phase, a recognition-practice phase, and a final test phase. (1)   (2)   (3)

12 categories included chairs,
lamps, bowties, & butterflies

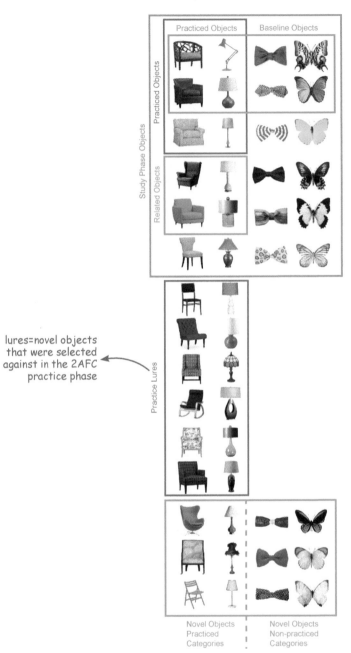

FIGURE 1

Example of a subset of stimuli. This is an example of the objects from four of the 12 categories for one subject. The red box indicates the objects that were presented in the study phase. The blue boxes show the objects in the practice phase. The green boxes delineate the objects from the test phase. Please see Figure S1 for a complete illustration of the entire stimulus set for one participant

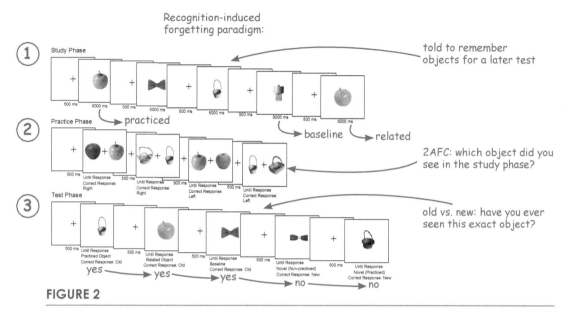

FIGURE 2

Example of the stimuli and procedure. The study phase consisted of 78 objects presented sequentially for 5 s interleaved by a 500 ms fixation cross. In the practice phase, participants were a subset of the objects from the study phase paired with a novel exemplar from the same category. Participants performed a two-alternative forced-choice recognition task, responding by button press to indicate which object (the object on the left or on the right) was the object they had seen in the study phase. Finally, in the test phase, participants made an old/new recognition judgment. Novel objects (i.e., new objects they had never seen before) were either drawn from practiced categories or non-practiced categories

Each session began with a study phase during which participants were shown one object at a time for 5 s, interleaved by a 500-ms center fixation cross, until 78 objects were shown. Participants were instructed to study the visual details of these objects for a later memory test. In order to minimize the influence of primacy and recency effects (Murdock, 1962), three filler objects from two additional categories were included in the beginning and end of the study phase but were not included in the analysis. Therefore, six of the 78 objects were excluded from analysis because of their status as filler objects.

① study phase

Next, participants completed a recognition-practice phase, during which they practiced recognizing half of the objects (three out of six) from half of the categories (six out of 12) they were shown in the study phase. Recognition practice involved completing a two-alternative forced-choice recognition task for each of these 18 objects. Specifically, participants were shown

② practice phase

two objects at a time on the screen, one to the left and one to the right of fixation. One of the objects was an object they were shown during the study phase (i.e., one of the 18 practiced objects). The other object was a novel object from the same category. Participants were instructed to determine which of the objects they had seen in the first block and respond with a two-alternative forced-choice button press. The specific objects practiced were counterbalanced across subjects, such that practiced objects for half of the subjects were not practiced for the other half of subjects. Consistent with previous studies, feedback was not provided during the recognition-practice phase, but performance on recognition practice was analyzed.

not told on each trial if they were correct

test phase

③ Finally, during the test phase, participants were shown one object at a time and asked to report whether they had ever seen the exact image previously in the experiment and respond by button press, from this point forward known as the old-versus-new judgment. These images fell into five categories. In three of the categories, the objects were old, and a correct response would be 'yes': (1) practiced objects were shown both during the study phase and practiced in the recognition-practice phase; (2) related objects were shown during the study phase and then were not practiced in the recognition-practice phase, but their category was practiced; and (3) baseline objects were shown during the study phase and then were not practiced in the recognition-practice phase, and their category was not practiced. The hit rates to the aforementioned three classes of objects were analyzed to determine whether recognition-induced forgetting exists for older adults, and whether practice improves memory for practiced objects relative to baseline objects. The final two categories consisted of new objects to which a correct response would be 'no': (4) novel objects from practiced categories were objects that were never seen before in the experiment but belong to practiced categories; and (5) novel objects from non-practiced categories were objects that were never seen before in the experiment and belong to non-practiced categories. The correct rejections to these two types novel objects were analyzed to determine whether recognition practice had a different effect on intrusion errors between practiced and non-practiced categories. Half of the

understanding these results depends on grasping these object conditions- be sure they make sense

research question 1

research question 2

Table 1. Results summary tables from the participants' responses to objects in the test phase

OLD OBJECTS			
	PRACTICED OBJECTS	BASELINE OBJECTS	RELATED OBJECTS
Hit	0.89	0.86	0.74
Miss	0.11	0.14	0.26
A′	0.9	0.89	0.84
B''_D	−0.41	−0.28	0.05

NEW OBJECTS		
	PRACTICED CATEGORY	NON-PRACTICED CATEGORY
False alarm	0.18	0.25
Correct rejection	0.82	0.75

Old objects are objects that were previously seen in the experiment and warranted a 'yes' response at test. New objects are objects that were novel and warranted a 'no' response at test.

Tables are often used to give the "whole story" but flipping to the next page you can see a figure that presents the hit rates so, skip ahead and come back to the table later if you're interested in these other values

objects in the memory test were old (36 total practiced, related and baseline objects), and half of the objects were new (36 total novel objects). Novel objects were equally divided into novel objects drawn from practiced categories and non-practiced categories. In between the three blocks, participants completed a 5-min filler task adopted from Maxcey and Woodman (2014).

yes and no answers were equally likely

Data analysis

The primary dependent variable for our recognition data was hit rate (i.e., hits for practiced, related and baseline objects, and correct rejections for test lures). We found the same pattern of results when we computed A′ (Snodgrass, Levy-Berger, & Haydon, 1985) and B''_D (Donaldson, 1992).[3] A complete list of analyses can be found in Table 1. We used a within-subjects analysis of variance and an alpha level of $p = 0.05$ for the

the value that depends on the independent variable (object type)

ANOVA use these stats terms to help refresh your memory of stats!

---

[3]Here, we report the analyses from hit rates for efficiency of presentation. However, the analyses of A′ and B''_D are also useful because they illustrate that recognition-induced forgetting is not simply due to participants becoming more conservative for categories with larger set sizes (as do practiced and related objects relative to baseline objects). This is clear because B''_D for practiced objects is not significantly different than B''_D for baseline objects, $t(29) = 1.265$, $p = .216$, scaled JZS Bayes factor 2.50 (see also Maxcey, 2016).

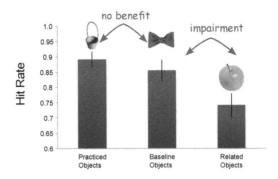

Stimulus Type at Test

FIGURE 3

Hit rates of the responses to the old memory test objects in the test phase. Practiced objects were recognized during the practice phase. Related objects are the objects that belong to practiced categories but were not themselves practiced. Baseline objects are categories of objects that were not practiced. The error bars show the 95% within-subjects confidence intervals as described by Cousineau (2005) with Morey's correction applied (Morey, 2008)

omnibus test. Preplanned, two-tailed repeated measures *t*-tests were used to determine whether there was a benefit of recognition practice for practiced objects (hit rate for practiced objects greater than hit rate for baseline objects) and any cost related to related objects (hit rate for related objects less than hit rate for baseline objects). The same follow-up t-tests examined any difference between correct rejection rates for novel objects from practiced versus non-practiced categories (% correct rejections for novel objects from practiced categories ≠ % correct rejections for novel objects from non-practiced categories). All t-tests are accompanied by measures of Cohen's *d* effect size. To provide a way of quantifying the support for the null hypothesis, we calculated the scaled JZS Bayes factor (as specified in Rouder, Speckman, Sun, Morey, & Iverson, 2009). Finally, we ran a Pearson's correlation to examine any correlation between age and the difference in correct rejection rates between novel objects from practiced relative to non-practiced categories. The two subgroups of participants (members of the Manchester University community and Montana State University community) performed similarly; thus, data were collapsed across these two subgroups in all of the aforementioned analysis conditions.

because age range was wide (65-91) this allows for our analysis of change as function of age.

RESULTS

Recognition-induced forgetting

The mean hit rates across the types of test objects are shown in Figure 3. These means show that, using pictures, older adults show only the impairment for related objects and not the benefit for practiced objects shown in college-age adults (Maxcey & Woodman, 2014). These findings resulted in a significant main effect of trial type in the analysis of variance, $F(2, 58) = 16.05$, $p < .001$. Specifically, participants were significantly better at identifying practiced objects (.89) than related objects (.74, $t(29) = 5.98$, $p < .001$, $d = 1.26$). However, participants showed no significant benefit for practiced objects (.89) over baseline objects (.86, $t(29) = 1.37$, $p = .182$). To provide another way of quantifying this similarity in performance across the practiced objects and baseline objects, we calculated the scaled JZS Bayes factor, which provided the estimate that the null hypothesis was 2.21 times more likely than the hypothesis that these means do differ (as specified in Rouder et al., 2009). This comparison between baseline and practiced objects is significant among college-age adults (Maxcey, 2016; Maxcey & Woodman, 2014) and is interpreted as the benefit of practice in recognition-induced forgetting paradigms (see also Maxcey & Bostic, 2015). The absence of a significant benefit for practiced objects is not due to poor performance during recognition practice because participants performed very well during recognition practice (.89).

> The benefit for practiced objects found in young adults is not present in these older adults

> analyzed practice phase to show lack of benefit is not due to poor performance during the practice phase

Despite this absence of a benefit of recognition practice for practiced objects, participants did show a significant cost for related objects. This emerged as reliably better performance in identifying baseline objects (.86) relative to related objects (.74), $t(29) = 3.67$, $p = .001$, $d = .83$. These results suggest that recognition practice did indeed hurt memory for related objects, even in the absence of a benefit for practiced objects. This finding serves as the first evidence of recognition-induced forgetting in older adults.

> do show recognition-induced forgetting (for the first time)

Intrusion errors for novel objects

We next sought to examine whether there was a cost to correctly rejecting novel objects from non-practiced categories, relative to novel objects from practiced categories. We found that correct rejections of novel objects from non-practiced categories (75%) were significantly lower than correct rejections of novel objects that were members of a practiced category (82%), $t(29) = 2.80$, $p = .009$, $d = .60$. These findings indicate that when older adults are presented with a new object from a semantic category to which they have previous experience with recognition practice, they are more accurate at identifying it as novel, compared with a new object from a semantic category with which they have less such experience. This latent effect of practice is also positively correlated with age, such that older participants showed a greater difference in correct rejection rates between novel objects from practiced relative to non-practiced categories, $r = +.463$, $p = .01$. In sum, older adults showed decreased intrusion errors to novel objects from practiced categories, a difference that increased with age. This demonstrates the surprising result that practice did not improve memory for the practiced objects but did improve the ability of the participants to reject other objects (e.g., as not the pill bottle I am looking for).

despite no benefit of practice improved correct rejections

latent-present but not visible

correlation showed changed with age

GENERAL DISCUSSION

Older adults incorrectly endorse novel stimuli as familiar under many circumstances, such as false seeing (Jacoby, Rogers, Bishara, & Shimizu, 2012), false hearing (Rogers, Jacoby, & Sommers, 2012), and false remembering (Jacoby, Bishara, Hessels, & Toth, 2005). However, the consequence of practicing object recognition in older adults was unknown. In the present study, we first sought to determine whether older adults exhibit recognition-induced forgetting. Indeed, older adults did exhibit a cost of recognition-induced forgetting. This cost emerged as reliably worse memory for related objects relative to baseline objects, as expected in this paradigm. Recognition practice did not significantly improve memory for practiced objects relative baseline. The absence of a benefit of recognition practice for practiced objects is in contrast to college-age adults who do show improved

high frequency of intrusion errors

① cost but not benefit

performance after recognition practice (Maxcey, 2016; Maxcey & Woodman, 2014). However, this lack of benefit for practiced objects is consistent with developmental evidence that children ages 6–8 years also do not show a benefit for practiced objects in the recognition-induced forgetting paradigm, while children ages 9–10 years do show better memory for practiced objects (Maxcey & Bostic, 2015).

relationship to work with children

We then sought to determine whether the memory impairment in recognition-induced forgetting had residual effects on intrusion errors for novel objects. We found significantly more intrusion errors to novel objects from non-practiced categories, relative to novel objects from practiced categories. Therefore, although there was no overt benefit of practice for practiced objects relative to baseline, practice clearly did have an effect on intrusion errors of novel objects. Specifically, practice boosted immunity to intrusion errors of novel objects from practiced categories. Interestingly, children ages 6–8 years who did not show an advantage for practiced objects (similar to the older adults herein) also show reliably more intrusion errors for novel objects from non-practiced categories relative to novel objects from practiced categories (Maxcey & Bostic, 2015).

Overt definition: open to view or knowledge

again, show how it relates to kids

Recent evidence from our lab has demonstrated that increased practiced in the recognition-induced forgetting paradigm in college-age adults increases memory for practice objects but does not worsen forgetting of related objects (Maxcey, 2016). In that study, intrusion errors did not differ across categories that were practiced two, four, or six times. However, the effect of parametrically manipulating the amount of practice objects receive on intrusion errors in the aging population is unknown. Future research is necessary to determine whether a similar parametric manipulation of recognition practice with older adults would further boost their immunity to intrusion errors, as well as reliably increase memory for practiced objects relative to baseline.

increase

what would more practice do?

generalizable results — The present study offers a paradigm that empirically demonstrates a generalizable improvement in older adults' correct rejections of novel items. Specifically, older adults were better able to correctly reject objects they had never seen before when they belonged to a practiced category, generalizing the effect of

potential future applications — recognition practice to new objects. This study sets the stage for future research to further examine these results in applied settings. For example, the development of apps that mimic the recognition-induced forgetting paradigm may help protect this vulnerable population from potentially dangerous intrusion errors.

ACKNOWLEDGEMENTS

Keith Hutchinson provided resources in support of this work. Geoffrey F. Woodman provided constructive comments on a previous version of this manuscript. We thank the following individuals for their useful online calculators: Jeffrey Rouder for his scaled JZS Bayes Factor calculator, Ian Neath for his online A' and B''_D calculator, and Lee Becker for his online Cohen's d calculator.

REFERENCES

Anderson, M. C. (2003). Rethinking interference theory: Executive control and the mechanisms of forgetting. *Journal of Memory and Language, 49,* 415–445. DOI:10.1016/j.jml.2003.08.006.

Anderson, M. C., Bjork, R. A., & Bjork, E. L. (1994). Remembering can cause forgetting: Retrieval dynamics in long-term memory. *Journal of Experimental Psychology: Learning, Memory, and Cognition, 20*(5), 1063–1087. DOI:10.1037//0278-7393.20.5.1063.

Aslan, A., Bäuml, K. H., & Pastotter, B. (2007). No inhibitory deficit in older adults' episodic memory. *Psychological Science, 18*(1), 72–78. DOI:10.1111/j.1467-9280.2007.01851.x.

Bartlett, J. C., & Fulton, A. (1991). Familiarity and recognition of faces in old age. *Memory & Cognition, 19,* 229–238. DOI:10.3758/BF03211147.

Bartlett, J. C., Leslie, J. E., Tubbs, A., & Fulton, A. (1989). Aging and memory for pictures of faces. *Psychology and Aging, 4*(3), 276–283. DOI:10.1037/0882-7974.4.3.276.

Bjorklund, D. F., & Harnishfeger, K. K. (1990). The resources construct in cognitive development: Diverse sources of evidence and a theory of inefficient inhibition. *Developmental Review, 10,* 48–71.

Borella, E., Carretti, B., Cornoldi, C., & De Beni, R. (2007). Working memory, control of interference and everyday experience of thought interference: When age makes the difference. *Aging Clinical and Experimental Research, 19*(3), 200–206. DOI:10.1007/BF03324690.

Borella, E., Carretti, B., & De Beni, R. (2008). Working memory and inhibition across the adult life-span. *Acta Psychologica*, 128(1), 33–44. DOI:10.1016/j.actpsy.2007.09.008.

Camp, G., Wesstein, H., & Bruin, A. B. (2012). Can questioning induce forgetting? Retrieval-induced forgetting of eyewitness information. *Applied Cognitive Psychology*, 26(3), 431–435. DOI:10.1002/acp.2815.

Carroll, M., Campbell-Ratcliffe, J., Murnane, H., & Perfect, T. (2007). Retrieval-induced forgetting in educational contexts: Monitoring, expertise, text integration, and test format. *European Journal of Cognitive Psychology*, 19(4-5), 580–606. DOI:10.1080/09541440701326071.

Coman, A., & Hirst, W. (2012). Cognition through a social network: The propagation of induced forgetting and practice effects. *Journal of Experimental Psychology: General*, 141(2), 321. DOI:10.1037/a0025247.

Coman, A., Manier, D., & Hirst, W. (2009). Forgetting the unforgettable through conversation socially shared retrieval-induced forgetting of September 11 memories. *Psychological Science*, 20(5), 627–633. DOI:10.1111/j.1467-9280.2009.02343.x.

Cousineau, D. (2005). Confidence intervals in within-subject designs: A simpler solution to Loftus and Masson's method. *Tutorial in Quantitative Methods for Psychology*, 1, 42–45.

De Beni, R., & Palladino, P. (2004). Decline in working memory updating through ageing: Intrusion error analyses. *Memory*, 12(1), 75–89. DOI:10.1080/09658210244000568.

Donaldson, W. (1992). Measuring recognition memory. *Journal of Experimental Psychology: General*, 121(3), 275–277. DOI:10.1037/0096-3445.121.3.275. Folstein, M. F., Folstein, S. E., & McHugh, P. R. (1975). "Mini-mental state". A practical method for grading the cognitive state of patients for the clinician. *Journal of Psychiatric Research*, 12(3), 189–198. DOI:10.1016/0022-3956(75)90026-6.

Friedman, O., & Leslie, A. M. (2004). Mechanisms of belief-desire reasoning inhibition and bias. *Psychological Science*, 15(8), 547–552.

Fulton, A., & Bartlett, J. C. (1991). Young and old faces in young and old heads: The factor of age in face recognition. *Psychology and Aging*, 6(4), 623–630. DOI:10.1037//0882-7974.6.4.623.

Gallo, D. A., Cotel, S. C., Moore, C. D., & Schacter, D. L. (2007). Aging can spare recollection-based retrieval monitoring: The importance of event distinctiveness. *Psychology and Aging*, 22(1), 209. DOI:10.1037/0882-7974.22.1.209.

Garcia-Bajos, E., Migueles, M., & Anderson, M. C. (2009). Script knowledge modulates retrieval-induced forgetting for eyewitness events. *Memory*, 17(1), 92–103. DOI:10.1080/09658210802572454.

Harris, C. B., Sharman, S. J., Barnier, A. J., & Moulds, M. L. (2010). Mood and retrieval-induced forgetting of positive and negative autobiographical memories. *Applied Cognitive Psychology*, 24(3), 399–413. DOI:10.1002/ acp.1685.

Hasher, L., & Zacks, R. T. (1988). Working memory, comprehension, and aging: A review and a new view. In G. H. Bower (Ed.), *The psychology of learning and motivation* (edn, Vol. 22, pp. 193–225). New York, NY: Academic Press.

Hauer, B. J., & Wessel, I. (2006). Retrieval-induced forgetting of auto-biographical memory details. *Cognition & Emotion*, 20(3–4), 430–447. DOI:10.1080/02699930500342464.

Hockley, W. E. (2008). The picture superiority effect in associative recognition. *Memory & Cognition*, 36(7), 1351–1359. DOI:10.3758/MC.36.7.1351.

Hogge, M., Adam, S., & Collette, F. (2008). Retrieval-induced forgetting in normal ageing. *Journal of Neuropsychology*, 2(Pt 2), 463–476. DOI:10.1348/174866407x268533.

Jacobs, D., Salmon, D. P., Troster, A. I., & Butters, N. (1990). Intrusion errors in the figural memory of patients with Alzheimer's and Huntington's disease. *Archives of Clinical Neuropsychology*, 5(1), 49–57. DOI:10.1093/arclin/5.1.49.

Jacoby, L. L., Bishara, A. J., Hessels, S., & Toth, J. P. (2005). Aging, subjective experience, and cognitive control: Dramatic false remembering by older adults. *Journal of Experimental Psychology: General*, 134, 131–148. DOI:10.1037/0096-3445.134.2.131.

Jacoby, L. L., Rogers, C. S., Bishara, A. J., & Shimizu, Y. (2012). Mistaking the recent past for the present: False seeing by older adults. *Psychology and Aging*, 27(1), 22–32. DOI:10.1037/a0025924.

Lamont, A. C., Stewart-Williams, S., & Podd, J. (2005). Face recognition and aging: effects of target age and memory load. *Memory and Cognition*, 33(6), 1017–1024. DOI:10.3758/BF03193209.

Little, J. L., Bjork, E. L., Bjork, R. A., & Angello, G. (2012). Multiple-choice tests exonerated, at least of some charges fostering test-induced learning and avoiding test-induced forgetting. *Psychological Science*, 23(11), 1337–1344. DOI:10.1177/0956797612443370.

Little, J. L., Storm, B. C., & Bjork, E. L. (2011). The costs and benefits of testing text materials. *Memory*, 19(4), 346–359. DOI:10.1080/09658211.2011.569725.

Lustig, C., May, C. P., & Hasher, L. (2001). Working memory span and the role of proactive interference. *Journal of Experimental Psychology: General*, 130(2), 199–207. DOI:10.1037/0096-3445.130.2.199.

MacLeod, M. (2002). Retrieval-induced forgetting in eyewitness memory: Forgetting as a consequence of remembering. *Applied Cognitive Psychology*, 16(2), 135–149. DOI:10.1002/acp.782.

Maxcey, A. M. (2016). Recognition-induced forgetting is not due to category-based set size. *Attention, Perception, & Psychophysics*, 78(1), 187–197. DOI:10.3758/s13414-015-1007-1.

Maxcey, A. M., & Bostic, J. (2015). Activating learned exemplars in children impairs memory for related exemplars in visual long-term memory. *Visual Cognition*, 23(5), 643–658. DOI:10.1080/13506285.2015.1064052.

Maxcey, A. M., & Woodman, G. F. (2014). Forgetting induced by recognition of visual images. *Visual Cognition*, 22(6), 789–808. DOI:10.1080/13506285.2014.917134.

Migueles, M., & García-Bajos, E. (2007). Selective retrieval and induced forgetting in eyewitness memory. *Applied Cognitive Psychology*, 21(9), 1157–1172. DOI:10.1002/acp.1323.

Morey, R. D. (2008). Confidence intervals from normalized data: A correction to Cousineau (2005). *Tutorial in Quantitative Methods for Psychology*, 4(2), 61–64.

study with
children explained

original paradigm
described here

Moulin, C. J., Perfect, T. J., Conway, M. A., North, A. S., Jones, R. W., & James, N. (2002). Retrieval-induced forgetting in Alzheimer's disease. *Neuropsychologia*, *40*(7), 862–867. DOI:10.1016/s0028-3932(01)00168-3.

Murdock, B. B. (1962). The serial position effect of free recall. *Journal of Experimental Psychology*, *64*(5), 482. DOI:10.1037/h0045106.

Paivio, A., Rogers, T. B., & Smythe, P. C. (1968). Why are pictures easier to recall than words? *Psychonomic Science*, *11*(4), 137–138. DOI:10.3758/BF03331011.

Park, D. C., & Gutchess, A. H. (2005). Long-term memory and aging: A cognitive neuroscience perspective. In R. Cabeza, L. Nyberh, & D. C.

Park (Eds.), *Cognitive neuroscience of aging: Linking cognitive and cerebral aging* (edn, pp. 218). New York: Oxford University Press.

Rogers, C. S., Jacoby, L. L., & Sommers, M. S. (2012). Frequent false hearing by older adults: The role of age differences in metacognition. *Psychology and Aging*, *27*(1), 33–45. DOI:10.1037/a0026231.

Rouder, J. N., Speckman, P. L., Sun, D., Morey, R. D., & Iverson, G. (2009). Bayesian *t*-tests for accepting and rejecting the null hypothesis. *Psychonomic Bulletin & Review*, *16*, 225–237. DOI:10.3758/PBR.16.2.225.

Schacter, D. L., Israel, L., & Racine, C. (1999). Suppressing false recognition in younger and older adults: The distinctiveness heuristic. *Journal of Memory and Language*, *40*(1), 1–24. DOI:10.1006/jmla.1998.2611.

Schneider, W., Eschman, A., & Zuccolotto, A. (2012). *E-prime reference guide*. Pittsburgh: Psychology Software Tools, Inc.

Searcy, J. H., Bartlett, J. C., & Memon, A. (1999). Age differences in accuracy and choosing in eyewitness identification and face recognition. *Memory and Cognition*, *27*(3), 538–552. DOI:10.3758/bf03211547. Shaw, J., Bjork, R., & Handal, A. (1995). Retrieval-induced forgetting in an eyewitness-memory paradigm. *Psychonomic Bulletin & Review*, *2*(2), 249–253. DOI:10.3758/bf03210965.

Smith, R. E., Hunt, R. R., & Dunlap, K. R. (2015). Why do pictures, but not visual words, reduce older adults' false memories? *Psychology and Aging*. DOI:10.1037/pag0000044.

Snodgrass, J. G., Levy-Berger, G., & Haydon, M. (1985). *Human experimental psychology*. Oxford: Oxford University Press.

Storm, B. C., & Angello, G. (2010). Overcoming fixation: Retrieval-induced forgetting and creative problem solving. *Psychological Science*, *21*, 1263–1265. DOI:10.1177/0956797610379864.

Storm, B. C., Angello, G., & Bjork, E. L. (2011). Thinking can cause forgetting: Memory dynamics in creative problem solving. *Journal of Experimental Psychology Learning Memory and Cognition*, *37*(5), 1287–1293. DOI:10.1037/a0023921.

Storm, B. C., Angello, G., Buchli, D. R., Koppel, R. H., Little, J. L., & Nestojko, J. F. (2015). A review of retrieval-induced forgetting in the contexts of learning, eye-witness memory, social cognition, autobiographical memory, and creative cognition. In B. Ross (Ed.), *The psychology of learning and motivation* (edn, pp. 141–194). Atlanta, GA: Academic Press, Elsevier Inc.

Storm, B. C., Bjork, E. L., & Bjork, R. A. (2005). Social metacognitive judgments: The role of retrieval-induced forgetting in person memory and impressions. *Journal of Memory and Language, 52*(4), 535–550. DOI:10.1016/j.jml.2005.01.008.

Storm, B. C., Bjork, E. L., & Bjork, R. A. (2008). Accelerated relearning after retrieval-induced forgetting: the benefit of being forgotten. *Journal of Experimental Psychology: Learning, Memory, and Cognition, 34*(1), 230–236. DOI:10.1037/0278-7393.34.1.230.

SUPPORTING INFORMATION

This is the supplemental material referred to in the text as "Figure S1"
Note: Supplemental information from journal articles is not included in this anthology.

Additional supporting information may be found in the online version of this article at publisher's website.

Why Aren't All Journal Articles I Read Following APA Style?

APA style is a writing standard set forth by the American Psychological Association. It is a standard that is commonly taught at the undergraduate level and is usually the required formatting for papers undergraduates write in psychology courses. However, the American Psychological Association does not own all journals, so not all articles you read will be in APA style. If you end up writing your own paper someday, you will need to consult the specific journal's website to ensure you are following its formatting requirements.

Give Yourself Enough Time

Reading a journal article is not going to take the same amount of time as reading your favorite novel, or even a textbook. In the beginning of the semester, it could easily take you hours to get through each article and the accompanying worksheets. Given that plenty of research suggests that doing short bursts of work is the most productive way to study, it would be wise to set a timer and allow yourself 30 minutes of time to work on an article, and then get up and do something else. Go for a walk, write a paper for another class, or grab some dinner. Then come back to the article for another 30 minutes. Budgeting your time wisely requires that you recognize that the article will take a while to get through, and that you shouldn't try to read it all in one sitting.

One major part of learning to read academic journals is realizing that the assignment to read an article is lengthy and will take more time than other assignments. I remember multiple reading quizzes that I felt like I wasn't prepared for because I either didn't give myself enough time to thoroughly read the paper or I thought, "Oh, I just have to read this, it won't take long" and I flew through it. As someone who has always been a fast reader, I would find myself getting upset that it would take me so long to read 15 pages. Being concerned about how long it takes to read one article while learning the ropes of academic writing hindered my ability to get a hang of it for a while. Recognize early on that it is in no way a quick and easy assignment, and do not beat yourself up because it can't be done 30 minutes.

Hannah Glenn, Cognitive Neuroscience Major, Manchester University, Class of 2016; PhD student, University of Wisconsin, Madison

HOW TO USE THIS BOOK

The chapters in this book are purposefully organized to guide you through a sequence of steps from reading and annotating the article, to completing elementary Reading Comprehension Questions that can be answered by skimming the paper, to answering deeper Comprehension Check Questions, and finally answering and writing True or False Statements. The intention behind this flow of tasks is that you will be able to successfully answer a variety of deep, applied questions about each article by the end of the chapter. The same questions follow each article because these are the questions you should be asking when you review an article or answering when you write your own manuscript. By repeating these same questions for each worksheet, you are learning the elements of any good article. Here I briefly describe how to tackle each of these tasks.

Annotate the Article

Annotate the article, using the suggestions I made above and referencing the sample article that I have marked to demonstrate this technique.

Reading Comprehension Questions

The Reading Comprehension Questions are on a worksheet that is the same for all the articles and serves as a guide to the types of questions you should be asking yourself as you read articles. It is general enough that it applies to all the articles you read and should apply to many others you may read in the future. These questions can be answered by skimming back over the article after you've given the article an initial read and annotating. These questions ask for information that is there in the article for you to find (rather than information you have to create on your own) and will help you better remember and understand the material.

I suggest making it a habit to answer these questions, or at least have these questions in mind, as you read any article in the future. They will help make sure you have a relatively comprehensive understanding of the purpose of the article, how it fits into the literature, and why its results matter. This activity prepares you for the more intellectually demanding Comprehension Check Questions.

Comprehension Check Questions

You will likely only be prepared to tackle the Comprehension Check Questions after you have read and annotated the article, and then skimmed back over the content searching for answers to the Reading Comprehension Questions. The Comprehension Check Questions serve as applied comprehension questions. The Comprehension Check Questions will be the same for each paper and really require that you tie together a number of larger issues regarding the work—ranging from proposing the next experiment the authors should run as if you were an author, to critiquing the paper like a reviewer. These questions require that you contemplate the material at a deeper level, which will both strengthen your memory for the paper and broaden your ability to see the larger themes and applications of the work. These exercises will help you learn to think critically and will help you to see the big picture in your own research someday.

True or False Statements

The Comprehension Check Questions are followed by space for you to write six True or False Statements. Although students often prefer multiple-choice questions to essay questions, true or false statements can be quite difficult. The intention is never to be *tricky* with these statements, but getting them correct does require a level of care and comprehension that you will hopefully develop and perfect as the semester continues. Your task is to write three true statements and three false statements, noting the page number of the article where the answer can be found. You will want to correct the three false statements by rewriting them to make them true in the space provided. In the meantime, here are some suggestions for issues to keep in mind for writing and answering true or false statements, based on my experience with students answering these types of statements in the past.

> True or false statements used to be my least favorite! Often, only one word is changed that makes it false. This forces you to become a more careful reader. After getting a couple of those wrong on tests, I learned I needed to change the way I read and studied articles. I now make sure I understand details. I now see a difference in the amount of time and focus I spend on a paper. Getting a couple true or false statements wrong made me a better reader and better student!
>
> Sarah Burens, Behavioral Neuroscience Major, The Ohio State University, Class of 2019

- First, look for key terms in the statement and make sure they are the correct key terms (e.g., if the question asks about *attentional blindness*, it's false because the phenomenon is called ***in**attentional blindness*).

- Read each word carefully and make sure they are internally consistent. Remember that taking a true statement and changing just one word could make it false.

- If you are doing a good job annotating the article, the answer should be in a section that you have marked. I'd actually mark the articles as you answer the questions as well, in order to be sure that you have emphasized those portions of the text. As you develop the skill of reading journal articles over time, you should find that you have already noted the sections in the text that correspond with good true or false statements. It will be very rewarding when you've properly anticipated appropriate question material and marked it in advance.

- If the statement is false, rewrite the question to make it true in the space provided.

A NOTE OF ENCOURAGEMENT

There is an E. L. Doctorow quote about writing that I love. I do not love it because it's about writing, but rather because the sentiment applies to so much of life. Here I'm going to use the analogy in terms of your embarking on learning how to read journal articles. He said, "[Writing is] like driving a car at night: you never see further than your headlights, but you can make the whole trip that way." This concept of successfully completing a long journey with very little information about what's ahead might encapsulate how you feel right now. Work your way through reading and thinking about these articles a little at time. Do not allow yourself to become overwhelmed or consumed by what may feel like the enormity of the journey or that you don't know each specific step that is going to get you to the finish line. Start each article allowing yourself to be comfortable with only working with what is right in front of you, that small part of the road in front of you which is illuminated by your headlights when driving at night, and realize that as you put more time into working through these articles, you will deepen your ability to read them and will accomplish the goal of honing this skill by the end of the semester.

Memory-Scanning

Mental Processes Revealed by Reaction-Time Experiments[1]

Saul Sternberg

O ne of the oldest ideas in experimental psychology is that the time between stimulus and response is occupied by a train of processes or *stages*—some being mental operations—which are so arranged that one process does not begin until the preceding one has ended. This *stage theory* implies that the reaction-time (RT) is a *sum*, composed of the durations of the stages in the series, and suggests that if one could determine the component times that add together to make up the RT, one might then be able to answer interesting questions about mental operations to which they correspond. The study of RT should therefore prove helpful to an understanding of the structure of mental activity.

The use of results from RT experiments to study stages of information processing began about a century ago with a paper, "On the Speed of Mental Processes," by F. C. Donders (1868). It was in this paper that Donders introduced the *subtraction method*—a method for analyzing the RT into its components and thereby studying the corresponding stages of processing.

1   Most of the research reported in this paper was supported by Bell Telephone Laboratories and conducted in its Behavioral and Statistical Research Center at Murray Hill, N.J. The work reported as Exp. 4 was done in collaboration with A. M. Treisman of the University of Oxford. I am grateful to C. S. Harris, T. K. Landauer, H. Rouanet, and R. Teghtsoonian for helpful criticisms of the manuscript, and to L. D. Harmon for discussion leading to Exp. 5. R. E. Main assisted with Exps. 4 and 5, B. Barkow with Exps. 7 and 8, and B. A. Nasto with Exps. 4, 5, 7, and 8.

1. DECOMPOSING RT BY THE SUBTRACTION METHOD

To use the subtraction method one constructs two different tasks in which RT can be measured, where the second task is thought to require all the mental operations of the first, plus an additional inserted operation. The difference between mean RTs in the two tasks is interpreted as an estimate of the duration of the inserted stage, as shown in Figure 1.1. This interpretation depends on the validity of both the stage theory and an *assumption of pure insertion* which states that changing from Task 1 to Task 2 merely inserts a new processing stage without altering the others.

For example, Wundt (1880, pp. 247–260) developed an application in which RTs were measured when a subject had to respond after he had identified a stimulus, and also when he had to respond after merely detecting its presence. The difference was used as an estimate of the identification time. In this instance the stages shown in Figure 1.1 might be (a) stimulus detection, (b) stimulus identification, and (c) response organization. In an earlier application, Donders (1868) had compared mean RTs in a simple-reaction task (one stimulus and response) and a choice-reaction task (multiple stimuli and responses); he regarded the difference as the duration of the stages of stimulus discrimination and response selection.

This kind of enterprise occupied many psychologists during the last quarter of the nineteenth century. Much of their work was summarized by J. Jastrow (1890) in a popular treatise on *The Time Relations of Mental Phenomena*.

Around the turn of the century the subtraction method became the subject of criticism for two main reasons. First, the differences in mean RT that were observed in some applications varied excessively from subject to subject, and from laboratory to laboratory. In retrospect, this seems to have been caused by the use of tasks and instructions that left the subject's choice of "processing strategy" relatively uncontrolled. [2] Second, introspective reports put into question the assumption of pure insertion, by suggesting that when the task was changed to insert a stage, other stages might also be altered. (For example, it was felt that changes in stimulus-processing requirements might also alter a response-organization stage.) If so, the difference between RTs could not be identified as the duration of the inserted stage. Because of these difficulties, Külpe, among others, urged caution in the interpretation of results from the subtraction method (1895, Secs. 69, 70). But it appears that no tests other

---

2 For example, Cattell (1886, p. 377) reported that "I have not been able myself to get results by [Wundt's] method. I apparently either distinguished the impression and made the motion simultaneously, or if I tried to avoid this by waiting until I had formed a distinct impression before I began to make the motion, I added to the simple reaction not only a perception, but a volition."

than introspection were proposed for distinguishing valid from invalid applications of the method.

A stronger stand was taken in later secondary sources. For example, in a section on the "discarding of the subtraction method" in his *Experimental Psychology* (1938, p. 309), R. S. Woodworth queried "[Since] we cannot break up the reaction into successive acts and obtain the time of each act, of what use is the reaction-time?" And, more recently, D. M. Johnson said in his *Psychology of Thought and Judgment* (1955, p. 5), "The reaction-time experiment suggests a method for the analysis of mental processes which turned out to be unworkable."

Nevertheless, the attempt to analyze RT into components goes on, and there has been a substantial revival in the last few years in the use of RT as a tool for the study of mental processes ranging from perceptual coding to mental

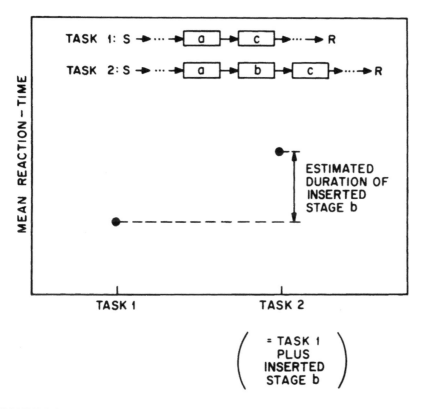

FIGURE 1.1

Donders' subtraction method. Hypothetical stages between stimulus (S) and response (R) are represented by *a, b,* and *c*.

arithmetic and problem-solving.[3] The work on memory retrieval described here is part of this revival, and is based heavily on Donders' stage theory. Modern styles of experimentation and data analysis lead to applications of the stage theory that seem to withstand the early criticisms, and to tests of validity other than introspection.

I shall describe experiments on retrieval from memory that have led to the discovery of some relatively simple search processes. My aim is to convey the general outline rather than the details of this work, so the picture I paint will be somewhat simplified; there will be little discussion of alternative explanations that have been considered and rejected. Such discussions can be found in Sternberg (1966, 1967a, b, and 1969).

The purpose of most of these experiments has been to study the ways in which information is retrieved from memory when learning and retention are essentially perfect. The method is to present a list of items for memorization that is short enough to be within the immediate-memory span. The subject is then asked a question about the memorized list; he answers as quickly as he can, and his delay in responding is measured. By examining the pattern of his RTs, while varying such factors as the number of items in the list and the kind of question asked, one can make inferences about the underlying retrieval processes. Since the aim has been to understand error-free performance, conditions and payoffs are arranged so that in most experiments the responses are almost always correct.

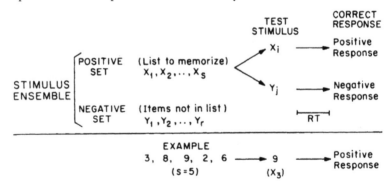

FIGURE 1.2

Paradigm of item-recognition task (Exps. 1-5).

2. JUDGING PRESENCE VERSUS ABSENCE IN A MEMORIZED LIST

The flavor of this approach will become clearer as we consider a particular experiment. Figure 1.2 shows the paradigm of an *item-recognition task*. The stimulus ensemble

3   See, e.g., Egeth, 1966; Hochberg, 1968; Nickerson, 1967; Posner & Mitchell, 1967; Restle & Davis, 1962; Smith, 1967; Suppes & Groen, 1966.

consists of all potential test stimuli. From among these, a set of *s* elements is selected arbitrarily and is defined as the *positive set*; these items are presented as a list for the subject to memorize. The remaining items are called the *negative set*. When a test stimulus is presented, the subject must decide whether it is a member of the positive set. If it is, he makes a *positive response* (e.g., saying "yes" or operating a particular lever). If not, he makes a *negative response*. The measured RT (sometimes referred to as *response latency*) is the time from test-stimulus onset to response.

Within the item-recognition paradigm, different procedures can be used. One of them, shown at the top of Figure 1.3, is the *varied-set procedure*. Here, the subject must memorize a different positive set on each trial. In one experiment (Exp. 1), for example, the stimulus ensemble consisted of the ten digits. On each trial a new positive set, ranging randomly over trials from one to six different digits, was presented sequentially at a rate of 1.2 seconds per digit. Two seconds after the last digit in the set was displayed, a warning signal appeared, followed by a visually-presented test digit. The subject pulled one lever, making a positive response, if the test stimulus was contained in the memorized list. He pulled the other lever, making a negative response, if it was not. After responding to the test stimulus the subject recalled the list. This forced him to retain the items in the presented order, and prevented him from working with the negative set rather than the positive. Regardless of the size of the positive set, the two responses were required equally often. As in the other experiments I shall describe, subjects were relatively unpracticed. The error rate in

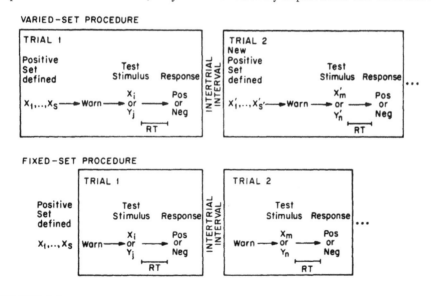

FIGURE 1.3

Varied-set and fixed-set procedures in item-recognition. A *Y* represents an item in the negative set. Primes are used in representing trial 2 of the varied-set procedure to show that both the items in the positive set *(X₁, ..., V₅)* and its size (*s*) may change from trial to trial.

this kind of experiment can be held to 1 or 2 percent by paying subjects in such a way as to penalize errors heavily while rewarding speed.

Averaged data from eight subjects are shown in Figure 1.4. Mean RT is plotted as a function of the number of symbols in memory—that is, the number of digits in the positive set that the subject committed to memory at the start of the trial.

These data are typical for item-recognition experiments. They show, first, a linear relation between mean RT and the size of the positive set. Second, the latencies of positive and negative responses increase at approximately the same rate. The slope of the line fitted to the means is 38 msec per item in memory; its zero-intercept is about 400 msec. (It happens to be true in these data that latencies of positive and negative responses have approximately the same *values:* the two latency functions have not only the same slope but also the same zero-intercept. This is not a general finding, but results from the particular conditions in this experiment. By varying the relative frequency with which positive and negative responses are required, for example, one can vary the relation between their latencies. But as relative frequency is varied the *slopes* of the two latency functions remain equal and unchanged.) Before considering the interpretation of these findings, we turn to some general matters regarding search processes.

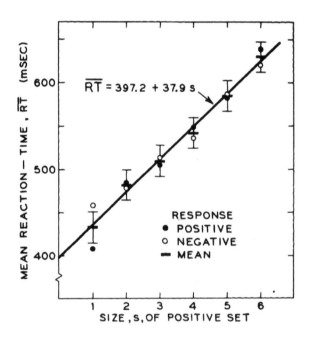

FIGURE 1.4

Results of Exp. 1: Item-recognition with varied-set procedure. Mean latencies of correct positive and negative responses, and their mean, as functions of size of positive set. Averaged data from eight subjects, with estimates of $\pm\sigma$ about means, and line fitted by least squares to means.

3. TWO TYPES OF SERIAL SEARCH

Let *serial search* (or *scanning*) be a process in which each of a set of items is compared one at a time, and no more than once, to a target item. Linear RT-functions, as in Figure 1.4, suggest that subjects in the item-recognition task use a serial search process whose mean duration increases by one unit for each additional comparison. The purpose of the search is to determine whether an agreement (or *match*) exists between the test item and any of the items in the memorized set. Two types of serial search that might serve this purpose need to be considered. In *self-terminating serial search*, the test stimulus is compared successively to one item in memory after another, either until a match occurs (leading to a positive response), or until all comparisons have been completed without a match (leading to a negative response). In *exhaustive serial search*, the test stimulus is compared successively to *all* the memorized items. Only then is a response made—positive if a match has occurred, and negative otherwise. A self-terminating search might require a separate test, after each comparison, to ascertain whether a match had occurred, rather than only one such test after the entire series. On the other hand, an exhaustive search must involve more comparisons, on the average, than a search that terminates when a match occurs.

Suppose that the average time from the beginning of one comparison to the beginning of the next is the same for each comparison in the series, and is not influenced by the number of comparisons to be made. Then the durations of both kinds of search will increase linearly with the number of memorized items (*list length*). There are, however, important differences. In an exhaustive search the test stimulus is compared to all items in memory before each positive response as well as before a negative response. Hence, the rate at which RT increases with list length—the slope of the RT-function—is the same for positive and negative responses. In contrast, a self-terminating search stops in the middle of the list, on the average, before positive responses, but continues through the entire list before negatives. The result is that as list length is increased, the latency of positive responses increases at half the rate of the increase for negatives. This difference between the two kinds of search is illustrated on the left side of Figure 1.5.

A second difference between the two types of search, illustrated on the right side of Figure 1.5, is in the serial-position functions for positive responses. In a simple exhaustive search neither the order of search nor the position of the matching item in the list should have any effect on the RT, since all items are compared. A self-terminating search that occurred in a random order, or started at a random point, also would produce flat serial-position curves. But if a self-terminating search started consistently with the first item, and proceeded serially, then the serial-position curves would increase linearly. (If, in addition, list length influenced *only* the search

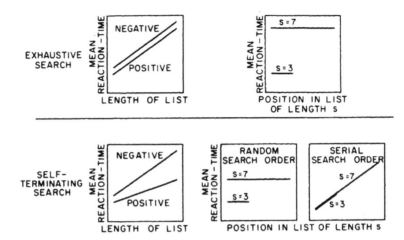

FIGURE 1.5

Some properties of exhaustive (top) and self-terminating (bottom) serial search. Left: Theoretical RT-functions (mean latencies of positive and negative responses as functions of length of list). Right: Theoretical serial-position functions (mean latency of positive responses as a function of serial position of test item in a list of given length).

process, then the curves for different list lengths would be superimposed: for example, the time to arrive at the second item in a memorized list would be independent of the length of the list.) Increasing serial-position functions are therefore sufficient (but not necessary) evidence for inferring that a search process is self-terminating.

4. HIGH-SPEED EXHAUSTIVE SCANNING

The serial-position curves actually observed in the item-recognition experiment described in Sec. 2 were relatively flat.[4] Together with this finding, the linearity of the latency functions and the equality of their slopes for positive and negative responses indicate an exhaustive search. The data show also that memory-scanning can proceed at a remarkably high rate. The slope of the mean RT-function, which is an estimate of the time per comparison, was 38 msec, indicating an average scanning rate between 25 and 30 digits per second.

---

4   Several investigators have, however, reported marked recency effects in item-recognition tasks: RTs were shorter for test stimuli later in the list (Corballis, 1967; Morin, DeRosa & Stultz, 1967; Morin, DeRosa & Ulm, 1967). Without embellishment a theory of exhaustive scanning cannot, of course, handle such findings. The salient procedural characteristics of experiments that produce such recency effects seem to be a fast rate of list presentation and a short interval (less than 1 sec) between the last item in the list and the test item. Findings of Posner, *et al.* (1969), indicate that in this range the time interval between successive stimuli may critically influence the nature and duration of comparison operations.

Perhaps because of its high speed, the scanning process seems not to have any obvious correlate in conscious experience. Subjects generally say either that they engage in a self-terminating search, or that they know immediately, with no search at all, whether the test stimulus is contained in the memorized list.

Is high-speed scanning used only when a list has just been memorized and is therefore relatively unfamiliar? The results discussed so far (Figure 1.4) are from the varied-set procedure (Figure 1.3), in which the subject must memorize a new positive set on each trial, and is tested only three seconds after its presentation. How is the retrieval process changed when a person is highly familiar with a particular positive set and has had a great deal of practice retrieving information from it? At the bottom of Figure 1.3 is shown *the fixed-set procedure* in the item-recognition paradigm, in which the same positive set is used for a long series of trials. For example, in one experiment (Exp. 2) subjects had 60 practice trials and 120 test trials for each positive set. On the average test trial, a subject had been working with the same positive set for ten minutes, rather than three seconds. The sets were sufficiently well learned that subjects could recall them several days later. Sets of one, two, and four digits were used. There were six subjects.

Results are shown in Figure 1.6, and are essentially identical to those from the varied-set procedure. The RT data are linear, the slopes for positive and negative responses are equal, and the average slope is 38 msec per digit. The small

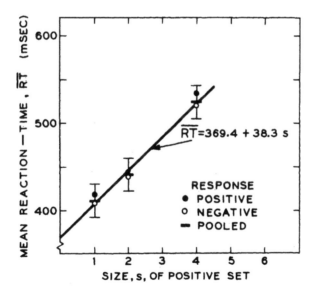

FIGURE 1.6

Results of Exp. 2: Item-recognition with fixed-set procedure. Mean latencies of correct positive, negative, and pooled responses as functions of size of positive set. Averaged data from six subjects, with estimates of ±σ about pooled means, and line fitted by least squares to those means. For each set size positive responses were required on 27% of the trials.

difference between the zero-intercepts in the two experiments is not statistically significant. The remarkable similarity of results from the two procedures indicates that the same retrieval process was used for both the unfamiliar and the well-learned lists.

5. ACTIVE AND INACTIVE MEMORY

Evidence has accumulated, particularly during the past decade, that there are at least two systems or states of memory for encoded verbal items (e.g., Broadbent, 1958; Waugh & Norman, 1965; Glanzer & Cunitz, 1966; Atkinson & Shiffrin, 1968). The picture that is emerging is roughly as follows: The *long-term store,* or *inactive memory,* is relatively permanent and of large capacity. It receives information from the *short-term store,* a temporary *active memory*[5] of small capacity from which information is rapidly lost unless an active retention process is operating. In the long-term store, the coding of verbal items includes semantic attributes; in the short-term store, however, such items are coded primarily as acoustic or articulatory representations of their spoken names, even when they have been presented visually (see Sperling, 1960; Conrad, 1964; Baddeley, 1966; Wickelgren, 1969). The active process that regenerates the rapidly-decaying traces of a list of items in the short-term store is *rehearsal,* the overtly- or silently-spoken cyclic serial recall of stored items (see Sanders, 1961; Sperling, 1963; Posner & Rossman, 1965; Cohen & Johansson, 1967; Crowder, 1967; Atkinson & Shiffrin, 1968). Rehearsal, which also causes information in the short-term store to be entered in the long-term store, has an approximate maximum rate of from three to seven items per second (Landauer, 1962).

Whereas in the varied-set procedure of Exp. 1 the positive set must have been stored in active memory only, it is reasonable to believe that the set had entered the long-term store in the fixed-set procedure of Exp. 2. However, the similarity of results from the two procedures suggests that the same memory system was being scanned: that is, when information in inactive memory has to be used, it may be entered also in active memory (where it is maintained by rehearsal) and thus become more readily available. An experiment that tests this conjecture is described below (Exp. 5).

It appears, then, that the memory of the positive sets in both tasks is maintained by a serial rehearsal process; supporting this notion, subjects reported silent rehearsal of the sets in both experiments. But the estimated rates of high-speed scanning and the fastest silent speech differ by a factor of at least four. Rehearsal is far too

5   An alternative term is "working memory," used by Newell & Simon, 1963, to refer to the arithmetic unit of a general-purpose computer. See also "Active verbal memory," Ch. 9 in Neisser, 1967, and "Operational memory," Sec. 4 in Posner, 1967.

slow to be identical to the scanning process. Instead, it should be thought of as a separate process whose only function in these tasks is to maintain the memory that is to be scanned.[6]

6. ENCODING OF THE TEST STIMULUS

In the scanning process inferred from these experiments, some internal representation of the test stimulus is compared to internal representations of the items in the positive set. What is the *nature* of the representations that can be compared at such high speed? Another way to phrase the question is to ask how much processing of the test stimulus occurs before it is compared to the memorized items.

Various considerations lead one to expect a good deal of preprocessing. For example, the idea that items held in active memory are retained as acoustic or articulatory representations of their spoken names introduces the possibility that the test stimulus is processed to the point of naming, and that the name of the test stimulus is compared to the names of the items in the positive set. But two points should be kept in mind regarding this possibility. First, it would require that stored names could be scanned much faster than they could be covertly articulated, since the scanning rate is about four times as fast as people can say names of digits to themselves. Second, unlike other forms of preprocessing, such as image-sharpening or feature-extraction, preprocessing a character to the point of identification or naming would itself require the retrieval of information from memory—that information which relates the character to its name.

In one experiment bearing on this question (Exp. 3), I degraded the test stimulus by superimposing a pattern that had been adjusted to increase the RT without substantially altering the error rate. I then examined the effect of stimulus quality on the function that relates mean RT and the size of the positive set. It is shown below that this effect would depend on the nature of the internal representation of the test-stimulus.

Figure 1.7 shows idealized data from a scanning experiment. The zero-intercept corresponds to the total duration of all processes that occur just once, regardless of the size of the positive set—such as the encoding of the test stimulus to form its representation, and the organization and execution of the motor response. The slope, on the other hand, measures the duration of processes that occur once for each member of the positive set—the comparison operation, and the time to switch

---

6 It is sometimes thought that the six or seven objects in the "span of apprehension" are immediately and simultaneously available, being contained in the "psychological present." And the information in active memory has occasionally been identified with this momentary capacity of consciousness (e.g., Miller, 1962, pp. 47-49; Waugh & Norman, 1965). The finding that one must scan one's active memory to ascertain its contents, rather than having immediate access to them, reveals a possible flaw in this argument.

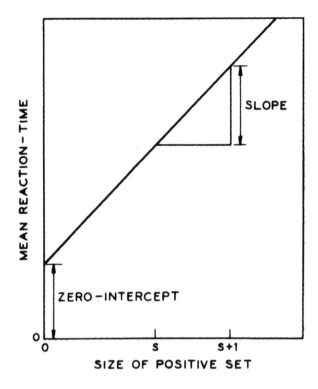

FIGURE 1.7

Idealization of mean RT-function from an item-recognition task.

from one item to the next.[7] Figure 1.8 shows a flow diagram of some hypothetical stages between test stimulus and response. The height of a box represents the mean duration of that stage. An effect of stimulus degradation on the *stimulus-encoding stage*, which generates the stimulus representation, would increase the zero-intercept of the RT-function. An effect on the *serial-comparison stage* would increase the slope, since a time increment would be added for each item compared.

Consider two extreme possibilities: First, suppose that the encoding stage did nothing other than transmit an unprocessed image, or direct copy, of the test stimulus. Then degradation could influence only the comparison operation, which occurs once for each member of the positive set; only the slope of the RT-function would change, as in Panel A of Figure 1.9. At the other extreme, suppose that the representation produced by the encoding stage was the *name* of the test stimulus.

---

7   This analysis assumes that the mean durations of comparisons leading to matches and to mismatches are equal. Without this assumption all the statements here (and elsewhere in the paper) are correct, except that the slope of the RT-function measures the mean duration of only those comparisons that lead to mismatches, together with the time to switch from one comparison to the next. Any difference between durations of the two kinds of comparison would contribute to a difference between zero intercepts of the latency functions for positive and negative responses.

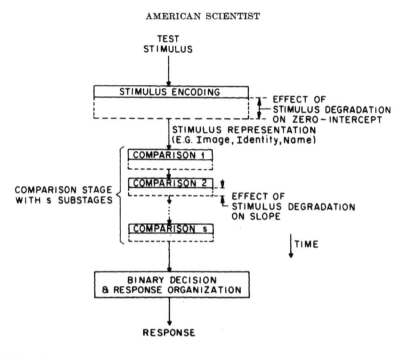

FIGURE 1.8

Some hypothetical stages and substages in item-recognition, and two possible effects of test-stimulus quality on stage and substage durations. Height of box represents mean duration of that stage or substage.

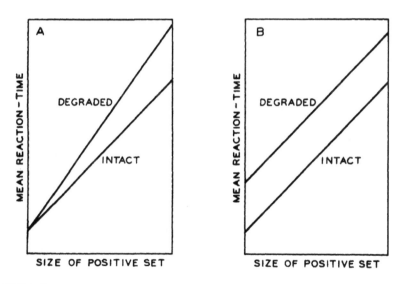

FIGURE 1.9

Two possibilities for the effect of test-stimulus quality on the RT-function. A: Quality influences comparison stage only. B: Quality influences encoding stage only.

The input to the serial-comparison stage would be the same, whether or not the test stimulus had been degraded by a superimposed visual pattern; hence degradation could not influence this stage. (For the serial-comparison stage to be influenced by visual degradation, its input would have to be visual, in the sense of embodying details of the physical stimulus pattern that are not present in the mere name of the stimulus.) Only the encoding stage, then, could be influenced by degradation; and since encoding takes place just once, only the zero-intercept of the RT-function would change, as in Panel B of Figure 1.9. (The absence of a change in slope, however, does not necessarily imply a nonvisual stimulus-representation; the representation could be visual, but highly processed.)

In Exp. 3 each of twelve subjects had positive sets of one, two, and four digits, with test stimuli *intact* in some blocks of trials, and in others *degraded* by a superimposed checkerboard pattern. Intact and degraded numerals are shown in Figure 1.10.

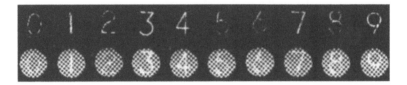

FIGURE 1.10

Photographs of intact and degraded numerals used in Exp. 3. Numerals were about 0.6 in. high and were viewed from a distance of about 29 in. Degraded numerals were somewhat more discriminable than they appear in the black-and-white photograph, possibly because of a slight color difference between numerals and checkerboard.

The fixed-set procedure was used. Results for the two sessions are shown separately in Figure 1.11. Consider first the data from the second session, on the right-hand side of the figure. Latencies of positive and negative responses have been averaged together. The functions for degraded and intact stimuli are almost parallel, but there is a large effect on the zero-intercept, closely approximating the pattern shown in Panel B of Figure 1.9. This indicates that degradation had a large influence on the stimulus-encoding stage, and that the representation generated was sufficiently processed that the serial-comparison stage could proceed as rapidly with degraded as with intact stimuli. The stimulus representation was either nonvisual or, if visual, sufficiently refined in the second session to eliminate any effect of degradation.

The data from this session are an instance of the *additivity* of two effects on RT. There is no interaction between the effect of set size and the effect of stimulus quality; instead, the effect of each of these factors on mean RT is independent of the level of the other. Such additivity supports the theory of a sequence of stages, one stage influenced by stimulus quality and the other by set size (see Sec. 7).

Now let us consider the data from the first session, shown on the left-hand side of Figure 1.11. Here, where subjects have not yet had much practice with the super-imposed checkerboard, there is a 20% increase in the slope of the RT-function, as well as an increase in its zero-intercept. This pattern agrees with neither of the pure cases of Figure 1.9. Stimulus quality apparently *can* influence the duration of comparison operations; hence, the output of the encoding stage must be sensitive to degradation. Findings from the two sessions imply, then, that although the stimulus representation is highly processed, it embodies physical attributes of the test stimulus, rather than being a name or identity. That is, the test-stimulus representation is visual. The memory representations of the positive set that are used in the serial-comparison stage must therefore also be visual, to make comparison possible. Hence, although items in the positive set appear to be represented as covertly-spoken names in the course of their rehearsal, this is not the only form in which they are available.

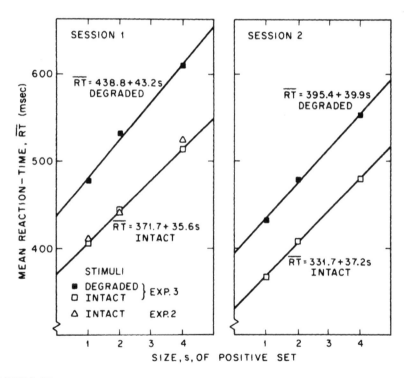

FIGURE 1.11

Results of Exp. 3: Effect of stimulus quality on item-recognition. Mean RT, based on pooled data from positive and negative responses, as a function of size of positive set for intact and degraded test stimuli. Left-hand and right-hand panels show data from Sessions 1 and 2, respectively. Averaged data from 12 subjects, with lines fitted by least squares. In all conditions positive responses were required on 27% of the trials. Triangles show results from Exp. 2 (Figure 1.6), which was similar.

What changed between the first and second sessions so as to virtually eliminate the influence of stimulus quality on the slope of the RT-function? Since the scanning rate with intact stimuli and the effect of degradation on the zero-intercept are approximately the same in the two sessions, it seems unlikely that the type of representation changed. For the present, my interpretation is that the encoding stage became more efficient at removing the effects of the fixed degrading pattern.

Additional support for the idea that the memory representations scanned in the item-recognition task have sensory characteristics, rather than being completely abstracted from the physical stimuli, comes from two other studies. In the first, Chase and Calfee (1969) created four different conditions in the varied-set procedure by representing both the positive set and the test stimulus either visually or aurally. When the set and test item were presented in different modalities, the slope of the RT-function increased by about 30%, indicating a slower scanning rate. If abstract representations were being compared in the same-modality conditions, then the change to different-modality conditions should have altered only the zero-intercept, as in Figure 1.9B. In the second study, Posner, *et al.* (1969), concluded that when a single letter is presented *aurally* for memorization, the decision whether a *visual* test-letter is the "same" is facilitated by the internal generation of a visual representation of the memorized letter, which obviates the need to identify the test letter. Still further evidence will be discussed below (Exp. 4).

7. A TEST OF THE STAGE THEORY

The work described above is grounded on Donders' stage theory. That is, as in his subtraction method, the effects on mean RT of changes in experimental conditions (factors) have been attributed to the selective effects of these factors on hypothetical processing stages between stimulus and response. How can we ensure that such inferences are not open to the classical criticism of the subtraction method, that even if information processing *is* organized in functionally different stages, factor effects may not be selective? One answer, of course, is that the test of a method's applicability is whether it produces results that fit together and make sense. But there are two other arguments as well.

The first stems from replacement of the assumption of pure insertion by a weaker and more plausible *assumption of selective influence*. Instead of requiring that a change in the task insert or delete an entire processing stage without altering others, the weaker assumption requires only that it influence the *duration* of some stage without altering others. One example is illustrated in Figure 1.12. To estimate the comparison time by the subtraction method, one would have studied Task 2, in which the positive set has one member, and compared it to a Task 1. Task 1 would have been constructed to measure the zero-intercept directly, by deleting the

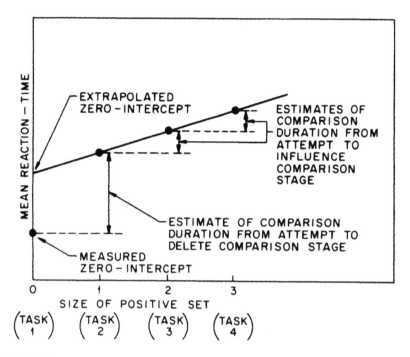

FIGURE 1.12

Example of error from hypothetical attempt to estimate comparison time by deleting the comparison stage altogether, as in the subtraction method, and to use a measured zero intercept. Attempt fails because *deletion* of comparison stage changes the demands placed on other stages, whereas *variation* of the number of comparisons, s, $(s \geq 1)$ does not.

entire comparison stage. But I suspect that there *is* no appropriate Task 1, in which deletion of all comparisons would leave the other stages of processing invariant. In this instance, then, the assumption of pure insertion is probably invalid. This is why the important RT-differences in the experiments described above were those between Tasks 2 and 3, 3 and 4, and so on, whose interpretation required only that the comparison stage be selectively *influenced* by set size. Similarly, in studying the preprocessing of the stimulus, instead of entirely eliminating the need to discriminate the stimulus (in an effort to *delete* the hypothetical encoding stage) I examined the effects of making its discrimination more or less difficult, thereby varying the amount of work the stage had to accomplish. Of course, one result of using a factor that influences but does not insert a stage is that we have no estimate of the stage's total duration. But that seems to be of less interest than whether there is such a stage, what influences it, what it accomplishes, and what its relation is to other stages.[8]

In a given experimental situation the validity of even the weaker assumption of selective influence must be checked, however. We can distinguish those situations where one of the assumptions—influence or insertion—holds, by testing the additivity of the effects of two or more factors on mean RT (Sternberg, 1969). It is this test that provides the second and most telling way of dealing with the classical criticism. Consider a pair of hypothetical stages and a pair of experimental factors, with each factor inserting or selectively influencing one of the stages. Because stage durations are additive (by definition), the changes in mean RT produced by such factors should be independent and additive. That is, the effect of one factor will be the same at all levels of the other, when the response is measured on a scale of time or its (arithmetic) mean.[9]

In experiments with the fixed-set procedure I have examined four factors, which are listed above the broken line in Figure 1.13. The additivity of five of the six possible factor pairs has been tested and confirmed (1&2, after a session of practice, 1&3, 2&3, 2&4, and 3&4). These instances of additivity support the assumption that the factors selectively influence different stages of processing and, *a fortiori*, confirm the existence of such stages. Another instance of additivity, and the one on which inferences about the structure of the comparison stage strongly depend, is represented by the linearity of the effect of set size: the effect of adding an item to the positive set is independent of the number of items already in the set. Together with other considerations (discussed in Sternberg, 1969) these findings lead to the analysis into processing stages and substages shown below the broken line in Figure. 1.13.[10]

---

8   This alternative was preferred by Cattell, 1886, who argued (p. 378) "I do not think it is possible to add a perception to the reaction without also adding a will-act. We can however change the nature of the perception without altering the will-time, and thus investigate with considerable thoroughness the length of the perception time." But he suggested no way to test these assertions.

9   Discussions of various other aspects and modern versions of the subtraction method, including considerations of validity, may be found in Hohle, 1967; McGill & Gibbon, 1965; McMahon, 1963; Smith, 1968; Sternberg, 1964; Sternberg, 1969; and Taylor, 1966.

10   The linear interaction between stimulus quality and set size in Session 1 is attributed to an "indirect" influence of stimulus quality on the duration of the second stage, by way of its effect on the output of the first stage (see Sec. 6, and Sternberg, 1967b). Thus one may sometimes infer a separate stage even when its output is not invariant with respect to a factor that influences its duration, and when as a consequence there is a failure of additivity. In this instance the inference is justified by the form of the interaction (a *linear* increase in the effect of degradation with set size), and the structure of the comparison stage (inferred to be a series of substages).

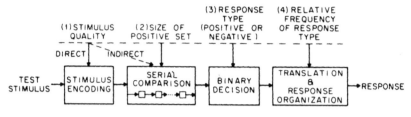

FIGURE 1.13

Four processing stages in item-recognition. Above the broken line are shown the four factors examined. Below the line is shown the decomposition of RT inferred from additive relations between factor pairs 1&2, 1&3, 2&3, 2&4, and 3&4, the linear effect of factor 2, and other considerations. (The indirect effect of factor 1 on the comparison stage, and the resulting interaction of factors 1&2, is seen in unpracticed subjects only.)

8. GENERALITY OF HIGH-SPEED SCANNING

Let us turn now to more substantive matters, and consider the generality of the high-speed exhaustive scanning process. Binary classification of digits into sets that are small, randomly-assembled, and relatively unfamiliar is hardly a typical example of memory retrieval. But it is useful to pin down one process fairly well, and explore techniques that reveal it in a relatively pure form, in order to use it as a baseline for the study of other mechanisms.[11]

For one example of a possible alternative to serial search, consider the case where the items in a memorized set share a physical feature whose presence distinguishes them from the rest of the stimulus ensemble. Here one might expect subjects to test the stimulus for the presence of the feature rather than compare it to the items in the set one by one. Surprisingly, using letters with a diagonal line-segment as the distinguishing feature, Yonas (1969) showed that subjects start by scanning the set; only after considerable practice do they use the feature test, thereby eliminating the effect of the number of letters in the set.

Another possible alternative to serial search is an "associative" process. Consider the case in which positive items are distinguished by membership in a well-learned category. (For example, the positive set might contain digits only, and the negative set, letters.) To each member of a category is associatively linked its category label, and the binary choice depends on which label is elicited by the test stimulus. The speed of such a process might be independent of the sizes of positive and negative

11   The function of such an experimental baseline is similar to the use of well-understood mathematical models as theoretical baselines (Sternberg, 1963, Sec. 6.6) in which it is the discrepancies between data and model that are of interest.

sets (although it might depend on various attributes of the categories that contained them, including *their* sizes; see Landauer & Freedman, 1968). On the other hand, the high speed of scanning might make it more efficient than an associative process, when one of the sets is small. In short, there may be alternative mechanisms for the same task, and which one is used may depend, in part, on which one is more efficient. If this is the case it is a great advantage to understand at least one of the alternatives in some detail.

9. RETRIEVAL OF NONSYMBOLIC VERSUS SYMBOLIC INFORMATION

Other questions about the generality of the scanning process are raised by its high speed, which precludes its being identified with the subvocalization of numeral names, and also by the influence of stimulus-quality on the scanning rate in Exp. 3 (Sec. 6), which indicates that the stimulus representation is not the name or identity of the numeral. The fact that numerals are patterns with extremely well-learned names may therefore be irrelevant to the scanning process. Of course, numerals have other special properties: they are highly familiar, they are symbols, they represent numerical quantities, and people are practiced at manipulating the numbers they represent. A. M. Treisman and I recently tested the importance of these properties for memory retrieval, using two different ensembles, one of non-sense forms, and the other of photographs of faces (Exp. 4). To our subjects, both ensembles were unfamiliar, non-symbolic, unordered, and without well-learned names. We used the fixed-set procedure with sets of size 1 to 4, but found it neces-sary to display the positive set before each trial in order to help the subjects, who were inexperienced, to maintain it in active memory.

RT data, shown in Figure 1.14, are qualitatively the same as those for digit sets. They show linearity, suggesting a serial process, and equality of slopes for positive and negative responses, indicating exhaustiveness of search. The main difference is in the scanning rate, which seems to depend to some extent on the nature of the stimuli. Even for faces, however, the estimated rate is high—about 18 faces per second. These findings indicate that high-speed exhaustive scanning does not depend on the special properties of numerals mentioned above. They also add further support to the conclusion that the test-stimulus representation in the case of numerals is not the name of the numeral, but is some sort of visual representation.

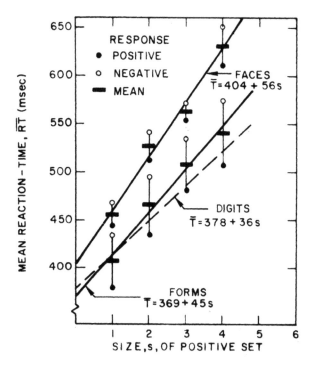

FIGURE 1.14

Results of Exp. 4: Item-recognition with nonsense forms and photographs of faces. Mean latencies of correct positive and negative responses, and their mean, as a function of size of positive set for the two stimulus ensembles. Averaged data from eight subjects for each ensemble, with lines fitted by least squares to means. Broken line was fitted to data from a similar experiment wtih an ensemble of numerals.

10. RETRIEVAL FROM INACTIVE VERSUS ACTIVE MEMORY

A further question about the generality of the high-speed scanning process is raised by the conjecture (Sec. 5) that it occurs only when information is being held in active memory. The similarity of results from the varied-set and fixed-set procedures led to the idea that even when a list is contained in long-term memory, it is transferred into active memory and maintained there by rehearsal in order to be used in the item-recognition task. If that is so, one would expect some change in the process if one prevented the relevant list from being rehearsed (for example, by occupying the active memory with other material). This kind of procedure moves us closer to studying the differences between retrieval from the short-term (active) and long-term (inactive) stores, and thereby understanding the latter by using the former as a baseline.

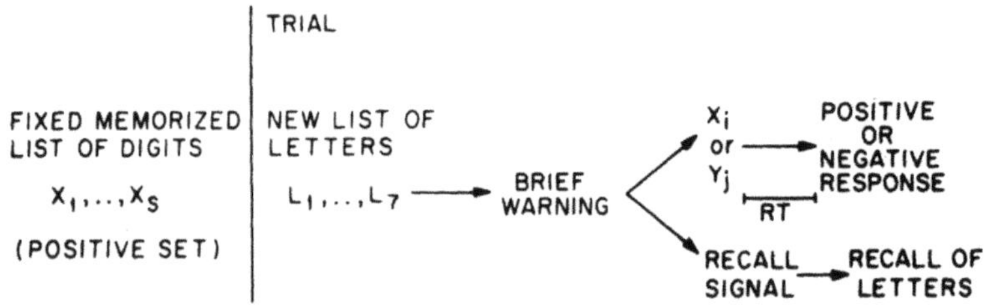

FIGURE 1.15

Paradigm of Exp. 5: Item-recognition from active and inactive memory. Only the inactive-memory condition is shown. In the active-memory condition, also involving a fixed-set procedure (Figure 1.3), no letters were presented.

The procedure in a small preliminary experiment (Exp. 5) is shown in Figure 1.15. At the start of a series of trials the subject memorized a list of 1, 3, or 5 digits, which defined the positive set for the entire series. On each trial a new list of seven letters was presented sequentially, at a rate of two letters per second. A short time after the last letter, there was a brief warning signal, and then one of two things could happen. On a random third of the trials the subject saw a recall signal, and attempted to recall the seven letters. These trials were used in order to encourage the subject to attend to the letters and retain them in memory until the test event. (Observing and retaining the list of letters was intended to occupy his active memory on all trials and prevent him from rehearsing the positive set.) On the remaining trials the subject saw a test digit. He was required to make a positive or negative response, based on the previously memorized digit set, as quickly as possible consistent with accuracy. This is a difficult task, and required a session of practice for smooth performance. In the series of control trials, which alternated with series of experimental trials, no lists of letters were presented.

Data averaged over the four subjects in this preliminary experiment are shown in Figure 1.16. The lower set of points represents performance in the control condition, which was similar in procedure to Exp. 2. Mainly because of one exceptional subject, the fitted line is somewhat steeper than usual, with a slope of 57 msec per digit. Otherwise the data are typical. In the experimental condition the fitted line is about twice as steep as in the control condition, with a slope of 105 msec per digit. Again, the latencies of positive and negative responses grow at equal rates as set size is increased. The zero-intercepts in the experimental and control conditions differ also, by over 100 msec.

Evidently, the retrieval process is radically altered, with the effective scanning rate halved, when the information to be retrieved is not being rehearsed and is therefore not in active memory. Current notions about the functions of

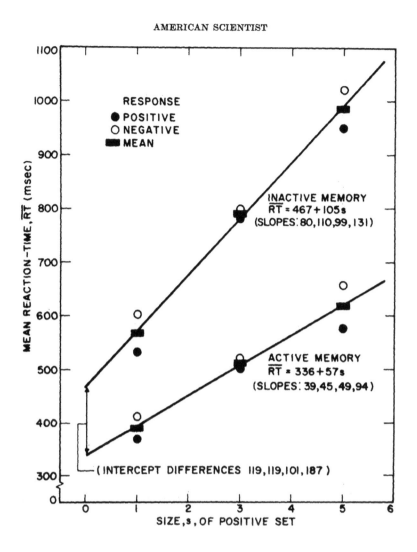

AMERICAN SCIENTIST

FIGURE 1.16

Results of Exp. 5: Item-recognition from active and inactive memory. Mean latencies of correct positive and negative responses, and their mean, as functions of size of positive set, in conditions of active and inactive memory. Averaged data from four subjects, with lines fitted by least squares to means. Intercept differences and slopes for the four subjects are listed, the order of subjects being the same in each list.

rehearsal include maintenance of short-term memory, and transfer of information into long-term memory (see Sec. 5). The results of Exp. 5 suggest a third role—that of making information already stored in long-term memory more rapidly accessible.

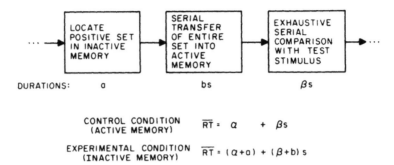

FIGURE 1.17

One explanation of results of Exp. 5. Left and middle boxes represent hypothetical stages that might be inserted in the inactive-memory condition. Also shown are hypothesized durations of these two stages and the comparison stage, and resulting theoretical RT-functions in which α represents the zero-intercept of the RT-function in the active-memory condition.

At this point there is little basis for selecting among potential explanations for the data from the experimental condition, but experiments are under way that may help to do so. The explanation that I favor, shown in Figure 1.17, is the one that makes plausible two striking aspects of the data: despite the large effect of condition, the linearity of the RT-function and the equality of slopes for positive and negative responses are both preserved. The first two boxes in the figure represent hypothetical stages that might be present in the experimental condition but not in the control. One might be searching for the positive set in inactive memory. This would take a fixed time, regardless of the size of the positive set, and could account for the increase in the zero-intercept. The second added stage might be the serial transfer of each item in the positive set into active memory, with a fixed average time per item transferred, estimated from the data to be about 50 msec. Since all items would be transferred, whether the required response was positive or negative, the slopes of the functions for both responses would be increased by the same amount. The high-speed scanning stage, which we already know to be exhaustive, would follow. The two added stages are plausible and would account for the important features of the data. But this explanation—particularly the concept of "transferring a set of items into active memory"—needs to be made more precise and then tested.

11. AN EXPLANATION OF EXHAUSTIVENESS

As mentioned in Sec. 3, an exhaustive search must involve more comparisons, on the average, than a search that terminates when a match occurs. The exhaustiveness of the high-speed scanning process therefore appears inefficient, and hence implausible. Why continue the comparison process beyond the point at which a match occurs? Figure 1.18 illustrates a system in which an exhaustive search could be more efficient than a self-terminating one for performance in an item-recognition task. A representation of the test stimulus is placed in a comparator. When the scanner is being operated by the "central processor" or "homunculus," H, it delivers memory representations of the items in the list, one after another, to the comparator. If and when a match occurs a signal is delivered to the match register. The important feature of the system is that the homunculus can *either* operate the scanner *or* examine the register. It cannot engage in both of these functions at once, and switching between them takes time.

In this kind of system, if the switching time is long relative to the scanning rate, and if the list is sufficiently short, then an exhaustive search (in which the match register must be examined only once) is more efficient than a self-terminating one (where the register would have to be examined after each comparison). The surprisingly high speed of the scanning process may therefore be made possible by its exhaustiveness. But such a system might have at least one important limitation.

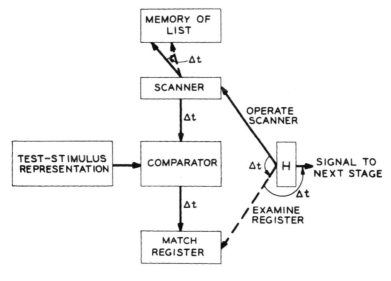

FIGURE 1.18

A system in which exhaustive scanning could be more efficient than self-terminating scanning. Some loci of possible time delays are represented by Δts.

After the search was completed, there might be no information available (without further reference to the memory of the list) as to the location in the list of the item that produced the match. The limitation would create no difficulty if the response required of the subject depended only on the presence or absence of an item in the list and not on its location, as in the item-recognition task. But the possibility that high-speed scanning does not yield location information does suggest an experiment to test this theory of exhaustiveness. Suppose we require a subject to give a response that *does* depend on where in the list a matching item is located. Then after each comparison, with information still available as to the location of the item just compared to the test stimulus (e.g., preserved by the position of the scanner in Figure 1.18), it would have to be determined whether this item produced a match (by the homunculus switching from scanner to register). Scanning should then be slower than when only presence or absence has to be judged; it should also be self-terminating, since further comparisons after a match had been detected would be superfluous. Such a process will be called *scanning to locate*.

12. RETRIEVAL OF CONTEXTUAL INFORMATION BY SCANNING TO LOCATE

In Figure 1.19 is shown the paradigm of a *context-recall task*, one of the experiments devised to test these ideas (Exp. 6). On each trial the subject memorized a new random list of from three to seven different digits, presented visually one after another. The length of the list was varied at random from trial to trial. After a delay and a

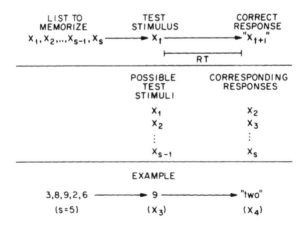

FIGURE 1.19

Paradigm of Exp. 6: Context-recall.

warning signal, a test item was presented, randomly selected from among all the digits in the list except the last. The test item, then, was always present in the list. The correct response was the spoken name of the item that followed the test item in the memorized list. The idea was that in order to make this response—that is, to recall an item defined by its contextual relation to the test item—the location of the test item in the list might first have to be determined. As in the other experiments described, subjects were encouraged to respond as rapidly as possible, while attempting to maintain a low error rate.

Two aspects of the data are of particular interest: the relation between mean RT and list length; and the relation, for a list of given length, between RT and the serial position of the test item in the list.

Data averaged over six subjects are shown in Figure 1.20. Consider first Panel A. The bars show the percentage of wrong responses, which rises to 25% for lists of length 7. This is much higher than one would like, given an interest in error-free performance. The effect of list-length on mean RT is roughly linear, suggesting a scanning process. (Even closer approximations to linearity have been found in other similar experiments.) With a slope of 124 msec per item, the fitted line is much steeper than the corresponding RT-function in the item-recognition task.

To interpret the slope, we have first to establish if the process is self-terminating, as expected. Evidence on this point is provided by the average serial-position functions shown in Panel B. For each list length, mean RT is plotted as a function of the serial position of the test item in the memorized list. These functions are all

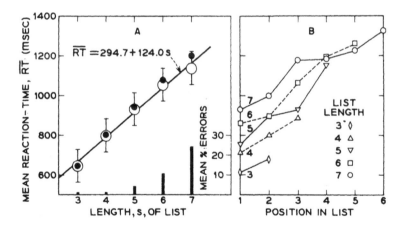

FIGURE 1.20

Results of Exp. 6: Context-recall. Averaged data from six subjects. A: Effect of list length on percent errors (bars), on mean latency of correct responses (open circles) with estimates of ±σ and line fitted by least squares, and on mean RT of all responses (filled circles). B: Relation between mean RT of correct responses and serial position of the test item in lists of five lengths.

increasing, suggesting a self-terminating process that tends to start at the beginning of the list and proceed in serial order.

Now we can interpret the slope of the function in Panel A, if we assume that list length influences only the scanning stage. (Evidence supporting this assumption of selective influence is presented below.) Since an average of about half the items in a list have to be scanned before a match occurs, the slope represents half of the time per item, and implies a scanning rate of about 250 msec per item, or four items per second, in scanning to locate an item in a memorized list. Scanning to locate is therefore about seven times as slow as the high-speed scanning process used to determine the presence of an item in a list. The slowness of the search, and the fact it is self-terminating, lend support to the explanation (Sec. 11) of the exhaustiveness of the high-speed process. Scanning to locate seems to be fundamentally different from scanning for presence.[12]

As mentioned earlier (Sec. 3), if a self-terminating process started consistently at the beginning of a list and proceeded serially, the serial-position functions would be steep and superimposed, whereas if it started at a random point they would be flat and separated. The functions shown in Panel B lie between these extremes. This is partly because they represent averages of data from several subjects. Data from two subjects in Exp. 6 who represent almost pure cases are shown in Figure 1.21. The estimated scanning rates for these two subjects are almost the same, but their starting strategies appear to be radically different. Subject 1 seems to have started at a random point. This could occur if the presentation of the test item interrupted an ongoing cyclic rehearsal process, and scanning then began at the serial position where rehearsal happened to have stopped. Subject 4, on the other hand, has the superimposed functions that would arise if he had started scanning consistently at the beginning of the list, perhaps by terminating his rehearsal before the test-stimulus appeared. Data from other subjects range between these extremes, presumably because of mixed starting strategies.

One explanation of these results is the following: In order to recall a contextual item, the subject must first determine the test item's location in the memorized list. This is achieved by a slow, self-terminating process of scanning to locate, in which the items in memory are compared successively to the test item until a match occurs. Each nonmatching item that participates contributes to the RT a component time

---

12 Alternative explanations of the dissimilarity of the two kinds of scanning are possible, of course. One interesting alternative (which existing data cannot reject) is that memory representations that can carry order information are different from those that need only carry item information, and that the observed differences in retrieval result from the fact that different kinds of memory representations are being scanned. However, for this alternative explanation to apply to Exp. 1 (in which subjects had to recognize an item and then recall the entire list in order), it must be possible for both kinds of memory representation to be maintained simultaneously.

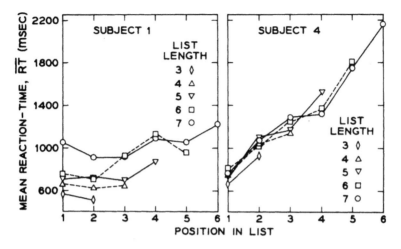

FIGURE 1.21

Individual data from Exp. 6: Context-recall. Contrasting sets of serial-position functions in lists of five lengths, one set relatively flat and separated, the other steep and, in general, superimposed.

that depends neither on list length nor on the item's position in the list. This component time is occupied by switching to the item, comparing it to the test stimulus, and determining that they have not matched. In the present context-recall task, the occurrence of a match is followed by a shift (e.g., a movement of the scanner in Figure 1.18) from the item that matches the test item to the adjacent response item. For superimposed serial-position functions (as in Figure 1.21) to be possible, we must assume that the duration of the shift operation (as well as other stages, such as stimulus-encoding and response-organization) is independent of the length of the list. Given this assumption, the slope of the RT-function is determined solely by the scanning rate.

The process of scanning to locate is a still more dramatic instance of having to hunt for information even when it is contained in a list that is being rehearsed. In some important sense one does not know what is in one's active memory, other than the single item to which attention is currently directed.[13]

---

13 One traditional view is that the structure of a memorized list is a chain of overlapping associated pairs of items: the subject's task in a context-recall experiment is thought of as the performance of one of the associations in the chain, and the RT measure as an index of associative strength. At the least, this view must be modified to recognize the existence of a search for the representation of the test item in the list. This search is an instance of the obligatory process (usually ignored by association theorists) that locates and activates the memory trace of a stimulus before an associative response to that stimulus can be performed (Rock, 1962). Furthermore, in this experiment, not only does the locating process produce the dominant effect, but also there appears to be *no* influence of associative strength (Sec. 13). One might therefore question whether the traditional view is at all appropriate, at least for lists contained in active memory. It has been challenged from other directions also in recent years (e.g., Slamecka, 1967).

13. INDEPENDENCE OF LEARNING AND RETRIEVAL FROM ACTIVE MEMORY

One problem with Exp. 6 is the high error rate, and its marked increase with list length (Figure 1.20A). This makes the RT data somewhat suspect and violates the aim of studying error-free processes. Moreover, it raises the possibility that the level of learning of the list, which is clearly lower for longer lists, might be contributing to the increase of RT with list length. (For example, suppose that a list embodies a chain of associations and that the recall of a contextual item involves the performance of one of the associations. If the associations in a longer list are weaker, then at least one of the sources of the effect of list length on RT might be an increased associative latency.) In an experiment (Exp. 7) devised to look into these matters, the list was presented once, twice, or three times, as shown in Figure 1.22, to vary how well it was learned. In the one-presentation condition, at the bottom of the figure, the list was presented, and there followed a test stimulus and response, just as in Exp. 6. Again, the list changed from trial to trial, and contained from 3 to 7 digits. In the two-presentation condition, each trial included an additional presentation of its list and an attempt to recall it. In the three-presentation condition there was still another presentation and recall of the list.

Results from six subjects are shown in Figure 1.23. At the bottom, the percentage of errors in naming the succeeding digit is shown as a function of list length, for each condition. Added presentations reduced the error rate by a factor of three. At the top of the figure, mean RT is shown as a function of list length, for each of the three conditions. Despite the change in level of learning indicated by the error data, the pattern of RTs shows no systematic change with number of presentations.

This invariance indicates that differences in level of learning that are associated with list length do not contribute to the influence of list length on mean RT; and further, that within the limits of the experiment, the rate of scanning to locate

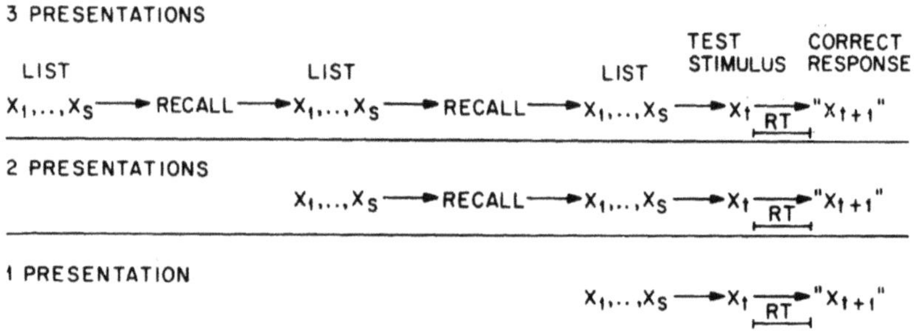

FIGURE 1.22

Conditions in Exp. 7: Effect of learning on context-recall.

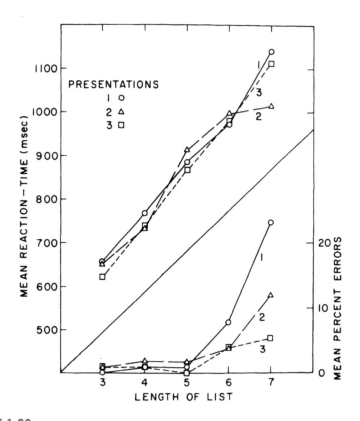

FIGURE 1.23

Results of Exp. 7: Effect of learning on context-recall. Averaged data from six subjects for one, two, and three presentations of the list. Bottom: mean percent errors in naming contextual item. Top: mean latency of correct responses.

is independent of how well a list has been learned.[14] The invariance with level of learning, which is similar to that of the high-speed scanning process over fixed-set and varied-set procedures, is consistent with the interpretation of the context-recall data presented in Sec. 11, and adds to the evidence that factors well known to influence learning may have no effect on active-memory functioning. Finally, given the invariance of the retrieval process, the strong influence of number of presentations on error rate suggests that the errors result primarily from faults in learning and retention, rather than in retrieval.

---

14   If a list could only be either perfectly learned or not learned at all, this conclusion would not be justified, since restricting the latencies analyzed to those of correct responses would entail the selection of lists that had been learned to the same degree (perfectly) in the three conditions. This objection does not apply here, mainly because correct responses in conjunction with *partially*-learned lists were frequent.

14. RECALL VERSUS RECOGNITION OF CONTEXTUAL INFORMATION

In explaining the difference between findings from the item-recognition and con-text-recall tasks (Exps. 1-5 *versus* Exps. 6-7) I have emphasized that in one case the response depends merely on presence of an item in the list, and in the other case on its exact location. For an explanation in these terms to be valid, however, certain other differences between the tasks must be shown to be unimportant: one task involves recall, and the other recognition; one requires that for production of the response a memory representation be converted into a particular form—its name—and the other does not; and whereas the number of response alternatives in one task grows with list length, the other always requires a binary choice.

The last experiment to be described (Exp. 8) was designed to evaluate the importance of these factors and to examine further the generality of the process of scanning to locate. A recognition procedure was used to study the retrieval of contextual information; the resulting *context-recognition task* is shown in Figure 1.24. On each trial the subject attempted to memorize a list of from 3 to 6 different digits, presented visually, one after another. To increase accuracy, the list was actually presented twice, with a recall attempt after the first presentation. The test stimulus was a pair of simultaneously presented digits that had appeared successively somewhere in the list. The subject's task was to decide whether the left-to-right order of the pair was the same as its temporal order in the list, or reversed. He made his response by pulling one of two levers (as in Exps. 1-5).

This experiment seemed to be somewhat risky, since there appeared to be a variety of strategies open to the subject. One possibility was that before its order could

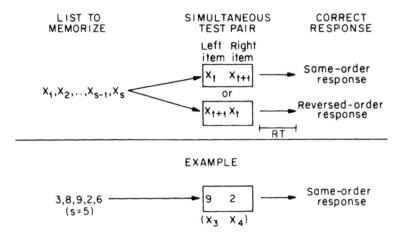

FIGURE 1.24

Paradigm of Exp. 8: Context-recognition.

be tested, the pair might have to be located in the list by means of a scanning process. This process would be revealed by the relation between RT and the length of the list. Suppose that the test pair is located in the list by scanning for the location of one of its members, according to the self-terminating process described in Sec. 11. One would then expect that in the context-recognition task mean RT for both same-order and reversed-order responses would increase linearly with list length, and at equal rates, and that the rate of increase would be the same as in the context-recall task.

The same six subjects who performed the context-recall task of Exp. 7 also served (in a balanced order) in the recognition task. RT-functions for both responses (Figure 1.25) are linear, supporting the notion that in this task, also, performance

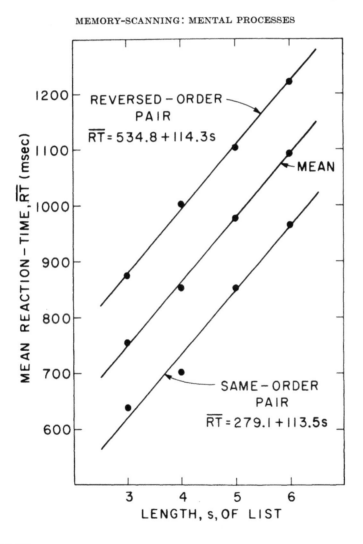

MEMORY-SCANNING: MENTAL PROCESSES

FIGURE 1.25

Results of Exp. 8: Context-recognition. Averaged data from six subjects. Mean latencies of correct same-order and reversed-order responses, and their mean, with lines fitted by least squares.

MEMORY-SCANNING: MENTAL PROCESSES

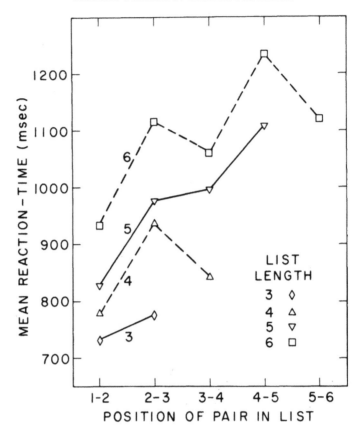

FIGURE 1.26

Further results of Exp. 8: Context-recognition. Relation between mean RT of correct responses and serial position of the test pair in lists of four lengths. Data were averaged over six subjects and over same-order and reversed-order responses.

involves a scanning process. For both responses the slope of the fitted line is 114 msec per item.[15] The equality of slopes is consistent with the idea that both responses depend on first locating one of the members of the pair in the list. That this is accomplished by means of a self-terminating process is suggested by the serial-position data: for all subjects, and for both responses, mean RT increased with the serial position of the pair in the list. Averaged serial-position data are shown in Figure 1.26.

RT-functions from the context-recognition and context-recall tasks (Exps. 7 and 8) are compared in Figure 1.27. The fitted lines are parallel, supporting the idea that

15   Although equal in slope, the RT-functions for the two kinds of response differ by about 250 msec in intercept. The several ways in which one might account for this difference are not discussed in this paper.

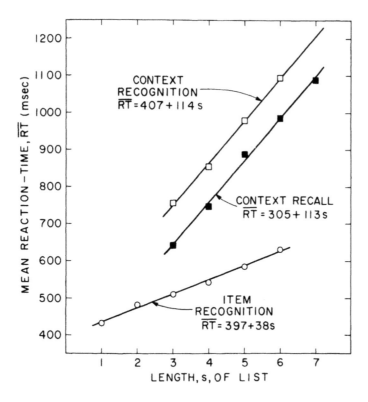

FIGURE 1.27

Comparison of results from context-recognition, context-recall, and item-recognition tasks. Top: Mean RTs from Exp. 8 (Figure 1.24), averaged over same-order and reversed-order responses. Middle: Mean RTs averaged over the three conditions in the context-recall task of Exp. 7 (Figure 1.22), which used the same subjects as Exp. 8. Bottom: Mean RTs from Exp. 1 (Figure 1.4).

the same search process (scanning to locate) underlies performance in both tasks. Also shown, for reference, is the RT-function from the item-recognition task of Exp. 1.

These parallel lines provide another striking instance of additive effects on mean RT. Here the additive factors are task (context-recognition *versus* recall) and list length; the absence of interaction indicates that these factors influence processing stages selectively, and helps to justify our interpretations of the data. Apparently, the change from recall to recognition does not influence the scanning stage, and, as assumed in Sec. 12, changes in list length do not influence perceptual and response stages.

One final substantive point about these results concerns their implications for the recognition-recall distinction. It is tempting to think that recognition involves less search, in some sense, than recall. These data reveal at least one search process that is as evident in a recognition task (Exp. 8) as in a recall task (Exp. 7).

SUMMARY

I have reviewed informally eight experiments on the retrieval of information from human memory, whose interpretation depended on inferences from the structure of RT data to the organization of mental processes. The experiments have led to the discovery of two kinds of memory search that people use in the retrieval of information from short memorized lists. One is a high-speed exhaustive scanning process, used to determine the *presence* of an item in the list; the other is a slow self-terminating scanning process used to determine the *location* of an item in the list. Among other substantive implications of the experiments are: (1) Apparently one *must* scan a list serially to retrieve information from it, even when it is contained in active memory. There is no evidence in any of these data that one can "think about" more than one thing at a time, and thereby simultaneously compare a set of memorized items to a test item. (2) On the other hand, even a well-learned list can be made more readily available by being maintained in active memory. (3) Despite the possibility that retention may depend on a rehearsal process involving covert speech, visual rather than auditory memory-representations are used for comparison to representations of visual stimuli. (4) The same search process can be involved in both recall and recognition tasks.

Many of the inferences from the data were based on a proposal first made by Donders (1868) that the time between stimulus and response be regarded as the sum of the durations of a series of processing stages. Donders' *subtraction method* depends on this *stage theory*, together with an *assumption of pure insertion* which states that a change in the subject's task can cause the insertion of an additional processing stage without altering the other stages. It was the questioning of this assumption, and the absence of any objective tests of its validity, that led to the decline of the subtraction method in the late nineteenth century.

The present paper advocates retaining the idea of stages of processing. But it shows how the insertion assumption can sometimes be replaced by a weaker *assumption of selective influence,* and how the validity of either assumption for a given experiment can be tested by determining whether the effects of experimental factors on RT are additive. The main ideas are: (1) if separate stages between stimulus and response have been correctly identified, then for each of these stages it may be easier to find a factor that *influences* it without altering other stages than to find one that *inserts* it without altering other stages; and (2) these factors would then have additive effects on mean RT. The discovery of several sets of such additive factors was critical in the interpretation of the experiments described.

REFERENCES

Atkinson, R. C. & Shiffrin, R. M. Human memory: a proposed system and its control processes. In K. W. Spence and J. T. Spence (Eds.), *The psychology of learning and motivation: Advances in research and theory.* Vol. 2. New York: Academic Press, 1968. Pp. 89–195.

Baddeley, A. D. The influence of acoustic and semantic similarity on long-term memory for word sequences. *Quart. J. exp. Psychol.,* 1966,18, 302–309.

Broadbent, D. E. *Perception and communication.* London: Pergamon Press, 1958.

Cattell, J. McK. The perception time. *Mind,* 1886, 11, 377–392. Reprinted in *James McKeen Cattell, Man of science.* Lancaster, Pa.: The Science Press, 1947. Pp. 64–79.

Chase, W. G. & Calfee, R. C. Modality and similarity effects in short-term recognition memory. *J. exp. Psychol.,* 1969, 81, 510–514.

Cohen, R. L. & Johansson, B. S. Some relevant factors in the transfer of material from short-term to long-term memory. *Quart. J. exp. Psychol.,* 1967, 19, 300–308.

Conrad, R. Acoustic confusions in immediate memory. *Brit. J. Psychol.,* 1964, 55, 75–84.

Corballis, M. C. Serial order in recognition and recall. *J. exp. Psychol.,* 1967, 74, 99–105.

Crowder, R. G. Short-term memory for words with a perceptual-motor interpolated activity. *J. verb. Learn, verb. Behav.,* 1967, 6, 753–761.

Donders, F. C. Over de snelheid van psychische processen. Onderzoekingen gedaan in het Physiologisch Laboratorium der Utrechtsche Hoogeschool, 1868-1869, Tweede reeks, II, 92–120. Transl. by W. G. Koster in W. G. Koster (Ed.), *Attention and performance II. Acta Psychol.,* 1969, 30, 412–431.

Egeth, H. E. Parallel versus serial processes in multidimensional stimulus discrimination. *Percept. & Psychophys.,* 1966,1, 245–252.

Glanzer, M. & Cunitz, A. R. Two storage mechanisms in free recall. *J. verb. Learn, verb. Behav.,* 1966, 5, 351–360.

Hochberg, J. In the mind's eye. In R. N. Haber (Ed.), *Contemporary theory and research in visual perception.* New York: Holt, Rinehart & Winston, 1968. Pp. 309–331.

Hohle, R. H. Component process latencies in reaction times of children and adults. In L. P. Lipsett and C. C. Spiker (Eds.), *Advances in child development and behavior.* Vol. 3. New York: Academic Press, 1967. Pp. 225–261.

Jastrow, J. *The time-relations of mental phenomena. Fact theory papers No. VI.* New York: N.D.C. Hodges, 1890.

Johnson, D. M. *The psychology of thought and judgment.* New York: Harper, 1955.

Külpe, O. *Outlines of psychology.* New York: MacMillan, 1895.

Landauer, T. K. Rate of implicit speech. *Percept, mot. Skills,* 1962, 15, 646.

Landauer, T. K. & Freedman, J. L. Information retrieval from long-term memory: category size and recognition time. *J. verb. Learn, verb. Behav.,* 1968, 7, 291–295.

McGill, W. J. & Gibbon, J. The general gamma distribution and reaction times. *J. math. Psychol.,* 1965, 2, 1–18.

McMahon, L. E. Grammatical analysis as part of understanding a sentence. Unpublished doctoral dissertation, Harvard University, 1963.

Miller, G. A. *Psychology, the science of mental life.* New York: Harper & Row, 1962.

Morin, R. E., DeRosa, D. V., & Stultz, V. Recognition memory and reaction time. In A. F. Sanders (Ed.), *Attention and performance. Acta Psychol.,* 1967, 27, 298–305.

Morin, R. E., DeRosa, D. V., & Ulm, R. Short-term recognition memory for spatially isolated items. *Psychon. Sci.,* 1967, 9, 617–618.

Neisser, U. *Cognitive psychology.* New York: Appleton-Century-Crofts, 1967.

Newell, A. & Simon, H. A. Computers in psychology. In R. D. Luce, R. R. Bush and E. Galanter (Eds.), *Handbook of mathematical psychology.* Vol. 1. New York: Wiley, 1963. Pp. 361–428.

Nickerson, R. S. Categorization time with categories defined by disjunctions and conjunctions of stimulus attributes. *J. exp. Psychol.,* 1967, 73, 211–219.

Posner, M. I. Short-term memory systems in human information processing. In A. F. Sanders (Ed.), *Attention and performance. Acta Psychol.*, 1967, *27*, 267–284.

Posner, M. I., Boies, S. J., Eichelman, W. H., & Taylor, R. L. Retention of visual and name codes of single letters. *J. exp. Psychol. Monogr.*, 1969, *79*, No. 1, Part 2, 1–16.

Posner, M. I. & Mitchell, R. F. Chronometric analysis of classification. *Psychol. Rev.*, 1967, *74*, 392–409.

Posner, M. I. & Rossman, E. Effect of size and location of informational transforms upon short-term retention. *J. exp. Psychol.*, 1965, *70*, 496–505.

Restle, F. & Davis, J. H. Success and speed of problem solving by individuals and groups. *Psychol. Rev.*, 1962, *69*, 520–536.

Rock, I. A neglected aspect of the problem of recall: The Höffding function. In J. M. Scher (Ed.), *Theories of the mind.* New York: Free Press, 1962. Pp. 645–659.

Sanders, A. F. Rehearsal and recall in immediate memory. *Ergonomics*, 1961, *4*, 25–34.

Slamecka, N. J. Serial learning and order information. *J. exp. Psychol.*, 1967, *74*, 62–66.

Smith, E. E. Effects of familiarity on stimulus recognition and categorization. *J. exp. Psychol.*, 1967, *74*, 324–332.

Smith, E. E. Choice reaction time: an analysis of the major theoretical positions. *Psychol. Bull.*, 1968, *69*, 77–110.

Sperling, G. The information available in brief visual presentations. *Psychol. Monogr.*, 1960, *75* (11, Whole No. 498).

Sperling, G. A model for visual memory tasks. *Hum. Factors*, 1963, *5*, 19–31.

Sternberg, S. Stochastic learning theory. In R. D. Luce, R. R. Bush and E. Galanter (Eds.), *Handbook of mathematical psychology.* Vol. 2. New York: Wiley, 1963. Pp. 1–120.

Sternberg, S. Estimating the distribution of additive reaction-time components. Paper presented at the meeting of the Psychometric Society, Niagara Falls, Ont., October 1964.

Sternberg, S. High-speed scanning in human memory. *Science*, 1966, *153*, 652–654.

Sternberg, S. Retrieval of contextual information from memory. *Psychon. Sci.*, 1967, *8*, 55–6. (a)

Sternberg, S. Two operations in character-recognition: Some evidence from reaction-time measurements. *Percept. & Psychophys.*, 1967, *2*, 45–53. (b)

Sternberg, S. The discovery of processing stages: Extensions of Donders' method. In W. G. Koster (Ed.), *Attention and performance II. Acta Psychol.*, 1969, *30*, 276–315.

Suppes, P. & Groen, G. Some counting models for first-grade performance data on simple addition facts. Technical Report 90, Institute for Mathematical Studies in the Social Sciences, Stanford University, 1966.

Taylor, D. H. Latency components in two-choice responding. *J. exp. Psychol.*, 1966, *72*, 481–488.

Waugh, N. C. & Norman, D. A. Primary memory. *Psychol. Rev.*, 1965, *72*, 89–104.

Wickelgren, W. A. Auditory or articulatory coding in verbal short-term memory. *Psychol. Rev.*, 1969, *76*, 232–235.

Woodworth, R. S. *Experimental psychology.* New York: Holt, 1938.

Wundt, W. *Grundzüge der physiologischen Psychologie*, Vol. II, 2nd ed. Leipzig: Engelmann, 1880.

Yonas, A. The acquisition of information-processing strategies in a time-dependent task. Unpublished doctoral dissertation, Cornell University, 1969.

Name:_____

READING COMPREHENSION QUESTIONS

Refer to the information you have just read to find the answers to these questions. Be sure that you do not simply copy what is already written in the article. Think about your answer and write it in your own words.

1. Write any words that you had to look up here, along with their definitions. If you did not need to look up any words, list and define several of the words you think the average college student may have found difficult. All students should have at least three words and definitions for this question.

2. Write the full reference for this article in APA style. For advice on APA style, consult www.apastyle.org.

3. Explain what is novel about this study that made it publishable. Be sure to describe exactly what previous studies lacked that this study offers. Simply describing this study, or simply describing previous studies, is insufficient.

Name:_____

4. Generally describe the methods used in the paper.

    • How many subjects were there? If there was more than one experiment, list the number of subjects in each experiment.

    • Who were the subjects (e.g., older adults, schizophrenic patients, college students)?

    • What was it like to be a subject (i.e., what were the subjects required to do)? Provide enough detail that the reader can truly imagine what it was like to be a subject.

5. What were the main findings of this paper?

Name:_____

COMPREHENSION CHECK QUESTIONS

Refer to the information you have just read to find the answers to these questions. Be sure that you do not simply copy what is already written in the article. Think about your answer and write it in your own words.

1. Experiment Proposal

Pretend that you are an author on this paper and are tasked with determining future directions. Taking into account what has already been done in the field (i.e., the information presented in the Introduction) and the present study, what is a novel next step in this research? If you were one of the authors of this study, what would you do next and why? Be sure to explain why you would perform this next step. For example, proposing to replicate the study sampling from a different subject population is not sufficient, unless you explain why it is a reasonable next step.

Name:_____

2. Writing Critique

Pretend that you are a reviewer on this paper and are required to make a substantial suggestion on how to improve the writing. For example, you could offer an alternative explanation of how to describe the importance of the work, explain why the real-world application is insufficient, or suggest how the authors could describe their work in a more interesting way. If you were a reviewer, what would you say to improve the writing (not the methods) of this paper? Be sure to provide concrete suggestions. For example, do not simply say that an aspect of the paper was confusing. Demonstrate that you took the time to understand the material and offer a better way to explain the portion you found confusing.

Name:_____

3. Application Question

Think about how the work in this paper applies to the real world. Describe a scenario (either real or imagined) under which this work applies to your life. Do not use the real-world application mentioned in the paper. Rather, consider how this work is relevant to you (again, it could be imagined). Be sure to demonstrate that you understand the results of the paper through your real-world application.

Name:_____

TRUE OR FALSE STATEMENTS

Write three *true* statements here, noting the page number where the answer can be located.

1. _____
   _____
   _____
   _____
   _____

   • Page number where answer can be located: _____

2. _____
   _____
   _____
   _____
   _____

   • Page number where answer can be located: _____

3. _____
   _____
   _____
   _____
   _____

   • Page number where answer can be located: _____

Name:_____

Write three *false* statements here, noting the page number where the answer can be located. Then rewrite each statement to make it true.

1. _____
   _____
   _____

   • Rewritten to be true:
   _____
   _____

   • Page number where answer can be located: _____

2. _____
   _____
   _____

   • Rewritten to be true:
   _____
   _____

   • Page number where answer can be located: _____

3. _____
   _____
   _____

   • Rewritten to be true:
   _____
   _____

   • Page number where answer can be located: _____

Studies of Interference in Serial Verbal Reactions

J. Ridley Stroop

INTRODUCTION

Interference or inhibition (the terms seem to have been used almost indiscriminately) has been given a large place in experimental literature. The investigation was begun by the physiologists prior to 1890 (Bowditch and Warren, J. W., 1890) and has been continued to the present, principally by psychologists (Lester, 1932). Of the numerous studies that have been published during this period only a limited number of the most relevant reports demand our attention here.

Münsterberg (1892) studied the inhibiting effects of changes in common daily habits such as opening the door of his room, dipping his pen in ink, and taking his watch out of his pocket. He concluded that a given association can function automatically even though some effect of a previous contrary association remains.

Müller and Schumann (1894) discovered that more time was necessary to relearn a series of nonsense syllables if the stimulus syllables had been associated with other syllables in the meantime. From their results they deduced the law of associative inhibition which is quoted by Kline (1921, p. 270) as follows: "If a is already connected with b, then it is difficult to connect it with k, b gets in the way." Nonsense syllables were also used by Shepard and Fogelsonger (1913) in a series of experiments in association and inhibition. Only three subjects were used in any experiment and the changes introduced to produce the inhibition were so great in many cases as to present novel situations. This latter fact was shown by

Stroop, J.R. (1935). Studies Of Interference In Serial Verbal Reactions. *Journal of Experimental Psychology*, 18(6), 643-662. American Psychological Association.

the introspections. The results showed an increase in time for the response which corresponded roughly to the increase in the complexity of the situation. The only conclusion was stated thus: "We have found then that in acquiring associations there is involved an inhibitory process which is not a mere result of divided paths but has some deeper basis yet unknown" (p. 311).

Kline (1921) used 'meaningful' material (states and capitals, counties and county seats, and books and authors) in a study of interference effects of associations. He found that if the first associative bond had a recall power of 10 percent or less it facilitated the second association, if it had a recall power of 15 percent to 40 percent the inhibitory power was small, if it had a recall power of 45 percent to 70 percent the inhibiting strength approached a maximum, if the recall power was 70 percent to 100 percent the inhibition was of medium strength and in some cases might disappear or even facilitate the learning of a new association.

In card sorting Bergström (1893 and 1894), Brown (1914), Bair (1902), and Culler (1912) found that changing the arrangement of compartments into which cards were being sorted produced interference effects. Bergström (1894, p. 441) concluded that "the interference effect of an association bears a constant relation to the practice effect, and is, in fact, equivalent to it." Both Bair and Culler found that the interference of the opposing habits disappeared if the habits were practiced alternately.

Culler (1912), in the paper already referred to, reported two other experiments. In one experiment the subjects associated each of a series of numbers with striking a particular key on the typewriter with a particular finger; then the keys were changed so that four of the numbers had to be written with fingers other than those formerly used to write them. In the other experiment the subjects were trained to react with the right hand to 'red' and with the left hand to 'blue'. Then the stimuli were interchanged. In the former experiment an interference was found which decreased rapidly with practice. In the latter experiment the interference was overbalanced by the practice effect.

Hunter and Yarbrough (1917), Pearce (1917), and Hunter (1922) in three closely related studies of habit interference in the white rat in a T-shaped discrimination box found that a previous habit interfered with the formation of an 'opposite' habit.

Several studies have been published which were not primarily studies of interference, but which employed materials that were similar in nature to those employed in this research, and which are concerned with why it takes more time to name colors than to read color names. Several of these studies have been reviewed recently by Telford (1930) and by Ligon (1932). Only the vital point of these studies will be mentioned here.

The difference in time for naming colors and reading color names has been variously explained. Cattell (1886) and Lund (1972) have attributed the difference to 'practice.' Woodworth and Wells (1911, p. 52) have suggested that, "The real mechanism here may very well be the mutual interference of the five names, all of which, from immediately preceding use, are 'on the tip of the tongue,' all are equally ready and likely to get in one another's way." Brown (1915, p. 51) concluded "that the difference in speed between color naming and word reading does not depend upon practice" but that (p. 34) "the association process in naming simple objects like colors is radically different from the association process in reading printed words."

Garrett and Lemmon (1924, p. 438) have accounted for their findings in these words, "Hence it seems reasonable to say that interferences which arise in naming colors are due not so much to an equal readiness of the color names as to an equal readiness of the color recognitive processes. Another factor present in interference is very probably the present strength of the associations between colors and their names, already determined by past use." Peterson (1918 and 1925) has attributed the difference to the fact that, "One particular response habit has become associated with each word while in the case of colors themselves a variety of response tendencies have developed." (1925, p. 281.) As pointed out by Telford (1930), the results published by Peterson (1925, p. 281) and also those published by Lund (1927, p. 425) confirm Peterson's interpretation.

Ligon (1932) has published results of a 'genetic study' of naming colors and reading color names in which he used 638 subjects from school grades 1 to 9 inclusive. In the light of his results he found all former explanations untenable (He included no examination of or reference to Peterson's data and interpretation.) and proceeded to set up a new hypothesis based upon a three factor theory, a common factor which he never definitely describes and special factors of word reading and color naming. He points out that the common factor is learned but the special factors are organic. He promises further evidence from studies now in progress.

The present problem grew out of experimental work in color naming and word reading conducted in Jesup Psychological Laboratory at George Peabody College For Teachers. The time for reading names of colors had been compared with the time for naming colors themselves. This suggested a comparison of the interfering effect of color stimuli upon reading names of colors (the two types of stimuli being presented simultaneously) with the interfering effect of word stimuli upon naming colors themselves. In other words, if the word 'red' is printed in blue ink how will the interference of the ink-color 'blue' upon reading the printed word 'red' compare with the interference of the printed word 'red' upon calling the name of the ink-color 'blue?' The increase in time for reacting to words caused by the presence of conflicting color stimuli is taken as the measure of the interference of color stimuli upon reading words. The increase in the time for reacting to colors caused by the presence of conflicting word stimuli is taken as the measure of the interference of word stimuli upon naming colors. A second problem grew out of the results of the first. The problem was, What effect would practice in reacting to the color stimuli in the presence of conflicting word stimuli have upon the reaction times in the two situations described in the first problem?

EXPERIMENTAL

The materials employed in these experiments are quite different from any that have been used to study interference. In former studies the subjects were given practice in responding to a set of stimuli until associative bonds were formed between the stimuli and the desired responses, then a change was made in the experimental 'set up' which demanded a different set of responses to the same set of stimuli. In the present study pairs of conflicting stimuli, both being inherent aspects of the same symbols, are presented simultaneously (a name of one color printed in the ink of another color—a word stimulus and a color stimulus). These stimuli are varied in such a manner as to maintain the potency of their interference effect. Detailed descriptions of the materials used in each of the three experiments are included in the reports of the respective experiments.

Experiment I: The Effect of Interfering Color Stimuli Upon Reading Names of Colors Serially

Materials

When this experiment was contemplated, the first task was to arrange suitable tests. The colors used on the Woodworth-Wells colorsheet were considered but two changes were deemed advisable. As the word test to be used in comparison with the color test was to be printed in black it seemed well to substitute another color for black as an interfering stimulus. Also, because of the difficulty of printing words in yellow that would approximate the stimulus intensity of the other colors used, yellow was discarded. After consulting with Dr. Peterson, black and yellow were replaced by brown and purple. Hence, the colors used were red, blue, green, brown, and purple. The colors were arranged so as to avoid any regularity of occurrence and so that each color would appear twice in each column and in each row, and that no color would immediately succeed itself in either column or row. The words were also arranged so that the name of each color would appear twice in each line. No word was printed in the color it named but an equal number of times in each of the other four colors; i.e. the word 'red' was printed in blue, green, brown, and purple inks; the word 'blue' was printed in red, green, brown, and purple inks; etc. No word immediately succeeded itself in either column or row. The test was printed from fourteen point Franklin lower case type. The word arrangement was duplicated in black print from same type. Each test was also printed in the reverse order which provided a second form. The tests will be known as "Reading color names where the color of the print and the word are different" (RCNd), and "Reading color names printed in black" (RCNb).

Subjects and Procedure

Seventy college undergraduates (14 males and 56 females) were used as subjects. Every subject read two whole sheets (the two forms) of each test at one sitting. One half of the subjects of each sex, selected at random, read the tests in the order RCNb (form 1), RCNd (form 2), RCNd (Form 1) and RCNb (form 2), while the other half reversed the order thus equating for practice and fatigue on each test and form. All subjects were seated so as to have good daylight illumination from the left side only. All subjects were in the experimental room a few minutes before beginning work to allow the eyes to adjust to light conditions. The subjects were volunteers and apparently the motivation was good.

A ten-word sample was read before the first reading of each test. The instructions were to read as quickly as possible and to leave no errors uncorrected. When an error was left the subject's attention was called to that fact as soon as the sheet was finished. On the signal "Ready! Go!" the sheet which the subject held face down was turned by the subject and read aloud. The words were followed on another sheet (in black print) by the experimenter and the time was taken with a stop watch to a fifth of a second. Contrary to instructions 14 subjects left a total of 24 errors uncorrected on the RCNd test, 4 was the maximum for any subject, and 4 other subjects left 1 error each on the RCNb test. As each subject made 200 reactions on each test this small number of errors was considered negligible. The work was done under good daylight illumination.

Results

Table 2.1 gives the means (m), standard deviations (σ), differences (D), probable error of the difference (PEd) , and the reliability of the difference (D/PEd) for the whole group and for each sex.

Table 2.1 The Mean Time in Seconds for Reading One Hundred Names of Colors Printed in Colors Different from That Named by the Word and for One Hundred Names of Colors Printed in Black

SEX	NO. SS.	RCNd	σ	RCNb	σ	D	PE_d	D/PE_d
Male	14	43.20	4.98	40.81	4.97	2.41	1.27	1.89
Female	56	43.32	6.42	41.04	4.78	2.28	.72	3.16
Male and Female	70	43.30	6.15	41.00	4.84	2.30	.63	3.64

Observation of the bottom line of the table shows that it took an average of 2.3 seconds longer to read 100 color names printed in colors different from that named by the word than to read the same names printed in black. This difference is not reliable which is in agreement with Peterson's prediction made when the test was first proposed. The means for the sex groups show no particular difference. An examination of the means and standard deviations for the two tests shows that the interference factor caused a slight increase in the variability for the whole group and for the female group, but a slight decrease for the male group.

Table 2.2 presents the same data arranged on the basis of college classification. Only college years one and two contain a sufficient number of cases for comparative purposes. They show no differences that approach reliability.

Table 2.2   Showing Data of Table 2.1 Arranged on the Basis of College Classification

COLLEGE YEAR	NO. SS.	RCNd	σ	RCNb	σ	D	D/PE_d
1st	35	43.9	6.31	41.7	5.58	2.2	.38
2nd	20	44.9	6.74	41.8	4.32	3.1	.57
3rd	8	39.8	4.62	39.2	3.73	.6	.16
4th	7	40.8	3.60	39.2	2.93	1.6	.51

Experiment 2: The Effect of Interfering Word Stimuli Upon Naming Colors Serially

Materials

For this experiment the colors of the words in the *RCNd* test, described in Experiment 1, were printed in the same order but in the form of solid squares (■) from 24 point type instead of words. This sort of problem will be referred to as the "Naming color test" (*NC*). The *RCNd* test was employed also but in a very different manner from that in Experiment 1. In this experiment the colors of the print of the series of names were to be called in succession ignoring the colors named by the words; *e.g.* where the word 'red' was printed in blue it was to be called 'blue,' where it was printed in green it was to be called 'green,' where the word 'brown' was printed in red it was to be called 'red,' etc. Thus color of the print was to be the controlling stimulus and not the name of the color spelled by the word. This is to be known as the "Naming color of word test where the color of the print and the word are different" (*NCWd*).

Subjects and Procedure

One hundred students (88 college undergraduates, 29 males and 59 females, and 12 graduate students, all females) served as subjects. Every subject read two whole sheets (the two forms) of each test at one sitting. Half of the subjects read in the order NC, NCWd, NCWd, NC, and the other half in the order NCWd, NC, NC, NCWd, thus equating for practice and fatigue on the two sets. All subjects were seated (in their individual tests) near the window so as to have good daylight illumination from the left side. Every subject seemed to make a real effort.

A ten-word sample of each test was read before reading the test the first time. The instructions were to name the colors as they appeared in regular reading line as quickly as possible and to correct all errors. The methods of starting, checking errors, and timing were the same as those used in Experiment 1. The errors were recorded and for each error not corrected, twice the average time per word for the reading of the sheet on which the error was made was added to the time taken by the stop watch. This plan of correction was arbitrary but seemed to be justified by the situation. There were two kinds of failures to be accounted for: first, the failure to see the error: and second, the failure to correct it. Each phase of the situation gave the subject a time advantage which deserved taking note of. Since no accurate objective measure was obtainable and the number of errors was small the arbitrary plan was adopted. Fifty-nine percent of the group left an average of 2.6 errors uncorrected on the NCWd test (200 reactions) and 32 percent of the group left an average of 1.2 errors uncorrected on the NC test (200 reactions). The correction changed the mean on the NCWd test from 108.7 to 110.3 and the mean of the NC test from 63.0 to 63.3.

Results

The means of the times for the NC and NCWd tests for the whole group and for each sex are presented in Table 2.3 along with the difference, the probable error of the difference, the reliability of the difference, and the difference divided by the mean time for the naming color test.

Table 2.3 The Mean Time for Naming One Hundred Colors Presented in Squares and in the Print of Words Which Name Other Colors

SEX	NO. SS.	NCWd	σ	NC	σ	D/NC	D	PE_d	D/PE_d
Male	29	111.1	21.6	69.2	10.8	.61	42.9	3.00	13.83
Female	71	107.5	17.3	61.0	10.5	.76	46.5	1.62	28.81
Male and Female	100	110.3	18.8	63.3	10.8	.74	47.0	1.50	31.38

The comparison of the results for the whole group on the NC and NCWd test given in the bottom line of the table indicates the strength of the interference of the habit of calling words upon the activity of naming colors. The mean time for 100 responses is increased from 63.3 seconds to 110.3 seconds or an increase of 74 percent. (The medians on the two tests are 61.9 and 110.4 seconds respectively.) The standard deviation is increased in approximately the same ratio from 10.8 to 18.8. The coefficient of variability remains the same to the third decimal place (σ/m = .171) . The difference between means may be better evaluated when expressed in terms of the variability of the group. The difference of 47 seconds is 2.5 standard deviation units in terms of the *NCWd* test or 4.35 standard deviation units on the *NC* test. The former shows that 99 percent of the group on the *NCWd* test was above the mean on the *NC* test (took more time); and the latter shows that the group as scored on the *NC* test was well below the mean on the *NCWd* test. These results are shown graphically in Figure 2.1 where histograms and normal curves (obtained by the Gaussian formula) of the two sets of data are superimposed. The small area in which the curves overlap and the 74 percent increase in the mean time for naming colors caused by the presence of word stimuli show the marked interference effect of the habitual response of calling words.

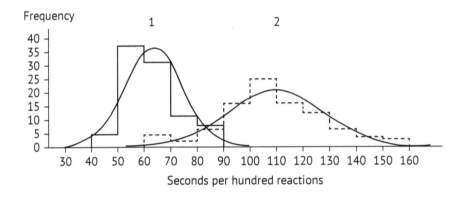

FIGURE 2.1

Showing the effect of interference on naming colors. (No interference [1]; interference [2].)

The means for the sex groups on the *NCWd* test show a difference of 3.6 seconds which is only 1.16 times its probable error; but the means on the *NC* test have a difference of 8.2 seconds which is 5.17 times its probable error. This reliable sex-difference favoring the females in naming colors agrees with the findings of Woodworth-Wells (1911), Brown (1915), Ligon (1932), etc.

The same data are arranged according to college classification in Table 2.4. There is some indication of improvement of the speed factor for both tests as the college rank improves. The relative difference between the two tests, however, remains generally the same except for fluctuations which are probably due to the variation in the number of cases.

Table 2.4 Showing the Data of Table III Arranged on the Basis of College Classification

CLASS	NO. SS.	NCWd	σ	NC	σ	D	D/NC	D/PE$_d$
1st yr	17	116.5	24.9	70.9	15.9	45.6	.64	22.7
2nd yr	37	114.4	18.0	66.1	10.6	48.3	.73	32.6
3rd yr	12	106.1	14.0	62.8	7.0	43.3	.69	41.2
4th yr	22	96.6	16.8	57.8	8.9	38.8	.67	30.3
Graduates	12	111.2	19.4	59.9	11.5	51.3	.86	37.6

Experiment 3: The Effects of Practice Upon Interference

Materials

The tests used were the same in character as those described in Experiments 1 and 2 (*RCNb*, *RCNd*, *NC*, and *NCWd*) with some revision. The *NC* test was printed in swastikas (卐) instead of squares (■). Such a modification allowed white to appear in the figure with the color, as is the case when the color is presented in the printed word. This change also made it possible to print the *NC* test in shades which more nearly match those in the *NCWd* test. The order of colors was determined under one restriction other than those given in section 2. Each line contained one color whose two appearances were separated by only one other color. This was done to equate, as much as possible, the difficulty of the different lines of the test so that any section of five lines would approximate the difficulty of any other section of five lines. Two forms of the tests were printed; in one the order was the inverse of that in the other.

Subjects and Procedure

Thirty-two undergraduates in the University of Arizona (17 males and 15 females), who offered their services, were the subjects. At each day's sitting 4 half-sheets of the same test were read, and the average time (after correction was made for errors according to the plan outlined in Experiment 2) was recorded as the day's score. Only a few errors were left uncorrected. The largest correction made on the practice test changed the mean from 49.3 to 49.6. The plan of experimentation was as follows:

Day	1	2	3	4	5	6	7
Test	RCNb	RCNd	NC	NCWd	NCWd	NCWd	NCWd
Day	8	9	10	11	12	13	14
Test	NCWd	NCWd	NCWd	NCWd	NC	RCNd	RCNd

On the 1st day the *RCNb* test was used to acquaint the subjects with the experimental procedure and improve the reliability of the 2nd day's test. The *RCNd* test was given the 2nd day and the 13th day to obtain a measure of the interference developed by practice on the *NC* and *NCWd* tests. The *RCNd* test was given the 14th day to get a measure of the effect of a day's practice upon the newly developed interference. The *NC* test was given the 3rd and 12th days, just before and just after the real practice series, so that actual change in interference on the *NCWd* test might be known. The test schedule was followed in regular daily order with two exceptions. There were two days between test days 3 and 4, and also two between test days 8 and 9, in which no work was done. These irregularities were occasioned by week-ends. Each subject was assigned a regular time of day for his work throughout the experiment. All but two subjects followed the schedule with very little irregularity. These two were finally dropped from the group and their data rejected.

All of the tests were given individually by the author. The subject was seated near a window so as to have good daylight illumination from the left side. There was no other source of light. Every subject was in the experimental room a few minutes

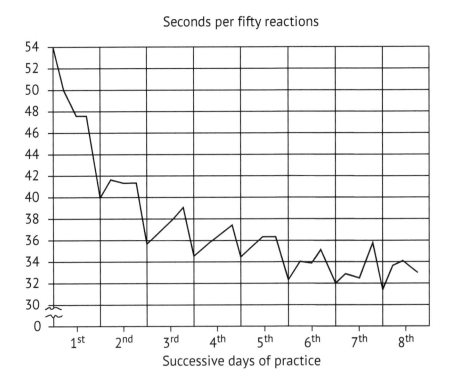

FIGURE 2.2

Mean scores for the group in each of the four half-sheets of the NCWd test, which constituted the daily practice

before beginning work to allow his eyes to adapt to the light conditions. To aid eye-adaptation and also to check for clearness of vision each subject read several lines in a current magazine. Every subject was given Dr. Ishihara's test for color vision. One subject was found to have some trouble with red-green color vision; and her results were discarded though they differed from others of her sex only in the number of errors made and corrected.

Results

The general results for the whole series of tests are shown in Table 2.5 which presents the means, standard deviations, and coefficients of variability for the whole group and for each sex separately, together with a measure of sex differences in terms of the probable error of the difference. Table 2.6, which is derived from Table 2.5, sum-marizes the practice effects upon the respective tests. The graphical representation of the results in the practice series gives the learning curve presented in Figure 2.2.

The Effect of Practice on the NCWd Test Upon Itself

The data to be considered here are those given in the section of Table 2.5 under the caption "Days of Practice on the NCWd Test." They are also presented in summary in the left section of Table 2.6 and graphically in Figure 2.2. From all three presentations it is evident that the time score is lowered considerably by practice. Reference to Table 2.6 shows a gain of 16.8 seconds or 33.9 percent of the mean of the 1st day's practice. The practice curve is found to resemble very much the 'typical' learning curve when constructed on time units. The coefficient of variability is increased from .14 ± .012 to .19 ± .015. This difference divided by its probable error gives 2.60 which indicates that it is not reliable. The probability of a real increase in variability, however, is 24 to 1. Hence, practice on the NCWd test serves to increase individual differences.

An examination of the data of the sex groups reveals a difference in speed on the NCWd test which favors the females. This is to be expected as there is a difference in favor of females in naming colors. Though the difference is not reliable in any one case it exists throughout the practice series; indicating that the relative improve-ment is approximately the same for the two groups. This latter fact is also shown by the ratio of the difference between the halves of practice series to the first half. It is .185 for the males and .180 for the females.

Table 2.5 Showing the Effects of Practice on the *NCWd* Text Upon itself Upon the NC Test, and Upon the RCNd Test in Terms of Mean Scores. Standard Deviations (σ), and Coefficients of Variability (σ/m) for Thirty-two College Students

SEX	NO. SS.	INITIAL TESTS						DAYS OF PRACTICE ON THE *NCWd* TEST							
		RCNb	σ	RCNd	σ	NC	σ	1	σ	2	σ	3	σ	4	σ
Male	17	19.8	1.8	19.6	2.5	30.6	3.6	51.2	8.5	41.6	7.8	38.2	7.6	37.3	8.0
Female	15	18.3	2.9	19.1	3.4	26.5	2.8	47.8	4.2	39.1	4.4	35.8	3.4	33.7	3.7
M & F	32	19.1	2.6	19.4	3.0	28.7	3.5	49.6	7.1	40.5	6.4	37.1	6.1	35.7	6.5
		SEX DIFFERENCES													
M & F		1.5		.5		4.1		3.4		2.5		2.4		3.6	
PE_d		.49		.70		.76		1.55		1.47		1.36		1.45	
D/PE_d		3.06		.71		5.39		2.19		1.70		1.76		2.48	
SEX		COEFFICIENTS OF VARIABILITY													
Male		.09 ±0.11		.13 ± .015		.12 ± .014		.17 ± .020		.19 ± .022		.20 ± .024		.22 ± .026	
Female		.16 ± .024		.18 ± .028		.11 ± .016		.09 ± .013		.11 ± .017		.09 ± .014		.11 ± .017	
M&F		.14 ± .012		.15 ± .013		.12 ± .010		.14 ± .012		.16 ± .014		.17 ± .014		.18 ± .016	

SEX	NO. SS.	DAYS OF PRACTICE ON THE *NCWd* TEST										FINAL TESTS			
		5	σ	6	σ	7	σ	8	σ	NC	σ	RCNd	σ	RCNd	σ
Male	17	36.3	7.4	33.9	7.3	33.5	6.7	33.4	7.1	25.9	4.2	37.3	13.7	22.2	4.8
Female	15	32.8	4.3	32.3	4.0	31.6	3.3	31.5	3.3	23.6	1.9	32.0	6.2	21.8	6.1
M&F	32	34.9	6.2	33.2	5.4	32.6	5.5	32.8	6.1	24.7	3.2	34.8	11.7	22.0	5.5
		SEX DIFFERENCES													
M & F		3.5		1.6		1.9		1.9		2.3		5.3		.4	
PE_d		1.41		1.34		1.23		1.30		.77		2.56		1.31	
D/PE_d		2.48		1.19		1.54		1.46		2.99		2.07		.31	
SEX		COEFFICIENTS OF VARIABILITY													
Male		.20 ± .024		.22 ± .026		.20 ± .024		.21 ± .025		.16 ± .019		.37 ± .048		.22 ± .026	
Female		.13 ± .020		.12 ± .019		.10 ±. 016		.11 ± .016		.08 ± .012		.19 ± .030		.28 ± .045	
M&F		.18 ± 0.16		.16 ± .014		.17 ±. 015		.19 ± .015		.13 ± .011		.34 ± .031		.25 ± .022	

The score is the average time for four trials of fifty reactions each.

Table 2.6 A Summary of the Means in Table 2.5. Showing the Effect of Practice in the *NCWd* Test Upon the *NCWd*, the NC, and the *RCNd* Tests

TEST	NCWd			NC			RCNd		
SEX	M	F	M & F	M	F	M&F	M	F	M&F
Initial Score	51.2	47.8	49.6	30.6	26.5	28.7	19.6	19.1	19.4
Final Score	33.4	31.5	32.8	25.9	23.6	24.7	37.3	32.0	34.8
Gain	17.8	16.3	16.8	4.7	2.9	4.0	−17.7	−12.9	−15.4
Percent Gain	34.8	34.1	33.9	15.4	10.9	13.9	−90.3	−67.5	−79.3

Minus sign shows loss.

The Effect of Practice on the NCWd Test upon the NC Test

The middle section of Table 2.6 shows a gain on the *NC* test of 4.0 seconds or 13.9 percent of the initial score. This is only 23.7 percent of the gain on the *NCWd* test which means that less than one fourth of the total gain on the *NCWd* test is due to increase in speed in naming colors. The improvement is greater for the males, which is accounted for by the fact that there is more difference between naming colors and reading names of colors for the males than for the females.

The Effect in the RCNd Test of Practice on the NCWd and NC Tests

The right section of Table 2.6 shows that the practice on the *NCWd* and *NC* tests resulted in heavy loss in speed on the *RCNd*. A comparison of the right and left sections of the table shows that the loss on the *RCNd* test, when measured in absolute units, is practically equal to the gain on the *NCWd* test; when measured in relative units it is much greater. It is interesting to find that in ten short practice periods the relative values of opposing stimuli can be modified so greatly. There is little relation, however, between the gain in one case and the loss in the other. The correlation between gain and loss in absolute units is .262 ± .11, while the correlation between percent of gain and percent of loss is .016 ± .17, or zero. This is what one might expect.

From a consideration of the results of the two applications of the *RCNd* test given in the final tests of Table 2.5 it is evident that the newly developed interference disappears very rapidly with practice. From one day to the next the mean decreases from 34.8 to 22.0 seconds. This indicates that renewing the effectiveness of old associations which are being opposed by newly formed ones is easier than strengthening new associations in opposition to old well established ones.

The variability of the group is increased by the increase in interference due to practice on the *NCWd* test. The coefficient of variability increases from .15 ± .013 to .34 ± .031, the difference divided by its probable error being 5.65. This is not surprising as the degree of the interference varies widely for different subjects. Its degree is determined by the learning on the practice series which is shown by the individual results to vary considerably. One day's practice on the *RCNd* test reduced the variability from .34 ± .031 to .25 ± .022. The decrease in variability is 2.3 times its probable error.

Table 2.7 The Effects of Practice on the NCWd Test and the RCNd Test Upon the Coefficient of Variability for the Group

TEST	NO. SS.	COEFFICIENTS OF VARIABILITY		D	PE_d	D/PE_d
		INITIAL	FINAL			
MCW	32	.14	.19	.05	.034	2.60
RCNd	32	.34	.25	.09	.037	2.33

The data from this experiment present interesting findings on the effect of practice upon individual differences. The results which have already been discussed separately are presented for comparison in Table 2.7.

These results show that practice increases individual differences where a stimulus to which the subjects have an habitual reaction pattern is interfering with reactions to a stimulus for which the subjects do not have an habitual reaction pattern (the word stimulus interfering with naming colors, NCWd test); but decreases individual differences where a stimulus to which the subjects do not have an habitual reaction pattern is interfering with reactions to a stimulus for which the subjects have an habitual reaction pattern (the color stimulus interfering with reading words—RCNd test). There are two other variables involved, however: initial variability and length of practice. Thus in the NCWd test the initial variability was less, the difficulty greater, and the practice greater than in the RCNd test. These findings lend some support to Peterson's hypothesis, "Subjects of normal heterogeneity would become more alike with practice on the simpler processes or activities, but more different on the more complex activities" (Peterson and Barlow, 1928, p. 228).

A sex difference in naming colors has been found by all who have studied color naming and has been generally attributed to the greater facility of women in verbal reactions than of men. There is some indication in our data that this sex difference may be due to the difference in the accustomed reaction of the two sexes to colors as stimuli. In other words responding to a color stimulus by naming the color may be more common with females than with males. This difference is probably built up through education. Education in color is much more intense for girls than for boys as observing, naming, and discussing colors relative to dress is much more common among girls than among boys. The practice in naming colors in the NCWd test decreased the difference between the sex groups on the NC test from a difference 5.38 times its probable error to a difference 2.99 times its probable error. This decrease in the difference due to practice favors the view that the difference has been acquired and is therefore a product of training.

SUMMARY

1. Interference in serial verbal reactions has been studied by means of newly devised experimental materials. The source of the interference is in the materials themselves. The words red, blue, green, brown, and purple are used on the test sheet. No word is printed in the color it names but an equal number of times in each of the other four colors; *i.e.* the word 'red' is printed in blue, green, brown, and purple inks; the word 'blue' is printed in red, green, brown, and purple inks; etc. Thus each word presents the name of one color printed in ink of another color. Hence, a word stimulus and a color stimulus both are presented simultaneously. The words of the test are duplicated in black print and the colors of the test are duplicated in squares or swastikas. The difference in the time for reading the words printed in colors and the same words printed in black is the measure of the interference of color stimuli upon reading words. The difference in the time for naming the colors in which the words are printed and the same colors printed in squares (or swastikas) is the measure of the interference of conflicting word stimuli upon naming colors.

2. The interference of conflicting color stimuli upon the time for reading 100 words (each word naming a color unlike the ink-color of its print) caused an increase of only 2.3 seconds or 5.6 percent over the normal time for reading the same words printed in black. This increase is not reliable. But the interference of conflicting word stimuli upon the time for naming 100 colors (each color being the print of a word which names another color) caused an increase of 47.0 seconds or 74.3 percent of the normal time for naming colors printed in squares. These tests provide a unique basis (the interference value) for comparing the effectiveness of the two types of associations. Since the presence of the color stimuli caused no reliable increase over the normal time for reading words ($D/PE_d = 3.64$) and the presence of word stimuli caused a considerable increase over the normal time for naming colors (4.35 standard deviation units) the associations that have been formed between the word stimuli and the reading response are evidently more effective than those that have been formed between the color stimuli and the naming response. Since these associations are products of training, and since the difference in their strength corresponds roughly to the difference in training in reading words and naming colors, it seems reasonable to conclude that the difference in speed in reading names of colors and in naming colors may be satisfactorily accounted for by the difference in training in the two activities. The word stimulus has been associated with the specific response 'to read,' while the color stimulus has been associated with various responses: 'to admire,' 'to name,' 'to reach for,' 'to avoid,' etc.

3. As a test of the permanency of the interference of conflicting word stimuli to naming colors eight days practice (200 reactions per day) were given in naming the colors of the print of words (each word naming a color unlike the inkcolor of its print). The effects of this practice were as follows: 1. It decreased the interference of conflicting word stimuli to naming colors but did not eliminate it. 2. It produced a practice curve comparable to that

obtained in many other learning experiments. 3. It increased the variability of the group. 4. It shortened the reaction time to colors presented in color squares. 5. It increased the interference of conflicting color stimuli upon reading words.

4. Practice was found either to increase or to decrease the variability of the group depending upon the nature of the material used.

5. Some indication was found that the sex difference in naming colors is due to the difference in the training of the two sexes.

NOTES

1. Descoeudres (1914) and also Goodenough and Brian (1929) presented color and form simultaneously in studying their relative values as stimuli.

2. In Appendix A will be found a key to all symbols and abbreviations used in this paper.

REFERENCES

Bair, J. H. The practice curve: A study of the formation of habits. *Psychol. Rev. Monog. Suppl.* (1902). (No. 19), pp. 1–70.

Bergström, J. A. Experiments upon physiological memory. *Amer. J. Psychol* (1893). 5, 356–359.

Bergström, J. A. The relation of the interference of the practice effect of an association. *Amer. J. Psychol.*, 1894, 6, 433–442.

Bowditch, H. P., & Warren, J. W. The knee-jerk and its physiological modifications. *J. Physiology,* 1890, 11, 25–46. Brown, Warner Practice in associating color names with colors. *Psychol. Rev* (1915). 22, 45–55.

Brown, Warner Habit interference in card sorting. *Univ. of Calif. Studies in Psychol* (1914). V(i, No 4)

Cattell, J. McK. The time it takes to see and name objects. *Mind* (1886). 11, 63–65.

Culler, A. J. Interference and adaptability. *Arch. of Psychol* (1912). 3(No. 24), 1–80.

Descoeudres, A.Couleur, forme, ou nombre,. *Arch. of Psychol* (1914). 14, 305–341.

Garrett, H. E., & Lemmon, V. W. An analysis of several wellknown tests. *J. Appld. Psychol* (1924). 8, 424–438.

Goodenough, F. L., & Brian, C. R. Certain factors underlying the acquisition of motor skill by pre-school children. *J. Exper. Psychol* (1929). 12, 127–155.

Hunter, W. S., & Yarbrough, J. U. The interference of auditory habits in the white rat. *J. Animal Behav* (1917). 7, 49–65.

Hunter, W. S. Habit interference in the white rat and in the human subject. *J. Comp. Physiol* (1922). 2, 29–59.

Kline, L. W. An experimental study of associative inhibition. *J. Exper. Psychol* (1921). 4, 270–299.

Lester, O. P. Mental set in relation to retroactive inhibition. *J. Exper. Psychol* (1932). 15, 681–699.

Ligon, E. M. A Genetic study of color naming and word reading. *Amer. J. Psychol* (1932). 44, 103–121.

Lund, F. H. The role of practice in speed of association. *J. Exper. Psychol* (1927). 10, 424–433.

Müller, G. E., & Schumann, F. Experimentelle Beiträge zu Untersuchung des Gedächtnisses. *Zsch. f. Psychol* (1894). 6, 81–190.

Münsterberg, HugoGedächtnisstudien. *Beiträge zur Experimentellen Psychologie* (1892). 4, 70.

Pearce, Bennie D.A note on the interference of visual habits in the white rat. *J. Animal Behav* (1917). *7*, 169–177.

Peterson, J., & Barlow, M. C. *The effects of practice on individual differences. The 27th Year Book of Nat. Soc. Study of Educ., Part II,*. (1928). pp. 211–230.

Peterson, J., Lanier, L. H., & Walker, H. M. Comparisons of white and negro children. *J. Comp. Psychol* (1925). *5*, 271–283.

Peterson, J., & David, Q. J. *The psychology of handling men in the army.* Minneapolis, Minn. Perine Book Co., 1918, pp. 146.

Shepard, J. F., & Fogelsonger, H. M.Association and inhibition. *Psychol. Rev* (1913). 20, 291–311.

Telford, C. W. Differences in responses to colors and their names. *J. Genet. Psychol* (1930). 37, 151–159.

Woodworth, R. S., & Wells, F. L. Association tests. *Psychol. Rev. Monog. Suppl* (1911). 13(No. 57), pp. 85.

APPENDIX

A Key to Symbols and Abbreviations

NC   Naming Colors.

NCWd   Naming the Colors of the Print of Word Where the Color of the Print and the Word are Different.

RCNb   Reading Color Names Printed in Black Ink.

RCNd   Reading Color Names Where the Color of the Print and the Word are Different.

D   Difference

D/PEd   Difference divided by the probable error of the difference.

M&F   Males and Females.

PEd   Probable error of the difference.

σ Sigma or standard deviation.

σ/m Standard deviation d ivided by the mean.

Name:_____

READING COMPREHENSION QUESTIONS

Refer to the information you have just read to find the answers to these questions. Be sure that you do not simply copy what is already written in the article. Think about your answer and write it in your own words.

1. Write any words that you had to look up here, along with their definitions. If you did not need to look up any words, list and define several of the words you think the average college student may have found difficult. All students should have at least three words and definitions for this question.

2. Write the full reference for this article in APA style. For advice on APA style, consult www.apastyle.org.

3. Explain what is novel about this study that made it publishable. Be sure to describe exactly what previous studies lacked that this study offers. Simply describing this study, or simply describing previous studies, is insufficient.

Name:_____

4. Generally describe the methods used in the paper.

   • How many subjects were there? If there was more than one experiment, list the number of subjects in each experiment.

   • Who were the subjects (e.g., older adults, schizophrenic patients, college students)?

   • What was it like to be a subject (i.e., what were the subjects required to do)? Provide enough detail that the reader can truly imagine what it was like to be a subject.

5. What were the main findings of this paper?

Name:_____

COMPREHENSION CHECK QUESTIONS

Refer to the information you have just read to find the answers to these questions. Be sure that you do not simply copy what is already written in the article. Think about your answer and write it in your own words.

1. Experiment Proposal

Pretend that you are an author on this paper and are tasked with determining future directions. Taking into account what has already been done in the field (i.e., the information presented in the Introduction) and the present study, what is a novel next step in this research? If you were one of the authors of this study, what would you do next and why? Be sure to explain why you would perform this next step. For example, proposing to replicate the study sampling from a different subject population is not sufficient, unless you explain why it is a reasonable next step.

Name:_____

2. Writing Critique

Pretend that you are a reviewer on this paper and are required to make a substantial suggestion on how to improve the writing. For example, you could offer an alternative explanation of how to describe the importance of the work, explain why the real-world application is insufficient, or suggest how the authors could describe their work in a more interesting way. If you were a reviewer, what would you say to improve the writing (not the methods) of this paper? Be sure to provide concrete suggestions. For example, do not simply say that an aspect of the paper was confusing. Demonstrate that you took the time to understand the material and offer a better way to explain the portion you found confusing.

Name:_____

3. Application Question

Think about how the work in this paper applies to the real world. Describe a scenario (either real or imagined) under which this work applies to your life. Do not use the real-world application mentioned in the paper. Rather, consider how this work is relevant to you (again, it could be imagined). Be sure to demonstrate that you understand the results of the paper through your real-world application.

Name:_____

TRUE OR FALSE STATEMENTS

Write three *true* statements here, noting the page number where the answer can be located.

1. _____
   _____
   _____
   _____
   _____

   * Page number where answer can be located: _____

2. _____
   _____
   _____
   _____
   _____

   * Page number where answer can be located: _____

3. _____
   _____
   _____
   _____
   _____

   * Page number where answer can be located: _____

Name:_____

Write three *false* statements here, noting the page number where the answer can be located. Then rewrite each statement to make it true.

1. _____
   _____
   _____

   • Rewritten to be true:
     _____
     _____

   • Page number where answer can be located: _____

2. _____
   _____
   _____

   • Rewritten to be true:
     _____
     _____

   • Page number where answer can be located: _____

3. _____
   _____
   _____

   • Rewritten to be true:
     _____
     _____

   • Page number where answer can be located: _____

Mental Rotation of Three-Dimensional Objects

Roger N. Shepard and Jacqueline Metzler

Abstract

The time required to recognize that two perspective drawings portray objects of the same three-dimensional shape is found to be (i) a linearly increasing function of the angular difference in the portrayed orientations of the two objects and (ii) no shorter for differences corresponding simply to a rigid rotation of one of the two-dimensional drawings in its own picture plane than for differences corresponding to a rotation of the three-dimensional object in depth.

Human subjects are often able to determine that two two-dimensional pictures portray objects of the same three-dimensional shape even though the objects are depicted in very different orientations. The experiment reported here was designed to measure the time that subjects require to determine such identity of shape as a function of the angular difference in the portrayed orientations of the two three-dimensional objects.

This angular difference was produced either by a rigid rotation of one of two identical pictures in its own picture plane or by a much more complex, nonrigid transformation, of one of the pictures, that corresponds to a (rigid) rotation of the three-dimensional object in depth.

Shepard, R. N., & Metzler, J. (1971). Mental Rotation of Three-Dimensional Objects. *Science*, 171(3972), 701-703.

This reaction time is found (i) to increase linearly with the angular difference in portrayed orientation and (ii) to be no longer for a rotation in depth than for a rotation merely in the picture plane. These findings appear to place rather severe constraints on possible explanations of how subjects go about determining identity of shape of differently oriented objects. They are, however, consistent with an explanation suggested by the subjects themselves. Although introspective reports must be interpreted with caution, all subjects claimed (i) that to make the required comparison they first had to imagine one object as rotated into the same orientation as the other and that they could carry out this "mental rotation" at no greater than a certain limiting rate; and (ii) that, since they perceived the two-dimensional pictures as objects in three-dimensional space, they could imagine the rotation around whichever axis was required with equal ease.

In the experiment each of eight adult subjects was presented with 1600 pairs of perspective line drawings. For each pair the subject was asked to pull a right-hand lever as soon as he determined that the two drawings portrayed objects that were congruent with respect to three-dimensional shape and to pull a left-hand lever as soon as he determined that the two drawings depicted objects of different three-dimensional shapes. According to a random sequence, in half of the pairs (the "same" pairs) the two objects could be rotated into congruence with each other (as in Figure 3.1, A and B), and in the other half (the "different" pairs) the two objects differed by a reflection as well as a rotation and could not be rotated into congruence (as in Figure 3.1C).

The choice of objects that were mirror images or "isomers" of each other for the "different" pairs was intended to prevent subjects from discovering some distinctive feature possessed by only one of the two objects and thereby reaching a decision of noncongruence without actually having to carry out any mental rotation. As a further precaution, the ten different three-dimensional objects depicted in the various perspective drawings were chosen to be relatively unfamiliar and meaningless in overall three-dimensional shape.

Each object consisted of ten solid cubes attached face-to-face to form a rigid armlike structure with exactly three right-angled "elbows" (see Figure 3.1). The set of all ten shapes included two subsets of five: within either subset, no shape could be transformed into itself or any other by any reflection or rotation (short of $360°$). However, each shape in either subset was the mirror image of one shape in the other subset, as required for the construction of the "different" pairs.

For each of the ten objects, 18 different perspective projections—corresponding to one complete turn around the vertical axis by $20°$ steps—were generated by digital computer and associated graphical output[1]. Seven of the 18 perspective views of each object were then selected so as (i) to avoid any views in which some part of the object was wholly occluded by another part and yet (ii) to permit the construction of two pairs that differed in orientation by each possible angle, in $20°$ steps, from $0°$ to

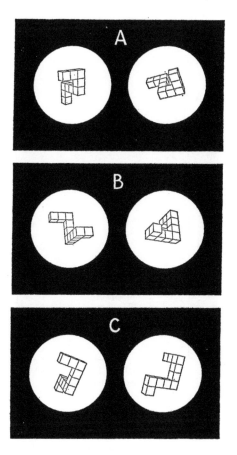

FIGURE 3.1

Examples of pairs of perspective line drawings presented to the subjects. (A) A "same" pair, which differs by an 80° rotation in the picture plane; (B) a "same" pair, which differs by an 80° rotation in depth; and (C) a "different" pair, which cannot be brought into congruence by *any* rotation.

180°. These 70 line drawings were then reproduced by photo-offset process and were attached to cards in pairs for presentation to the subjects.

Half of the "same" pairs (the "depth" pairs) represented two objects that differed by some multiple of a 20° rotation about a vertical axis (Figure 3.1B). For each of these pairs, copies of two appropriately different perspective views were simply attached to the cards in the orientation in which they were originally generated. The other half of the "same" pairs (the "picture-plane" pairs) represented two objects that differed by some multiple of a 20° rotation in the plane of the drawings themselves (Figure 3.1A). For each of these, one of the seven perspective views was selected for each object and two copies of this picture were attached to the card in appropriately different orientations. Altogether, the 1600 pairs presented to each subject included 800 "same" pairs, which consisted of 400 unique pairs (20 "depth" and 20 "picture-plane" pairs at each of the ten angular differences from 0° to 180°), each

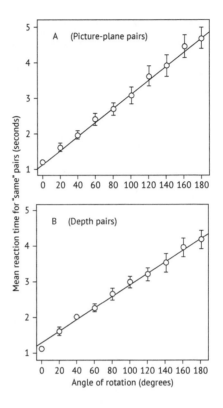

FIGURE 3.2

Mean reaction times to two perspective line drawings portraying objects of the same three-dimensional shape. Times are plotted as a function of angular difference in portrayed orientation: (A) for pairs differing by a rotation in the picture plane only; and (B) for pairs differing by a rotation in depth. (The centers of the circles indicate the means and, when they extend far enough to show outside these circles, the vertical bars around each circle indicate a conservative estimate of the standard error of that mean based on the distribution of the eight component means contributed by the individual subjects.)

of which was presented twice. The remaining 800 pairs, randomly intermixed with these, consisted of 400 unique "different" pairs, each of which (again) was presented twice. Each of these "different" pairs corresponded to one "same" pair (of either the "depth" or "picture-plane" variety) in which, however, one of the three-dimensional objects had been reflected about some plane in three-dimensional space. Thus the two objects in each "different" pair differed, in general, by both a reflection and a rotation.

The 1600 pairs were grouped into blocks of not more than 200 and presented over eight to ten 1-hour sessions (depending upon the subject). Also, although it is only of incidental interest here, each such block of presentations was either "pure," in that all pairs involved rotations of the same type ("depth" or "picture-plane"), or "mixed," in that the two types of rotation were randomly intermixed within the same block.

Each trial began with a warning tone, which was followed half a second later by the presentation of a stimulus pair and the simultaneous onset of a timer. The lever-pulling response stopped the timer, recorded the subject's reaction time and terminated the visual display. The line drawings, which averaged between 4 and 5 cm in maximum linear extent, appeared at a viewing distance of about 60 cm. They were positioned, with a center-to-center spacing that subtended a visual angle of 9°, in two circular apertures in a vertical black surface (see Figure 3.1, A to C).

The subjects were instructed to respond as quickly as possible while keeping errors to a minimum. On the average only 3.2 percent of the responses were incorrect (ranging from 0.6 to 5.7 percent for individual subjects). The reaction-time data presented below include only the 96.8 percent correct responses. However, the data for the incorrect responses exhibit a similar pattern.

In Figure 3.2, the overall means of the reaction times as a function of angular difference in orientation for all correct (right-hand) responses to "same" pairs are plotted separately for the pairs differing by a rotation in the picture plane (Figure 3.2A) and for the pairs differing by a rotation in depth (Figure 3.2B). In both cases, reaction time is a strikingly linear function of the angular difference between the two three-dimensional objects portrayed. The mean reaction times for individual subjects increased from a value of about 1 second at 0° of rotation for all subjects to values ranging from 4 to 6 seconds at 180° of rotation, depending upon the particular individual. Moreover, despite such variations in slope, the *linearity* of the function is clearly evident when the data are plotted separately for individual three-dimensional objects or for individual subjects. Polynomial regression lines were computed separately for each subject under each type of rotation. In all 16 cases the functions were found to have a highly significant linear component ($P < .001$) when tested against deviations from linearity. No significant quadratic or higher-order effects were found ($P > .05$, in all cases).

The angle through which different three-dimensional shapes must be rotated to achieve congruence is not, of course, defined. Therefore, a function like those plotted in Figure 3.2 cannot be constructed in any straightforward manner for the "different" pairs. The *overall* mean reaction time for these pairs was found, however, to be 3.8 seconds—nearly a second longer than the corresponding overall means for the "same" pairs. (In the postexperimental interview, the subjects typically reported that they attempted to rotate one end of one object into congruence with the corresponding end of the other object; they discovered that the two objects were *different* when, after this "rotation," the two free ends still remained noncongruent.)

Not only are the two functions shown in Figure 3.2 both linear but they are very similar to each other with respect to intercept and slope. Indeed, for the larger angular differences the reaction times were, if anything, somewhat shorter for rotation in depth than for rotation in the picture plane. However, since this small difference is either absent or reversed in four of the eight subjects, it is of doubtful significance. The determination of identity of shape may therefore be based, in both cases, upon a process of the same general kind. If we can describe this process as some sort of "mental rotation in three-dimensional space," then the slope of the obtained functions indicates that the average rate at which these particular objects can be thus "rotated" is roughly 60° per second.

Of course the plotted reaction times necessarily include any times taken by the subjects to decide how to process the pictures in each presented pair as well as the time taken actually to carry out the process, once it was chosen. However, even for these highly practiced subjects, the reaction times were still linear and were no more than 20 percent lower in the "pure" blocks of presentations (in which the subjects knew both the axis and the direction of the required rotation in advance of each presentation) than in the "mixed" blocks (in which the axis of rotation was unpredictable). Tentatively, this suggests that 80 percent of a typical one of these reaction times may represent some such process as "mental rotation" itself, rather than a preliminary process of preparation or search. Nevertheless, in further research now underway, we are seeking clarification of this point and others.

ROGER N. SHEPARD
JACQUELINE METZLER

Department of Psychology,
Stanford University,
Stanford, California 94305

REFERENCES AND NOTES

1. Mrs. Jih-Jie Chang of the Bell Telephone Laboratories generated the 180 perspective projections for us by means of the Bell Laboratories' Stromberg-Carlson 4020 microfilm recorder and the computer program for constructing such projections developed there by A. M. Noll. See, for example, A. M. Noll, *Computers Automation* 14, 20 (1965).
2. We thank Mrs. Chang [see 1]; and we also thank Dr. J. D. Elashoff for her suggestions concerning the statistical analyses. Assistance in the computer graphics was provided by the Bell Telephone Laboratories. Supported by NSF grant GS-2283 to R.N.S.

Name:_____

READING COMPREHENSION QUESTIONS

Refer to the information you have just read to find the answers to these questions. Be sure that you do not simply copy what is already written in the article. Think about your answer and write it in your own words.

1. Write any words that you had to look up here, along with their definitions. If you did not need to look up any words, list and define several of the words you think the average college student may have found difficult. All students should have at least three words and definitions for this question.

2. Write the full reference for this article in APA style. For advice on APA style, consult www.apastyle.org.

3. Explain what is novel about this study that made it publishable. Be sure to describe exactly what previous studies lacked that this study offers. Simply describing this study, or simply describing previous studies, is insufficient.

Name:_____

4. Generally describe the methods used in the paper.

- How many subjects were there? If there was more than one experiment, list the number4 of subjects in each experiment.

- Who were the subjects (e.g., older adults, schizophrenic patients, college students)?

- What was it like to be a subject (i.e., what were the subjects required to do)? Provide enough detail that the 45reader can truly imagine what it was like to be a subject.

5. What were the main findings of this paper?

Name:_____

COMPREHENSION CHECK QUESTIONS

Refer to the information you have just read to find the answers to these questions. Be sure that you do not simply copy what is already written in the article. Think about your answer and write it in your own words.

1. Experiment Proposal

Pretend that you are an author on this paper and are tasked with determining future directions. Taking into account what has already been done in the field (i.e., the information presented in the Introduction) and the present study, what is a novel next step in this research? If you were one of the authors of this study, what would you do next and why? Be sure to explain why you would perform this next step. For example, proposing to replicate the study sampling from a different subject population is not sufficient, unless you explain why it is a reasonable next step.

Name:_____

2. Writing Critique

Pretend that you are a reviewer on this paper and are required to make a substantial suggestion on how to improve the writing. For example, you could offer an alternative explanation of how to describe the importance of the work, explain why the real-world application is insufficient, or suggest how the authors could describe their work in a more interesting way. If you were a reviewer, what would you say to improve the writing (not the methods) of this paper? Be sure to provide concrete suggestions. For example, do not simply say that an aspect of the paper was confusing. Demonstrate that you took the time to understand the material and offer a better way to explain the portion you found confusing.

Name:_____

3. Application Question

Think about how the work in this paper applies to the real world. Describe a scenario (either real or imagined) under which this work applies to your life. Do not use the real-world application mentioned in the paper. Rather, consider how this work is relevant to you (again, it could be imagined). Be sure to demonstrate that you understand the results of the paper through your real-world application.

Name:_____

TRUE OR FALSE STATEMENTS

Write three *true* statements here, noting the page number where the answer can be located.

1. _____
   _____
   _____
   _____
   _____

   • Page number where answer can be located: _____

2. _____
   _____
   _____
   _____
   _____

   • Page number where answer can be located: _____

3. _____
   _____
   _____
   _____
   _____

   • Page number where answer can be located: _____

Name:_____

Write three *false* statements here, noting the page number where the answer can be located. Then rewrite each statement to make it true.

1. _____
    _____
    _____

    - Rewritten to be true:
      _____
      _____

    - Page number where answer can be located: _____

2. _____
    _____
    _____

    - Rewritten to be true:
      _____
      _____

    - Page number where answer can be located: _____

3. _____
    _____
    _____

    - Rewritten to be true:
      _____
      _____

    - Page number where answer can be located: _____

Word Length and the Structure of Short-Term Memory

Alan D. Baddeley, Neil Thomson, and Mary Buchanan

Abstract

A number of experiments explored the hypothesis that immediate memory span is not constant, but varies with the length of the words to be recalled. Results showed: (1) Memory span is inversely related to word length across a wide range of materials; (2) When number of syllables and number of phonemes are held constant, words of short temporal duration are better recalled than words of long duration; (3) Span could be predicted on the basis of the number of words which the subject can read in approximately 2 sec; (4) When articulation is suppressed by requiring the subject to articulate an irrelevant sound, the word length effect disappears with visual presentation, but remains when the presentation is auditory. The results are interpreted in terms of a phonemically-based store of limited temporal capacity, which may function as an output buffer for speech production, and as a supplement to a more central working memory system.

Miller (1956) has suggested that the capacity of short-term memory is constant when measured in terms of number of chunks, a chunk being a subjectively meaningful unit. Because of the subjective definition of a chunk, this hypothesis is essentially irrefutable unless an independent measure of the

Baddeley, A. D., Thomson, N., & Buchanan, M. (1975). Word Length and the Structure of Short-Term Memory. *Journal of Verbal Learning and Verbal Behavior*, 14(6), 575-589. Copyright © by Elsevier B.V. Reprinted with permission.

nature of a chunk is available. Typically this problem has been avoided by making the simplifying assumption that such experimenter-defined units as words, digits, and letters constitute chunks to the subject. Hence, although Miller's hypothesis is not refutable in the absence of an independent measure of a chunk, it is meaningful to test a weaker version, namely that the capacity of short-term memory is a constant number of items, where items are defined experimental units. Words represent one commonly accepted type of item, and in this case, the chunking hypothesis would predict that the capacity of short-term memory, as measured in words, should be constant regardless of the size or duration of the words used.

A number of studies testing this hypothesis have used the recency effect in free recall as an estimate of short-term memory capacity. Craik (1968) found no reliable effect of word length on performance in the free recall of separate groups of words comprising one to five syllables. This invariance held true whether performance was measured in terms of either raw scores, or estimates of primary memory and secondary memory components. This result was replicated and extended by Glanzer and Razel (1974) who observed a recency effect which was constant when measured in number of items, even when an item comprised a whole proverb rather than a single word. They concluded from their study that short-term or primary memory has a capacity of two items regardless of item duration or complexity.

Miller's generalization, however, was based on the memory span paradigm, and it is questionable whether recency and span depend on the same memory mechanisms. There is indeed a growing body of evidence suggesting that the recency effect in free recall is basically unrelated to short-term memory as measured by memory span. Such evidence includes:

1. Craik's (1970) observation that a subject's memory span correlates more highly with the secondary memory than the primary memory component of free recall.
2. Memory span shows clear evidence of speech coding, being impaired by both phonemic similarity (Conrad, 1964; Baddeley, 1966) and articulatory suppression (Levy, 1971). This is not the case for the recency effect in free recall which is unaffected by either phonemic similarity (Craik & Levy, 1970; Glanzer, Koppenaal, & Nelson, 1972) or articulatory suppression (Richardson & Baddeley, 1975).
3. Baddeley and Hitch (1974) have shown unimpaired recency in free recall for subjects performing a concurrent memory span task involving the retention of a sequence of six digits. Since the memory span task did not interfere with recency, it is difficult to maintain the view that the two tasks are based on the same limited-capacity system.

Studies investigating the effect of word length on memory span do not in general support the weak version of Miller's hypothesis. Thus, unpublished work by Laughery,

Lachman, and Dansereau (Note 1) and by Standing, Bond, and Smith (Note 2) have reported poorer performance in a memory span task when longer words are used. Mackworth (1963) found a high correlation between reading rate and memory span for a wide range of materials, including pictures, letters, digits, shapes, and colors. This result could be interpreted in terms of word length as a determinant of memory span, with reading rate providing an indirect measure of word length. The situation is, however, complicated by the fact that subjects in some cases were asked to label pictures, and in others to read words so that it is not clear whether the result is due to articulation time or to difficulty in retrieving the correct verbal label. Watkins and Watkins (1973) present the clearest published evidence for an effect of word length on memory span, in a study primarily concerned with the modality effect. They found evidence for a word length effect on earlier serial positions, but observed that the modality effect (the enhanced recall of auditorily presented items) did not interact with word length. They suggest that the word length effect observed may have been due to the greater difficulty of perceiving their four-syllable words which were presented at a 1/sec rate.

These studies do not support the hypothesis that memory span capacity is a constant number of items. However, it is always possible to save the item-based hypothesis by questioning the assumption that words constitute items. Given evidence that short-term memory is a speech-based system, it could be reasonably argued that its capacity should be measured in more basic speech units such as syllables or phonemes. The experiments that follow aim first to study the influence of word-length on memory span, secondly to explore the relative importance of number of syllables and temporal duration of a word as determinants of span, and thirdly to explore the implications of this for the question of whether the underlying memory system is time-based or item-based.

EXPERIMENT I

This study compared the memory span of subjects for sets of long and short words of comparable frequency of occurrence in English. One set comprised eight mono-syllables, namely, *sum, hate, harm, wit, bond, yield, worst,* and *twice.* The other set comprised eight five-syllable words, namely *association, opportunity, representative, organization, considerable, immediately, university,* and *individual.*

Method

Five list lengths were used, comprising sequences of four, five, six, seven, and eight words. Eight sequences of each length were made up from the pool of short words, and eight from the pool of long words. In both cases, sequences were generated by sampling at random without replacement from the appropriate pool of words. All subjects were tested on both long and short words, and all received the sequences in ascending order of list length, beginning with sequences of four words and proceeding up to the point at which they failed on all eight sequences, whereupon testing on the pool of words in question was discontinued. Half the subjects began with the pool of long words, and half with the short words.

The words were read to the subject at a 1.5-sec rate, with each list being preceded by the spoken warning "Ready." Subjects were allowed 15 sec to recall the words verbally in the order presented. Subjects were allowed to familiarize themselves with the two pools of words at the beginning of the experiment, and these two pools remained visible to the subjects on prompt cards throughout the experiment. Several different prompt cards with the words in differing orders were used in this and subsequent experiments so as to prevent the subjects from using location on the card as a cue. The subjects were eight undergraduate or postgraduate students from the University of Stirling.

Results and Discussion

Performance was scored in terms of number of sequences recalled completely correctly (i.e., all the items correct and in the correct order). Figure 4.1 shows the level of performance at each sequence length for the long and the short words. There is a very clear advantage to the short word set which occurs at all sequence lengths and is characteristic of all eight subjects tested.

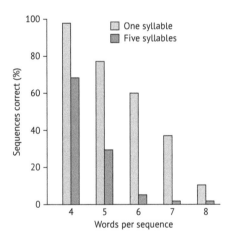

FIGURE 4.1

Effect of word length on memory span. Mean percentage recall of long and short words as a function of sequence length.

There is little doubt that the sample of short words used results in better memory span performance than the sample of long words. However, it is arguable that polysyllabic words tend to be linguistically different from monosyllables. In particular, our polysyllables tended to be of Latin origin, compared to the monosyllables which seemed to comprise simpler words of Anglo-Saxon origin. Experiment II attempted to avoid this problem by using words from a single category, country names, a sample of material unlikely to come from any single language source.

EXPERIMENT II
Method

Sequences of five words were constructed by sampling without replacement from each of two pools. The pool of short words comprised the country names *Chad, Chile, Greece, Tonga, Kenya, Burma, Cuba, Malta,* while the long names were *Somaliland, Afghanistan, Venezuela, Czechoslovakia, Yugoslavia, Ethiopia, Nicaragua,* and *Australia.* The names were selected on the basis of their probable familiarity to the subjects, and because they had a similar frequency of repetition of initial and final letters within the pool. Subjects were tested on a total of eight sequences of five short names and eight sequences of five long names. Eight undergraduate subjects were tested using the same presentation procedure as Experiment I.

Results and Discussion

Table 4.1 shows the mean number of sequences recalled completely correctly, and the mean number of items recalled in the appropriate serial position, for long and short names. On both these scores all eight subjects showed a clear word length effect. Since the material in this study was very different at a linguistic level from the material used in the previous study, and since the effect is very large in both cases, it is clear that the word length effect is a robust phenomenon of some generality. However, in these and all previous experiments investigating the effect of word length, two major variables are confounded, namely a word's spoken duration and the number of syllables it contains. The results could therefore indicate either that memory span is limited in the number of items it can hold, with the item being the syllable, or that the temporal duration of the words determines the size of memory span. The latter possibility might be predicted by decay theory (Broadbent, 1958) which assumes that forgetting occurs as a function of time. Many studies have attempted to test the theory by measuring performance as a function of presentation rate, and while some studies report enhanced performance with rapid presentation as predicted by decay theory (Conrad & Hille, 1958), others have found the opposite (Sperling & Speelman, 1970). However, in none of these studies was the subject prevented from rehearsing, and this makes interpretation of the results difficult as the subject is effectively re-presenting the list to himself at a rate of his own choosing. This problem can be avoided by allowing the subject to rehearse while using lists of long- and short-duration words. As less long words than short words can be rehearsed in a given period of time, a word duration effect will be predicted by decay theory (Sperling, 1963). On the other hand, a simple displacement or interference model would predict an effect of number of items, but not duration. Thus, the hypothesis that short-term memory capacity is a constant number of items, where the syllable is the item, predicts no word length effect for words matched for syllable number, but differing in spoken duration. Decay theory, on the other hand, predicts that the amount recalled will be a function of word duration. The next experiment tests these predictions.

Table 4.1 Mean Number of Sequences and Items Correctly Recalled as a Function of Word Length in Experiment II

	SHORT NAMES		LONG NAMES	
	MEAN	SD	MEAN	SD
Sequences correct				
Max = 8	4.50	2.00	.88	1.27
Items correct				
Max = 5	4.17	.71	2.80	.24

EXPERIMENT III

Method

Two pools of disyllabic words, matched for frequency, were produced such that one set tended to have a longer duration when spoken normally. The long word set comprised: *Friday, coerce, humane, harpoon, nitrate, cyclone, morphine, tycoon, voodoo,* and *zygote,* and the short words were *bishop, pectin, ember, wicket, wiggle, pewter, tipple, hackle, decor,* and *phallic.* The words were recorded by a female experimenter onto magnetic tape, which was then played through an oscillograph. This plots the wave-form of the signal against time, allowing the duration of the utterance to be measured. The mean duration of the long words was 0.77 sec, and of the short words, 0.46 sec.

From each pool of words, 10 lists of five words were constructed by sampling at random without replacement. The twenty lists were divided into four blocks of five, two comprising lists of short duration words and two of long duration words. A Latin square design was then used to present the blocks in counterbalanced order to each of the 12 subjects. Words were read at a 2-sec rate, and subjects were required to recall verbally at the same rate, paced by a metronome. Recall was paced so as to ensure that the mean delay between input and recall was comparable for long and short words (Conrad & Hille, 1958). Subjects were familiarized with the set of words and with the procedure, and were instructed to commence recall as soon as the last item in each list had been presented. Twelve undergraduates from the University of Stirling served as subjects.

Results and Discussion

Figure 4.2 shows the mean number of words correctly recalled as a function of serial position. A three-way analysis of variance involving subjects, word length, and serial position showed significant effects of word length, $F(1, 11) = 11.33$, $p < .01$, serial position, $F(4, 44) = 36.82$, $p < .001$, and a significant interaction between word length and serial position, $F(4, 44) = 3.28$, $p < .05$. Analysis by t test showed that the word length effect was significant for serial positions 1, 2, and 3, but not for positions 4 and 5.

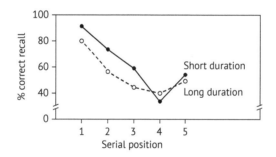

FIGURE 4.2

Mean recall of disyllabic words of long and short temporal duration.

These results are very similar to those of Watkins and Watkins (1973) showing a word length effect only for the earlier serial positions; this could reflect the masking of an underlying word length effect by the modality effect. However, the experiment differs from the Watkins and Watkins study in using words which are matched for number of syllables, but differ in spoken duration. As such, the results are consistent with decay theory, and are inconsistent with the hypothesis that short-term memory holds a constant number of syllables.

The last version of Miller's weakened hypothesis to be investigated is that short-term memory holds a constant number of phonemes. In the last experiment, there was a clear tendency for the long words to have more constituent phonemes, thus the result is open to the interpretation that the word length effect represents a limit to the number of phonemes that can be held. Experiment IV compares performance on sets of words which are matched for number of constituent phonemes, but which differ in duration. Decay theory again predicts a difference in performance in favor of the short duration words.

EXPERIMENT IV

Two sets of words were generated with the following constraints: They differed in spoken duration; they were equal in number of syllables; they were matched for word frequency; and they were equal in number of phonemes (with Scottish pronunciation). Given all these constraints, the previous sets of words reduced from 10 to five; details are given in Table 4.2. Sequences of five words were produced, and the experiment performed using a procedure identical to that used in Experiment III, except that the presentation and paced recall rate was increased to 1 sec per word. Eight Scottish undergraduates served as subjects.

Table 4.2 Details of Words Used in Experiment IV

	WORDS	FREQUENCY	NUMBER OF PHONEMES	DURATION (SEC)
Long	Coerce	1	5	.80
	Harpoon	1	6	.75
	Friday	40	5	.70
	Cyclone	3	6	.88
	Zygote	—	5	.90
Short	Wicket	1	5	.50
	Pectin	1	6	.60
	Bishop	40	5	.28
	Pewter	3	6	.40
	Phallic	—	5	.42

Results and Discussion

Subjects recalled a mean of 61.6% of the long words and 72.2 % of the short. A three-way analysis of variance showed a significant effect of word length, $F(1, 7) = 18.9$, $p < .01$, and of serial position, $F(4, 28) = 38.06$, $p < .001$, but no interaction between serial position and word length, $F(4, 28) = 0.55$, $p > .05$.

It is clear then that word duration may influence span when the number of both syllables and phonemes is held constant. The absence of an interaction between word length and serial position is puzzling in view of the previous result, it may be due to either the change in material, or more likely, the change in presentation and recall rate. However, despite this minor discrepancy between experiments III and IV, both seem to concur in suggesting that the temporal duration of items is a powerful determinant of memory span. Before finally dismissing the hypothesis that short-term memory capacity is a constant number of items, a procedural point that could have distorted the results should be mentioned. In both experiments the same experimenter read out the words and it is possible that some incidental feature of her mode of delivery produced the observed effect. To avoid this possibility, the experiment was repeated using visual presentation at a 2-sec rate and to our dismay, a statistically reliable word length effect was not observed.

However, a closer examination of the data revealed that most subjects did show the predicted effect, but that two out of eight did substantially better on the long words. On testing a further set of subjects and asking them how they remembered the material, it was found that those who did best on the short words reported using a rehearsal strategy, whilst those who did better on the long words reported using an imagery strategy. Use of this latter strategy was facilitated by the fact that the presentation rate had been reduced to 2 sec/word in order to obviate perceptual difficulties. As the subject of investigation is the articulatory short-term memory system, it is reasonable to instruct subjects to use a rehearsal strategy in order to avoid this difficulty. The next experiment, then, is a replication of the previous one, but using visual presentation with an instruction to the subjects to rehearse.

EXPERIMENT V

The same material and design were used as in the previous experiment, except that the material was presented visually on flash cards at a 2-sec rate, and recall was un-paced. The duration of the words was also measured in a different way. The duration of a word is determined by two sets of variables, the acoustic nature of the word and the subjects' articulatory rate. The latter variable has been shown to be very stable over a wide range of conditions within a subject, but to vary considerably between subjects (Goldman-Eisler, 1961), and, as decay theory assumes rehearsal rate determines performance, the subject's rather than the experimenter's pronounciation of the words was used.

Two different estimates of rehearsal rate were made. In the first of these, subjects were timed for reading the 10, five-word lists in each condition, as quickly as they could out loud, the 50 words being typed out in two columns. This was done four times for each word length after the memory task, times being recorded by stopwatch. The times so obtained were transformed into reading rate (RR) scores in units of words per second. The second estimate of rehearsal rate involved requiring the subject to repeat continuously three of the words from one of the pools out loud. Subjects did this as quickly as they could, and were timed by stopwatch for 10 repetitions of the three words. For each condition, they did this four times, always with a different set of three words, and always after the memory task. These times were transformed into articulatory rate scores (AR) in units of words per second. Half the subjects did the reading rate test first, and half the articulatory rate test first. The subjects, who were instructed to remember the lists by repeating the words to themselves, were eight members of the Applied Psychology Unit subject panel who were paid for their services.

Results and Discussion

Subjects recalled a mean of 53.4% of the long words correctly and in the right order, and 71.7% of the short words. Analysis of variance showed that there was a significant effect of word length, $F(1, 7) = 15.14$, $p < .01$, indicating that the word duration effect is not dependent on auditory presentation. There was again a significant effect of serial position, $F(4, 28) = 14.79$, $p < .001$, but the interaction between word length and serial position failed to reach significance, $F(4, 28) = 2.43$, $.05 < p < .1$. These results are again inconsistent with the hypothesis that short-term memory capacity is a constant number of items. An alternative view, that short-term memory is a time-based system, will next be explored and the adequacy of decay theory in this context empirically investigated.

Let us assume that the memory system underlying the word length effect exhibits trace decay, but that rehearsal may revive a decaying trace. It then follows that the amount recalled will be a function of rehearsal rate. Thus, if it can be assumed that reading rate (RR) and articulation rate (AR) are good estimates of rehearsal rate, then it should be possible to use them as predictors of memory span. Table 4.3 shows the ratio of memory span to reading rate and to articulation rate across conditions. A Wilcoxon matched pairs test showed that there was no effect of conditions for either the memory span-reading rate ratio, $T = 9$, $N = 8$, $p > .05$, or for the memory span-articulation rate ratio, $T = 10$, $N = 6$, $p > .05$. In short, Table 4.3 indicates that a subject can recall as many words as he can read in 1.6 sec, or can articulate in 1.3 sec. The next experiment explored this relationship in more detail using five different word lengths rather than two.

Table 4.3 Ratio of Memory Score to Reading Rate and to Articulation Rate for Subjects in Experiment V.

SUBJECT	MEMORY SCORE READING RATE		MEMORY SCORE ARTICULATION RATE	
	K_L^a	K_S^b	K_L^a	K_S^b
1	1.78	1.70	1.48	1.43
2	1.72	1.42	.93	.93
3	1.55	1.80	1.15	1.14
4	1.43	1.83	1.34	1.48
5	1.30	1.46	1.14	1.32
6	1.68	1.95	1.40	1.79
7	1.38	1.59	1.24	1.00
8	2.15	1.63	1.95	1.36
Mean	1.62	1.67	1.33	1.31

[a]K_L = Constant for long words.
[b]K_S = Constant for short words.

EXPERIMENT VI

Method

Five pools of 10 words were constructed. Each pool comprised one word from each of 10 semantic categories, the items being matched as closely as possible for familiarity to the subjects. The sets differed in comprising words of either one, two, three, four, or five syllables, as may be seen in Table 4.4.

Table 4.4 Pools of Words, Matched for Conceptual Class; Used in Experiment VI

NUMBER OF SYLLABLES				
1	2	3	4	5
Stoat	Puma	Gorilla	Rhinoceros	Hippopotamus
Mumps	Measles	Leprosy	Diphtheria	Tuberculosis
School	College	Nursery	Academy	University
Greece	Peru	Mexico	Australia	Yugoslavia
Crewe	Blackpool	Exeter	Wolverhampton	Weston-Super-Mare
Switch	Kettle	Radio	Television	Refrigerator
Maths	Physics	Botany	Biology	Physiology
Maine	Utah	Wyoming	Alabama	Louisiana
Scroll	Essay	Bulletin	Dictionary	Periodical
Zinc	Carbon	Calcium	Uranium	Aluminium

From each pool, 10 lists of five words were produced by sampling at random without replacement. The 50 lists were then presented visually on video tape in completely random order; hence subjects were unaware on any given trial what set would be used and so were unlikely to use a different strategy for words of different length. Half the subjects received Lists 1–25 first, and half Lists 26–50 first. Words were written on cards and presented at a 2-sec rate by a card changer which was viewed by a video camera and recorded. A card containing a row of asterisks served as a warning that the list was about to appear. Twelve seconds were allowed for spoken recall.

Reading rate was measured in this experiment by requiring the subjects to read lists of 50 words comprising five occurrences of each item in a given set. The words were typed in uppercase in random order in two columns on a sheet of paper. Subjects were instructed to read the lists aloud as quickly as they could, consistent with pronouncing each word correctly. Their reading times were measured by stopwatch. Subjects read each list a total of four times, twice before beginning the memory task and twice after completing it. Half the subjects began both tests by reading the one-syllable list and proceeding up to the five-syllable list, while the remainder of the subjects were tested in the reverse order. The subjects, who were tested individually, comprised 14 members of the Applied Psychology Unit's panel who were paid for their services.

Results

Figure 4.3 shows the effect of word length on mean percentage of words correctly recalled in the appropriate position, and mean reading rate.

Memory scores. Analysis of variance showed a significant effect of conditions, $F(4, 52) = 36.70, p < .001$, and of subjects, $F(13, 52) = 11.84, p < .001$. A Newman-Keuls test between conditions showed that words of one or two syllables were better recalled than words of three or four, which in turn were better than five-syllable words ($p < .05$ in each case).

Reading rate. Analysis of variance showed a significant effect of conditions, $F(4, 52) = 244.02, p < .001$. A Newman-Keuls test between conditions showed that each condition was significantly different from every other one ($p < .01$ in each case).

The next set of analyses tested the prediction made by decay theory, that the ratio memory span to reading rate is constant across conditions. Figure 4.4 shows memory span plotted as a function of reading rate, the line being fitted by the method of least squares. The slope of the line is 1.87, and the intercept on the ordinate 0.17. The standard error of the estimate is 0.10. The value of the intercept differs significantly from zero, $t(3) = 3.71, p < .05$. Thus the results are well described by the

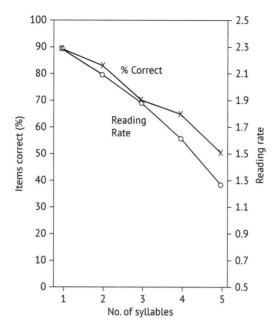

FIGURE 4.3

Mean reading rate and percentage correct recall of sequences of five words as a function of word length.

function $S = c + kR$, where S is the memory span, R is reading rate, and k and c are constants.

One final question of interest is whether such a relationship holds across subjects as well as across word samples, or in other words as to whether fast readers are also good memorizers. This proved to be the case; there was a substantial correlation between memory span and reading rate, $r(13) = .685, p < .005$.

Discussion

The results show that the manipulations were effective in producing sets of words of different spoken duration, and that memory score for these words was well predicted by their duration. It has also been shown that fast readers tend to be good memorizers. The relationship between reading rate and memory span thus appears to be remarkably straightforward. Again the ratio of reading rate to span is approximately constant, indicating in the present study that subjects are able to remember as much as they can read out in 1.8 sec. At this stage of research, however, it is probably imprudent to generalize this result too widely. There are many variables which change memory span, but which are unlikely to change reading rate

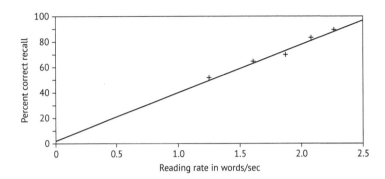

FIGURE 4.4

The relationship between reading rate and recall observed in Experiment VI.

(e.g., list length, word meaningfulness, interpolated delay). It would be of interest to know whether these variables have an effect on the slope, as predicted by decay theory, or on the intercept of the function. Only if the intercept stays consistently near to zero for a variety of conditions can the simple form of decay theory under discussion be accepted. The main result of the experiment however, when seen in conjunction with the previous studies, is that short-term memory capacity, as measured by memory span, is constant when measured in units of *time*, not in units of structure.

The time-based system, which presumably underlies the effects observed, is broadly consistent with a decay theory component of short-term forgetting. Decay theory ascribes to rehearsal the role of reviving a decaying trace, and it is this function of rehearsal that requires the prediction of a word length effect. It follows that if rehearsal could be prevented then, providing the presentation rate was the same for both long and short words, no word length effect should occur. The next experiment was designed to test this prediction. The technique used to stop rehearsal was that of articulatory suppression (Murray, 1968) in which the subject is required to articulate an irrelevant item during presentation of the list.

EXPERIMENT VII

In this experiment, the recall of visually presented lists of long and short words was compared under two conditions: (1) with the subject remaining silent during list input and being free to rehearse, and (2) with the subject required to articulate an irrelevant sequence of items. The design thus involved four conditions, comprising two word lengths in each of two presentation conditions.

Method

Two pools of 10 words each were produced, one of one-syllable words and one of five-syllable words, matched for word frequency. From each pool, 16 five-word lists were constructed by sampling at random without replacement. Each set of 16 lists was divided into two equal blocks and a Latin square used to determine order of presentation of the blocks. All subjects did all conditions. The lists were presented at a 1.5-sec rate on a memory drum, and subjects were instructed to recall the items in the order presented. In the suppression conditions, subjects counted repeatedly from one to eight, keeping rate of articulation as constant as possible at about three digits per second. They began counting before the list appeared and stopped to recall as soon as the last item had been presented. In the no-suppression condition, subjects were simply told to try to remember the words. The subjects, 12 undergraduate students from the University of Stirling, were familiarized with the pools of words before being tested.

Results and Discussion

Figure 4.5 shows the mean percentage of words recalled in the correct serial position as a function of word length for the two presentation conditions. Analysis of variance showed a significant effect of word length, $F(1, 11) = 17.73$, $p < .005$, of suppression, $F(1, 11) = 67.89$, $p < .001$, and a significant interaction between word length and suppression, $F(1, 11) = 16.30$, $p < .005$. The data may be summarized by saying that the word length effect disappears under suppression. Thus, these results are consistent with decay theory if it can be assumed that suppression stops rehearsal. Unfortunately, this latter assumption is open to dispute, since the effects of suppression seem to be dependent on presentation modality (Levy, 1971; Peterson & Johnson, 1971). In particular, suppression has been shown to have a large effect on visually presented material, but little effect on auditorily presented material. It would seem unlikely that suppression stops rehearsal with visual presentation, but not with auditory. An alternative explanation might be to assume that suppression stops the transformation of a visual stimulus into a phonemic code. Thus, given that the word length effect is mediated by a system employing a speech code, and that under suppression, visually presented material does not enter this system, we have an alternative explanation for the above results. Experiment VIII was designed to throw light on this issue.

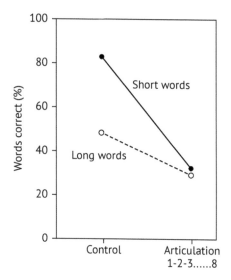

FIGURE 4.5

Effect of articulatory suppression on the word length effect. The influence of articulatory suppression on the recall of auditorily presented long and short words.

EXPERIMENT VIII

This was essentially a replication of the previous experiment, with the addition of a condition involving auditory presentation. This expanded the design into a 2 × 2 × 2 design, with two levels of word length (one and five syllables), two articulatory conditions (suppression and no suppression), and two presentation modes (auditory and visual). All subjects did all conditions, with the number of replications per condition being reduced to five. The experiment was run in two halves, with the four conditions of one modality in each half. Half the subjects did the visual conditions first, and half the auditory conditions first. Within a modality, the order of the conditions was determined by a Latin square. New pools of words were used, taken from the one- and five-syllable pools of Experiment VI. Presentation rate was slowed to 2 sec; in the auditory condition, the lists were read to the subject, whilst in the visual condition, the lists were presented on a memory drum. In all conditions, recall was verbal. In all other respects the procedure was as for the previous experiment; the subjects were 16 members of the Applied Psychology Unit panel who were paid for their services.

Results and Discussion

The mean percentage of words correctly recalled in the appropriate serial position is shown in Figure 4.6. Analysis of variance showed significant effects of word length, $F(1, 15) = 14.02$, $p < .005$, suppression, $F(1, 15) = 85.68$, $p < .001$, and modality, $F(1, 15) = 39.66$, $p < .001$. The interaction between word length and modality was significant, $F(1, 15) = 8.81$, $p < .01$, as was the suppression × modality interaction, $F(1, 15) = 33.13$, $p < .001$. The remaining two-way interaction, word length x suppression, just failed to reach significance $F(1, 15) = 4.49$, $.05 < p < .10$. The three-way interaction did reach significance, $F(1, 15) = 6.23$, $p < .05$. This last result indicates that the change in the word length effect produced by suppression is different in the two presentation modalities. Specifically, the word length effect is abolished by suppression in the visual modality, but is unchanged in the auditory modality.

The results demonstrate very clearly how the effects of suppression change with presentation modality and provide support for the view that suppression stops the visual to auditory transformation. These results can still be fitted into the simple decay and rehearsal hypothesis, but only if the assumption is made that articulatory suppression does not prevent rehearsal, but simply inhibits the translation of visual material into a phonemic code.

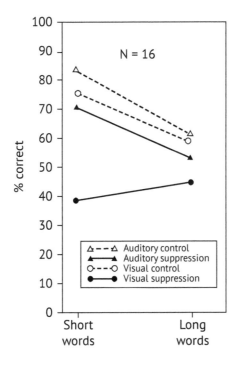

FIGURE 4.6

The influence of articulatory suppression on the recall of long and short words as a function of modality of presentation.

GENERAL DISCUSSION

The experiments described have shown: (1) That memory span is sensitive to word length across a range of verbal materials. (2) That when number of syllables and number of phonemes are held constant, the word length effect remains. (3) A systematic relationship between articulation time and memory span, such that memory span is equivalent to the number of words which can be read out in approximately 2 sec. (4) That memory span is correlated with reading rate across subjects. (5) That articulatory suppression abolishes the word length effect when material is presented visually.

We shall discuss the implications of these results for existing empirical generalizations about memory, and will then attempt to fit them into a conceptual framework.

The most obvious implication of these results is for Miller's (1956) suggestion that memory span is limited in terms of number of chunks of information, rather than their duration. It suggests a limit to the generality of the phenomenon which Miller discusses, but does not, of course, completely negate it. The question remains as to how much of the data subsumed under Miller's original generalization can be accounted for in terms of temporal rather than structural limitations. Consider, for example, the tendency for subjects' memory span for letter sequences to vary with order of approximation to English. McNulty (1966) has shown that higher orders of approximation to English lead to higher memory span performance when measured in terms of number of letters recalled, but not when measured in terms of number of adopted chunks. It seems highly probable that sequences which can be reduced to a relatively small number of chunks (e.g., THEMILEAKE) will be not only well remembered, but also spoken much more rapidly than sequences which cannot be reduced in this way (e.g., YVSPCWUECR). Such a view has, of course, been explored in some detail by Glanzer and Clark (1962) in connection with the recall of verbally recodable visual patterns. Both letter sequences and the types of pattern used by Glanzer and Clark are encodable into articulatory sequences which can be produced within the 1- to 2-sec limit implied by our results. It would clearly be desirable to explore the relationship between articulation time and memory for materials such as approximations to English prose, which are broadly consistent with Miller's chunking hypothesis (Tulving & Patkau, 1962), but which would seem likely to involve articulation times considerably in excess of 2 sec.

A second general point arises from the contrast between the recency effect in free recall, which apparently shows no word length effect (Craik, 1968; Glanzer & Razel, 1974), and the memory span task, which clearly does show such an effect. This fits in with the general pattern of results mentioned in the Introduction, suggesting that memory span relies on phonemic coding, whereas recency does not. This provides further evidence for the suggestion that the two reflect quite different underlying memory processes. Since most current views of the nature of short-term memory assumed a common primary memory system underlying both, it is unclear how they would interpret the word length effect.

One approach which does not have this drawback is the framework suggested by Baddeley and Hitch (1974), who explicitly postulate a working memory system which is responsible for performance on memory span tasks, but is not responsible for the recency effect in free recall. The formulation is based on a range of experiments in which subjects were required to perform reasoning, prose comprehension, or free recall learning tasks while simultaneously holding sequences of up to six random digits in short-term memory. In general, the results suggested that subjects could hold up to three items with virtually no effect on performance, but when required to remember six items, a decrement appeared. A tentative formulation was suggested in terms of a working memory system which acts as a central executive, and a supplementary articulatory rehearsal loop with a capacity of about three items.

Most of the experiments in the present series fit neatly into this broad framework, on the assumption that the word-length effect is the result of the limited capacity of the rehearsal loop. Looked at from this viewpoint, our data suggest that the articulatory loop system is time-based, and hence has a temporally limited capacity. When access to the loop is prevented by articulatory suppression, memory depends entirely on the capacity of the executive working memory system, which is not phonemically based, and does not have the same temporal limitation as the articulatory loop. The tendency for memory span to be impaired by phonemic similarity among the items to be remembered can also be attributed to the operation of the articulatory rehearsal system. As in the case of the word-length effect, the phonemic similarity effect disappears when articulatory suppression occurs with visually presented material (Levy, 1971). Finally, the existence of patients who have drastically impaired digit span, and yet who appear to show none of the general cognitive impairments that might be anticipated from most views of the role of short-term memory (Shallice & Warrington, 1970), can readily be accounted for within this framework if it is assumed that such patients are defective in the operation of the articulatory rehearsal system, while having the executive component of the working memory system intact.

One of our results however does present a problem for such a view. This is raised by the observation that the word-length effect does occur despite articulatory suppression, provided the material is presented auditorally. Levy (1971) has shown a similar pattern of results for phonemic similarity, with the similarity effect disappearing under suppression when visual presentation is used, but not when the presentation is auditory. On the straightforward assumption of an articulatory rehearsal loop which is entirely synonymous with subvocalization, it should follow that suppression effects could not be avoided by auditory presentation. Experiment

VIII, however, suggests that although articulatory suppression produces an overall impairment in performance with auditory presentation, it does not influence the word-length effect. This would therefore seem to point to articulation as being a means of converting the visual stimulus into a phonemic code which may be accepted by some form of storage system. With auditory presentation, the material is presumably already encoded in an appropriate form, and can be fed into the supplementary system without the need for articulation. The fact that articulatory suppression still impairs performance, even with auditory presentation, may imply either that there is an additional advantage to be gained by articulation, or simply that the task of suppression provides a secondary task which takes up some of the general processing capacity which might otherwise be devoted to remembering the items presented.

Suppose one tentatively assumes a supplementary phonemically based store, what might its other characteristics be? Could it, for example, be equivalent to the precategorical acoustic store suggested by Crowder and Morton (1969)? This seems unlikely for two reasons: First because the word length effect occurs with visual presentation, provided suppression is avoided, whereas the precategorical acoustic store does not appear to be operative unless auditory presentation is used. Secondly, Watkins and Watkins (1973) have presented evidence suggesting that the precategorical acoustic store is not sensitive to the effect of word length; if this is so, it can clearly not be used to explain the word-length effect. An alternative is to suggest that the system is an output buffer of some type: A limited-capacity store for holding the motor program necessary for the verbal production of letter names has been suggested by Sperling (1963). It seems plausible to assume that some form of buffer store is necessary for the smooth production of speech; and indeed the existence of the eye-voice span in reading points to some such temporary storage process (Morton, 1964), since what the reader is saying when reading aloud lags consistently behind the point at which he is fixating. Such a buffer system would need to be separate from the act of articulation, since it is presumably necessary to set up new articulatory programs while existing programs are operating. On this interpretation, therefore, articulatory programs can be set up or at least primed, either by the act of overt or covert articulation, or indirectly through auditory stimulation. It is tentatively suggested that such a system may be necessary for fluent speech, and may have the supplementary advantage of providing an additional backup system for the immediate retention of phonemically codable material. Such a view is clearly very tentative and leaves unspecified the complex problem of how such a store might be interfaced with the other components of the system so as to account for even the basic phenomena of the memory span. It does, however, have the advantage of linking together the existing data in a way which is both internally consistent and also likely to generate testable hypotheses.

REFERENCES

Baddeley, A. D. Short-term memory for word sequences as a function of acoustic, semantic and formal similarity. *Quarterly Journal of Experimental Psychology*, 1966, **18**, 362–365.

Baddeley, A. D., & Hitch, G. Working memory. In G. A. Bower (Ed.), *The psychology of learning and motivation*. New York: Academic Press, 1968, Vol. 8.

Broadbent, D. E. *Perception and communication*. London: Pergamon Press, 1958.

Conrad, R. Acoustic confusion in immediate memory. *British Journal of Psychology*, 1964, **55**, 75–84.

Conrad, R., & Hille, B. A. The decay theory of immediate memory and paced recall. *Canadian Journal of Psychology*, 1958, **12**, 1–6.

Craik, F. I. M. Two components in free recall. *Journal of Verbal Learning and Verbal Behavior*, 1968, **7**, 996–1004.

Craik, F. 1. M. The fate of primary memory items in free recall. *Journal of Verbal Learning and Verbal Behavior*, 1970, **9**, 143–148.

Craik, F. I. M., & Levy, B. A. Semantic and acoustic information in primary memory. *Journal of Experimental Psychology*, 1970, **86**, 77–82.

Crowder, R. G., & Morton, J. Precategorical acoustic storage (PAS). *Perception & Psychophysics*, 1969, **5**, 365–373.

Glanzer, M., & Clark, W. H. Accuracy of perceptual recall: An analysis of organization. *Journal of Verbal Learning and Verbal Behavior*, 1962, **1**, 289–299.

Glanzer, M., Koppenaal, L., & Nelson, R. Effects of relations between words on short-term storage and long-term storage. *Journal of Verbal Learning and Verbal Behavior*, 1972, **8**, 435–447.

Glanzer, M., & Razel, M. The size of the unit in short-term storage. *Journal of Verbal Learning and Verbal Behavior*, 1974, **13**, 114–131.

Goldman-Eisler, F. The significance of changes in rate of articulation. *Language and Speech*, 1961, **4**, 171–174.

Levy, B. A. The role of articulation in auditory and visual short-term memory. *Journal of Verbal Learning and Verbal Behavior*, 1971, **10**, 123–132.

Mackworth, J. F. The relation between the visual image and post-perceptual immediate memory. *Journal of Verbal Learning and Verbal Behavior*, 1963, **2**, 75–85.

McNulty, J. A. The measurement of "adopted chunks" in free recall learning. *Psychonomic Science*, 1966, **4**, 71–72.

Miller, G. A. The magical number seven, plus or minus two: Some limits to our capacity for processing information. *Psychological Review*, 1956, **63**, 81–97.

Morton, J. The effects of context upon speed of reading, eye movements and eye-voice span. *Quarterly Journal of Experimental Psychology*, 1964, **16**, 340–354.

Murray, D. J. Articulation and Acoustic confusability in short-term memory. *Journal of Experimental Psychology*, 1968, **78**, 679–684.

Murray, D. J. Articulation and Acoustic confusability in short-term memory. *Journal of Experimental Psychology*, 1968, **78**, 679–684.

Peterson, L. R., & Johnson, S. F. Some effects of minimising articulation on short-term retention. *Journal of Verbal Learning and Verbal Behavior*, 1971, **10**, 346–354.

Richardson, J. T. E., & Baddeley, A. D. The effect of articulatory suppression in free recall. *Journal of Verbal Learning and Verbal Behavior*, 1975, **14**, 623–629.

Shallice, T. & Warrington, E. K. Independent functioning of verbal memory stores: A neuropsychological study. *Quarterly Journal of Experimental Psychology*, 1970, **22**, 261–273.

Sperling, G. A model for visual memory tasks. *Human Factors*, 1963, **5**, 19–31.

Sperling, G., & Speelman, R. G. Acoustic similarity and auditory short-term memory: Experiments and a model. In D. A. Norman (Ed.), *Models of human memory*. New York: Academic Press, 1970.

Tulving, E., & Patkau, J. E. Concurrent effects of contextual constraint and word frequency on immediate recall and learning of verbal material. *Canadian Journal of Psychology*, 1962, **16,** 83–95.

Watkins, M. J., & Watkins, O. C. The postcategorical status of the modality effect in serial recall. *Journal of Experimental Psychology*, 1973, **99,** 226–230.

REFERENCE NOTES

1. Laughery, K. R., Lachman, R., & Dansereau, D. D. Short-term memory: Effects of item-pronunciation time. (Unpublished.)

2. Standing, L., Bond, B., & Smith, P. The memory span. (Unpublished.)

Name:_____

READING COMPREHENSION QUESTIONS

Refer to the information you have just read to find the answers to these questions. Be sure that you do not simply copy what is already written in the article. Think about your answer and write it in your own words.

1. Write any words that you had to look up here, along with their definitions. If you did not need to look up any words, list and define several of the words you think the average college student may have found difficult. All students should have at least three words and definitions for this question.

2. Write the full reference for this article in APA style. For advice on APA style, consult www.apastyle.org.

3. Explain what is novel about this study that made it publishable. Be sure to describe exactly what previous studies lacked that this study offers. Simply describing this study, or simply describing previous studies, is insufficient.

Name:_____

4. Generally describe the methods used in the paper.

    •   How many subjects were there? If there was more than one experiment, list the number of subjects in each experiment.

    •   Who were the subjects (e.g., older adults, schizophrenic patients, college students)?

    •   What was it like to be a subject (i.e., what were the subjects required to do)? Provide enough detail that the reader can truly imagine what it was like to be a subject.

5. What were the main findings of this paper?

Name:_____

COMPREHENSION CHECK QUESTIONS

Refer to the information you have just read to find the answers to these questions. Be sure that you do not simply copy what is already written in the article. Think about your answer and write it in your own words.

1. Experiment Proposal

Pretend that you are an author on this paper and are tasked with determining future directions. Taking into account what has already been done in the field (i.e., the information presented in the Introduction) and the present study, what is a novel next step in this research? If you were one of the authors of this study, what would you do next and why? Be sure to explain why you would perform this next step. For example, proposing to replicate the study sampling from a different subject population is not sufficient, unless you explain why it is a reasonable next step.

Name:_____

2. Writing Critique

Pretend that you are a reviewer on this paper and are required to make a substantial suggestion on how to improve the writing. For example, you could offer an alternative explanation of how to describe the importance of the work, explain why the real-world application is insufficient, or suggest how the authors could describe their work in a more interesting way. If you were a reviewer, what would you say to improve the writing (not the methods) of this paper? Be sure to provide concrete suggestions. For example, do not simply say that an aspect of the paper was confusing. Demonstrate that you took the time to understand the material and offer a better way to explain the portion you found confusing.

Name:_____

3. Application Question

Think about how the work in this paper applies to the real world. Describe a scenario (either real or imagined) under which this work applies to your life. Do not use the real-world application mentioned in the paper. Rather, consider how this work is relevant to you (again, it could be imagined). Be sure to demonstrate that you understand the results of the paper through your real-world application.

Name:_____

TRUE OR FALSE STATEMENTS

Write three *true* statements here, noting the page number where the answer can be located.

1. _____
   _____
   _____
   _____
   _____

   • Page number where answer can be located: _____

2. _____
   _____
   _____
   _____
   _____

   • Page number where answer can be located: _____

3. _____
   _____
   _____
   _____
   _____

   • Page number where answer can be located: _____

Name:_____

Write three *false* statements here, noting the page number where the answer can be located. Then rewrite each statement to make it true.

1. _____
   _____
   _____

   - Rewritten to be true:
     _____
     _____

   - Page number where answer can be located: _____

2. _____
   _____
   _____

   - Rewritten to be true:
     _____
     _____

   - Page number where answer can be located: _____

3. _____
   _____
   _____

   - Rewritten to be true:
     _____
     _____

   - Page number where answer can be located: _____

Creating False Memories
Remembering Words Not Presented in Lists

Henry L. Roediger and Kathleen B. McDermott

Abstract

Two experiments (modeled after J. Deese's 1959 study) revealed remarkable levels of false recall and false recognition in a list learning paradigm. In Experiment 1, subjects studied lists of 12 words (e.g. *bed*, *rest*, *awake*); each list was composed of associates of 1 nonpresented word (e.g. *sleep*). On immediate free recall tests, the nonpresented associates were recalled 40% of the time and were later recognized with high confidence. In Experiment 2, a false recall rate of 55% was obtained with an expanded set of lists, and on a later recognition test, subjects produced false alarms to these items at a rate comparable to the hit rate. The act of recall enhanced later remembering of both studied and nonstudied material. The results reveal a powerful illusion of memory: People remember events that never happened.

False memories—either remembering events that never happened, or remembering them quite differently from the way they happened—have recently captured the attention of both psychologists and the public at large. The primary impetus for this recent surge of interest is the increase in the number of cases in which memories of previously unrecognized abuse are reported during the course of therapy. Some researchers have argued that certain therapeutic practices

Roediger, H. L., & McDermott, K. B. (1995). Creating False Memories: Remembering Words Not Presented In Lists. *Journal of Experimental Psychology: Learning, Memory, and Cognition*, 21(4), 803-814. Copyright © by American Psychological Association. Reprinted with permission.

can cause the creation of false memories, and therefore, the apparent "recovery" of memories during the course of therapy may actually represent the creation of memories (Lindsay & Read, 1994; Loftus, 1993). Although the concept of false memories is currently enjoying an increase in publicity, it is not new; psychologists have been studying false memories in several laboratory paradigms for years. Schacter (in press) provides an historical overview of the study of memory distortions.

Bartlett (1932) is usually credited with conducting the first experimental investigation of false memories; he had subjects read an Indian folktale, "The War of the Ghosts," and recall it repeatedly. Although he reported no aggregate data, but only sample protocols, his results seemed to show distortions in subjects' memories over repeated attempts to recall the story. Interestingly, Bartlett's repeated reproduction results never have been successfully replicated by later researchers (see Gauld & Stephenson, 1967; Roediger, Wheeler, & Rajaram, 1993); indeed, Wheeler and Roediger (1992) showed that recall of prose passages (including "The War of the Ghosts") actually improved over repeated tests (with very few errors) if short delays occurred between study and test.[1]

Nonetheless, Bartlett's (1932) contribution was an enduring one because he distinguished between *reproductive* and *reconstructive* memory. Reproductive memory refers to accurate, rote production of material from memory, whereas reconstructive memory emphasizes the active process of filling in missing elements while remembering, with errors frequently occurring. It generally has been assumed that the act of remembering materials rich in meaning (e.g., stories and real-life events) gives rise to reconstructive processes (and therefore errors), whereas the act of remembering more simplified materials (e.g., nonsense syllables, word lists) gives rise to reproductive (and thus accurate) memory. Bartlett (1932) wrote that "I discarded nonsense materials because, among other difficulties, its use almost always weights the evidence in favour of mere rote recapitulation" (p. 204).

The investigators of false memories have generally followed Bartlett's (1932) lead. Most evidence has been collected in paradigms that use sentences (Bransford & Franks, 1971; Brewer, 1977), prose passages (Sulin & Dooling, 1974), slide sequences (Loftus, Miller, & Burns, 1978), or videotapes (Loftus & Palmer, 1974). In all these paradigms, evidence of false memories has been obtained, although the magnitude of the effect depends on the method of testing (McCloskey & Zaragoza, 1985; Payne, Toglia, & Anastasi, 1994). The predominance of materials that tell a story (or can be

---

1 Bartlett's (1932) results from the serial reproduction paradigm—in which one subject recalls an event, the next subject reads and then recalls the first subject's report, and so on—replicates quite well (e.g., I. H. Paul, 1959). However, the repeated reproduction research, in which a subject is tested repeatedly on the same material, is more germane to the study of false memories in an individual over time. To our knowledge, no one has successfuly replicated Bartlett's observations in this paradigm with instructions that emphasize remembering (see Gauld & Stevenson, 1967).

represented by a script or schema) can probably be attributed to the belief that only such materials will cause false memories to occur.

There is one well-known case of false memories being produced in a list learning paradigm: Underwood (1965) introduced a technique to study false recognition of words in lists. He gave subjects a continuous recognition task in which they decided if each presented word had been given previously in the list. Later words bore various relations to previously studied words. Underwood showed that words associatively related to previously presented words were falsely recognized. Anisfeld and Knapp (1968), among others, replicated the phenomenon. Although there have been a few reports of robust false recognition effects (Hintzman, 1988), in many experiments the false recognition effect was either rather small or did not occur at all. For example, in a study by L. M. Paul (1979), in which synonyms were presented at various lags along with other, unrelated lures, the false recognition effect was only 3% (a 20% false-alarm rate for synonyms and a 17% rate for unrelated lures). Gillund and Shiffrin (1984) failed to find any false recognition effect for semantically related lures in a similar paradigm. In general, most research on the false recognition effect in list learning does little to discourage the belief that more natural, coherent materials are needed to demonstrate powerful false memory effects. Interestingly, most research revealing false memory effects has used recognition measures; this is true both of the prose memory literature (e.g., Bransford & Franks, 1971; Sulin & Dooling, 1974) and the eyewitness memory paradigm (Loftus et al., 1978; McCloskey & Zaragoza, 1985). Reports of robust levels of false recall are rarer.

We have discovered a potentially important exception to these claims, one that reveals false recall in a standard list learning paradigm. It is represented in an experimental report published by Deese in 1959 that has been largely overlooked for the intervening 36 years, despite the fact that his observations would seem to bear importantly on the study of false memories. Deese's procedure was remarkably straightforward; he tested memory for word lists in a single-trial, free-recall paradigm. Because this paradigm was just gaining favor among experimental psychologists at that time and was the focus of much attention during the 1960s, the neglect of Deese's report is even more surprising. However, since the Social Science Citation Index began publication in 1969, the article has been cited only 14 times, and only once since 1983. Most authors mentioned it only in passing, several authors apparently cited it by mistake, and no one has followed up Deese's interesting observations until now, although Cramer (1965) reported similar observations and did appropriately cite Deese's (1959) article. (While working on this article, we learned that Don Read was conducting similar research which is described briefly in Lindsay & Read, 1994, p. 291.)[2]

Deese (1959) was interested in predicting the occurrence of extralist intrusions in single-trial free recall. To this end, he developed 36 lists, with 12 words per list. Each list was composed of the 12 primary associates of a critical (nonpresented) word. For example, for the critical word *needle,* the list words were *thread, pin, eye, sewing, sharp, point, pricked, thimble, haystack, pain, hurt,* and *injection.* He found that some of the lists reliably induced subjects to produce the critical nonpresented word as an intrusion on the immediate free recall test. Deese's interest was in determining why some lists gave rise to this effect, whereas others did not. His general conclusion was that the lists for which the associations went in a backward (as well as forward) direction tended to elicit false recall. That is, he measured the average probability with which people produced the critical word from which the list was generated when they were asked to associate to the individual words in the list. For example, subjects were given *sewing, point, thimble,* and so on, and the average probability of producing *needle* as an associate was measured. Deese obtained a correlation of .87 between the probability of an intrusion in recall (from one group of subjects) and the probability of occurrence of the word as an associate to members of the list (from a different group). Our interest in Deese's materials was in using his best lists and developing his paradigm as a way to examine false memory phenomena.

Our first goal was to try to replicate Deese's (1959) finding of reliable, predictable extralist intrusions in a single-trial, free-recall paradigm. We found his result to be surprising in light of the literature showing that subjects are often extremely accurate in recalling lists after a single trial, making few intrusions unless instructed to guess (see Cofer, 1967; Roediger & Payne, 1985). As previously noted, most prior research on false memory phenomena has employed measures of recognition memory or cued recall. Deese's paradigm potentially offers a method to study false recollections in free recall. However, we also extended Deese's paradigm to recognition tests. In Experiment 1, we examined false recall and false recognition of the critical non-presented words and the confidence with which subjects accepted or rejected the critical nonpresented words as having been in the study lists. In Experiment 2, we tested other lists constructed to produce extralist intrusions in single-trial free recall, to generalize the finding across a wider set of materials. In addition, we examined the extent to which the initial false recall of items led to later false recognition of those same items. Finally, we employed the remember–know procedure developed by Tulving (1985) to examine subjects' phenomenological experience during false

---

2 Some people know of Deese's (1959) paper indirectly because Appleby (1986) used it as the basis of a suggested classroom demonstration of déjà vu.

recognition of the critical nonpresented items. We describe this procedure more fully below.

EXPERIMENT 1

The purpose of Experiment 1 was to replicate Deese's (1959) observations of false recall by using six lists that produced among the highest levels of erroneous recall in his experiments. Students heard and recalled the lists and then received a recognition test over both studied and nonstudied items, including the critical nonpresented words.

Method

Subjects

Subjects were 36 Rice University undergraduates who participated as part of a course project during a regular meeting of the class, Psychology 308, Human Memory.

Materials

We developed six lists from the materials listed in Deese's (1959) article. With one exception, we chose the six targets that produced the highest intrusion rates in Deese's experiment: *chair, mountain, needle, rough, sleep,* and *sweet.* As in Deese's experiment, for each critical word, we constructed the corresponding list by obtaining the first 12 associates listed in Russell and Jenkins's (1954) word association norms. For example, the list corresponding to *chair* was *table, sit, legs, seat, soft, desk, arm, sofa, wood, cushion, rest,* and *stool.* In a few instances, we replaced 1 of the first 12 associates with a word that seemed, in our judgment, more likely to elicit the critical word. (The lists for Experiment 1 are included in the expanded set of lists for Experiment 2 reported in the Appendix.)

The 42-item recognition test included 12 studied and 30 nonstudied items. There were three types of nonstudied items, or lures: (a) the 6 critical words, from which the lists were generated (e.g., *chair*), (b) 12 words generally unrelated to any items on the six lists, and (c) 12 words weakly related to the lists (2 per list). We drew the weakly related words from Positions 13 and below in the association norms; for example, we chose *couch* and *floor* for the *chair* list. We constructed the test sequence in blocks; there were 7 items per block, and each block corresponded to a studied list (2 studied words, 2 related words, 2 unrelated words, and the critical nonstudied lure). The order of the blocks corresponded to the order in which lists had been studied. Each block of test items always began with a studied word and ended with the critical lure; the other items were arranged haphazardly in between. One of the

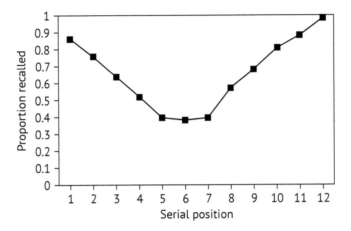

FIGURE 5.1

Probability of correct recall in Experiment 1 as a function of serial position. Probability of recall of the studied words was .65, and probability of recall of the critical nonpresented item was .40.

two studied words that were tested occurred in the first position of the study list (and therefore was the strongest associate to the critical item); the other occurred somewhere in the first 6 positions of the study list.

Procedure

Subjects were tested in a group during a regular class meeting. They were instructed that they would hear lists of words and that they would be tested immediately after each list by writing the words on successive pages of examination booklets. They were told to write the last few items first (a standard instruction for this task) and then to recall the rest of the words in any order. They were also told to write down all the words they could remember but to be reasonably confident that each word they wrote down did in fact occur in the list (i.e., they were told not to guess). The lists were read aloud by the first author at the approximate rate of 1 word per 1.5 s. Before reading each list, the experimenter said "List 1, List 2," and so on, and he said "recall" at the end of the list. Subjects were given 2.5 min to recall each list.

After the sixth list, there was brief conversation lasting 2–3 min prior to instructions for the recognition test. At this point, subjects were told that they would receive another test in which they would see words on a sheet and that they were to rate each as to their confidence that it had occurred on the list. The 4-point rating scale was 4 for *sure that the item was old* (or studied), 3 for *probably old,* 2 for *probably new,* and 1 for *sure it was new.* Subjects worked through the recognition test at their own pace.

At the end of the experiment, subjects were asked to raise their hands if they had recognized six particular items on the test, and the critical lures were read aloud.

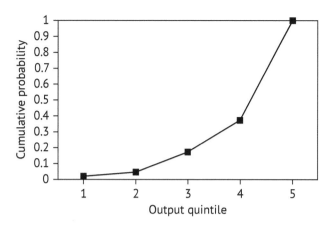

FIGURE 5.2

Recall of the critical intrusion as a function of output position in recall. Quintiles refer to the first 20% of responses, the second 20%, and so on.

Most subjects raised their hands for several items. The experimenter then informed them that none of the words just read had actually been on the list and the subjects were debriefed about the purpose of the experiment, which was a central topic in the course.

Results

Recall

The mean probability of recall of the studied words was .65, and the serial position curve is shown in Figure 5.1. The curve was smoothed by averaging data from three adjacent points for each position because the raw data were noisy with only six lists. For example, data from the third, fourth, and fifth points contributed to the fourth position in the graph. The first and the last positions, however, were based only on the raw data. The serial position curve shows marked recency, indicating that subjects followed directions in recalling the last items first. A strong primacy effect is also apparent, probably because the strongest associates to the critical target words occurred early in the list. The critical omitted word was recalled with a probability of .40, or with about the same probability as items that had been presented in the middle of the list (see Figure 5.1). Therefore, items that were not presented were recalled at about the same rate as those that were presented, albeit those in the least favorable serial positions.

The average output position for recall of the critical nonpresented word was 6.9 (out of 8.6 words written down in lists in which there was a critical intrusion).

The cumulative production levels of the critical intrusion for those trials on which they occurred is shown in Figure 5.2 across quintiles of subjects' responses. The critical intrusion appeared only 2% of the time in the first fifth of subjects' output but 63% of the time in the last quintile. Thus, on average, subjects recalled the critical nonstudied item in the last fifth of their output, at the 80th percentile of recalled words (6.9 ÷ 8.6 × 100).

Other intrusions also occurred in recall, albeit at a rather low rate. Subjects intruded the critical lure on 40% of the lists, but any other word in the English language was intruded on only 14% of the lists. Therefore, subjects were not guessing wildly in the experiment; as usual in single-trial free recall, the general intrusion rate was quite low. Nonetheless, subjects falsely recalled the critical items at a high rate.

Recognition

The recognition test was given following study and recall of all six lists, and thus the results were likely affected by prior recall. (We consider this issue in Experiment 2.) The proportion of responses for each of the four confidence ratings are presented in Table 5.1 for studied (old) items and for the three different types of lures: unrelated words, weakly related words, and the critical words from which the lists were derived. Consider first the proportion of items subjects called old by assigning a rating of 3 (*probably old*) or 4 (*sure old*). The hit rate was 86% and the false-alarm rate for the standard type of unrelated lures was only 2%, so by usual criteria subjects showed high accuracy. The rate of false alarms was higher for the weakly related lures (.21) than for the unrelated lures, $t(35) = 7.40$, $SEM = .026$, $p < .001$. This outcome replicates the standard false-recognition effect first reported by Underwood (1965). The false-recognition rate for weakly related lures was greater than obtained in many prior studies (e.g., L. M. Paul, 1979), and the rate for the critical nonpresented words was dramatically larger than the rate for the weakly related words. As shown in Table 5.1, the false-alarm rate for the critical nonstudied lures (.84) approached the hit rate (.86), $t(35) < 1$, $SEM = .036$, ns.

Table 5.1 Recognition Results for Experiment 1: The Proportion of Items Classified As Sure Old (a Rating of 4), Probably Old (3), Probably New (2), or Sure New (1) and the Mean Ratings of Items As a Function of Study Status

STUDY STATUS	OLD		NEW		MEAN RATING
	4	3	2	1	
Studied	.75	.11	.09	.05	3.6
Nonstudied					
Unrelated lure	.00	.02	.18	.80	1.2
Weakly related lure	.04	.17	.35	.44	1.8
Critical lure	.58	.26	.08	.08	3.3

Consider next the results based on subjects high-confidence responses (i.e., when they were sure the item had appeared in the study list and rated it a "4"). The proportion of unrelated and weakly related lures falling into this category approached zero. However, subjects were still sure that the critical nonstudied items had been studied over half the time (.58). The hit rate for the studied items remained quite high (.75) and was reliably greater than the false-alarm rate for the critical lures, t (35) = 3.85, SEM = .044, p < .001. It is also interesting to look at the rates at which subjects classified items as *sure new*. Unrelated lures were correctly rejected with high confidence 80% of the time. Related lures received this classification only 44% of the time, and critical lures were confidently rejected at an even lower rate, 8%, which is similar to the rate for studied words (5%).

Table 5.1 also presents the mean ratings for the four types of items on the 4-point scale. This measure seems to tell the same story as the other two: The mean rating of the critical lures (3.3) approached that of studied items (3.6); the difference did reach significance, t (35) = 2.52, SEM = .09, p < .05. In general, the judgments subjects provided for the critical lures appeared much more similar to those of studied items than to the other types of lures.

Discussion

The results of Experiment 1 confirmed Deese's (1959) observation of high levels of false recall in a single-trial, free-recall task, albeit with six lists that were among his best. We found that the critical nonpresented items were recalled at about the same level as items actually presented in the middle of the lists. This high rate of false recall was not due to subjects guessing wildly. Other intrusions occurred at a very low rate. In addition, we extended Deese's results to a recognition test and showed that the critical nonpresented items were called old at almost the same level as studied items (i.e., the false-alarm rate for the critical nonpresented items approximated the hit rate for the studied items). The false-alarm rate for the critical nonpresented items was much higher than for other related words that had not been presented. Finally, more than half the time subjects reported that they were sure that the critical nonstudied item had appeared on the list. Given these results, this paradigm seems a promising method to study false memories. Experiment 2 was designed to further explore these false memories.

EXPERIMENT 2

We had four aims in designing Experiment 2. First, we wanted to replicate and extend the recall and recognition results of Experiment 1 to a wider set of materials. Therefore, we developed twenty-four 15-item lists similar to those used in Experiment 1 and in Deese's (1959) experiment. (We included expanded versions of the six lists used in Experiment 1.) Second, we wanted to examine the effect of recall on the subsequent recognition test. In Experiment 1 we obtained a high level of false recognition for the critical nonpresented words, but the lists had been recalled prior to the recognition test, and in 40% of the cases the critical item had been falsely recalled, too. In Experiment 2, we examined false recognition both for lists that had been previously recalled and for those that had not been recalled. Third, we wanted to determine the false-alarm rates for the critical nonpresented items when the relevant list had not been presented previously (e.g., to determine the false-alarm rate for *chair* when related words had not been presented in the list). Although we considered it remote, the possibility existed that the critical nonpresented items simply elicit a high number of false alarms whether or not the related words had been previously presented.

The fourth reason—and actually the most important one—for conducting the second experiment was to obtain subjects' judgments about their phenomenological experience while recognizing nonpresented items. We applied the procedure developed by Tulving (1985) in which subjects are asked to distinguish between two states of awareness about the past: remembering and knowing. When this procedure is applied in conjunction with a recognition test, subjects are told (a) to judge each item to be old (studied) or new (nonstudied) and (b) to make an additional judgment for each item judged to be old: whether they remember or know that the item occurred in the study list. A *remember* experience is defined as one in which the subject can mentally relive the experience (perhaps by recalling its neighbors, what it made them think of, what they were doing when they heard the word, or physical characteristics associated with its presentation). A *know* judgment is made when subjects are confident that the item occurred on the list but are unable to reexperience (i.e., remember) its occurrence. In short, remember judgments reflect a mental reliving of the experience, whereas know judgments do not. There is now a sizable literature on remember and know judgments (see Gardiner & Java, 1993; Rajaram & Roediger, in press), but we will not review it here except to say that evidence exists that remember–know judgments do not simply reflect two states of confidence (high and low) because variables can affect remember–know and confidence (sure–unsure) judgments differently (e.g., Rajaram, 1993).

Our purpose in using remember–know judgments in Experiment 2 was to see if subjects who falsely recognized the critical nonpresented words would report accompanying remember experiences, showing that they were mentally reexperiencing events that never occurred. In virtually all prior work on false memories, it has been assumed that subjects' incorrect responses indicated false remembering. However, if Tulving's (1985) distinction is accepted, then responding on a memory test should not be equated with remembering. Further metamemorial judgments such as those obtained with the remember–know procedure are required to determine if subjects are remembering the events. In fact, in most experiments using the remember–know procedure, false alarms predominantly have been judged as know responses (e.g., Gardiner, 1988; Jones & Roediger, 1995). This outcome would be predicted in our experiment, too, if one attributes false recognition to a high sense of familiarity that arises (perhaps) through spreading activation in an associative network. Therefore, in Experiment 2 we examined subjects' metamemorial judgments with respect to their false memories to see whether they would classify these memories as being remembered or known to have occurred.

In Experiment 2, subjects were presented with 16 lists; after half they received an immediate free recall test, and after the other half they did math problems. After all lists had been presented, subjects received a recognition test containing items from the 16 studied lists and 8 comparable lists that had not been studied. During the recognition test, subjects made old–new judgments, followed by remember–know judgments for items judged to be old.

Method

Subjects

Thirty Rice University undergraduates participated in a one hour session as part of a course requirement.

Materials

We developed 24 lists from Russell and Jenkins's (1954) norms in a manner similar to that used for Experiment 1. For each of 24 target words, 15 associates were selected for the list. These were usually the 15 words appearing first in the norms, but occasionally we substituted other related words when these seemed more appropriate (i.e., more likely to elicit the nonpresented target as an associate). The ordering of words within lists was held constant; the strongest associates generally occurred first. An example of a list for the target word *sleep* is: *bed, rest, awake, tired, dream, wake, night, blanket, doze, slumber, snore, pillow, peace, yawn, drowsy.* All the lists, corrected for a problem noted in the next paragraph, appear in the Appendix.

The 24 lists were arbitrarily divided into three sets for counterbalancing purposes. Each set served equally often in the three experimental conditions, as described below. The reported results are based on only 7 of the 8 lists in each set because the critical items in 2 of the lists inadvertently appeared as studied items in other lists; dropping 1 list in each of two sets eliminated this problem and another randomly picked list from the third set was also dropped, so that each scored set was based on 7 lists. With these exceptions, none of the critical items occurred in any of the lists.

Design

The three conditions were tested in a within-subjects design. Subjects studied 16 lists; 8 lists were followed by an immediate free recall test, and 8 others were not followed by an initial test. The remaining 8 lists were not studied. Items from all 24 lists appeared on the later recognition test. On the recognition test, subjects judged items as old (studied) or new (nonstudied) and, when old, they also judged if they remembered the item from the list or rather knew that it had occurred.

Procedure

Subjects were told that they would be participating in a memory experiment in which they would hear lists of words presented by means of a tape player. They were told that after each list they would hear a sound (either a tone or a knock, with examples given) that would indicate whether they should recall items from the list or do math problems. For half of the subjects, the tone indicated that they should recall the list, and the knock meant they should perform math problems; for the other half of the subjects, the signals were reversed. They were told to listen carefully to each list and that the signal would occur after the list had been presented; therefore, subjects never knew during list presentation whether the list would be recalled. Words were recorded in a male voice and presented approximately at a 1.5-s rate. Subjects were given 2 min after each list to recall the words or to perform multiplication and division problems. Recall occurred on 4 inch by 11 inch sheets of paper, and subjects turned over each sheet after the recall period, so the recalled items were no longer in view. The first part of the experiment took about 45 min.

The recognition test occurred about 5 min after the test or math period for the 16th list. During this time, subjects were given instructions about making old–new and remember–know judgments. They were told that they would see a long list of words, some of which they had heard during the earlier phase of the experiment. They were to circle either the word *old* or *new* next to each test item to indicate whether the item had been presented by means of the tape player. If an item was judged old, subjects were instructed that they should further distinguish between remembering and knowing by writing an *R* or *K* in the space beside the item. Detailed instructions on the remember–know distinction were given, modeled after those of Rajaram (1993). Essentially, subjects were told that a remember judgment should be made for items for which they had a vivid memory of the actual presentation; know judgments were reserved for items that they were sure had been presented but for which they lacked the feeling of remembering the actual occurrence of the words. They were told that a remember judgment would be made in cases in which they remembered something distinctive in the speaker's voice when he said the word, or perhaps they remembered the item presented before or after it, or what they were thinking when they heard the word. They were always told to make the remember–know judgment about a word with respect to its presentation on the tape recorder, not whether they remembered or knew they had written it down on the free recall test. In addition, they were instructed to make remember–know judgments immediately after judging the item to be old, before they considered the next test item.

The recognition test was composed of 96 items, 48 of which had been studied and 48 of which had not. The 48 studied items were obtained by selecting 3 items from each of the 16 presented lists (always those in Serial Positions 1, 8, and 10). The lures, or nonstudied items, on the recognition test were 24 critical lures from all 24 lists (16 studied, 8 not) and the 24 items from the 8 nonstudied lists (again, from Serial Positions 1, 8, and 10). The 96 items were randomly arranged on the test sheet and beside each item were the words *old* and *new;* if subjects circled old, they made the remember–know judgment by writing *R* or *K* in the space next to the word. All subjects received exactly the same test sheet; counterbalancing of lists was achieved by having lists rotated through the three conditions (study + recall, study + arithmetic, and nonstudied) across subsets of 10 subjects.

After the recognition test, the experimenter asked subjects an open-ended question: whether they "knew what the experiment was about." Most subjects just said something similar to "memory for lists of words," but 1 subject said that she noticed that the lists seemed designed to make her think of a nonpresented word. She was the only subject who had no false recalls of the critical nonpresented words; her results were excluded from those reported below and replaced by the results obtained from a new subject. After the experiment, subjects were debriefed.

Results

Recall

Subjects recalled the critical nonpresented word on 55% of the lists, which is a rate even higher than for the 6 lists used in Experiment 1. The higher rate of false recall in Experiment 2 may have been due to the longer lists, to their slightly different construction, to the fact that 16 lists were presented rather than only 6, or to different signals used to recall the lists. In addition, in Experiment 1 the lists were read aloud by the experimenter, whereas in Experiment 2 they were presented by means of a tape player. Regardless of the reason or reasons for the difference, the

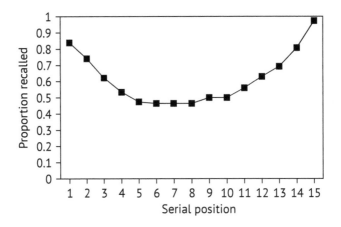

FIGURE 5.3

Probability of correct recall in Experiment 2 as a function of serial position. Probability of recall of the studied words was .62, and probability of recall of the critical nonpresented item was .55.

false-recall effect was quite robust and seems even stronger under the conditions of Experiment 2.

The smoothed serial position curve for studied words is shown in Figure 5.3, where marked primacy and recency effects are again seen. As in Experiment 1, subjects recalled the critical nonpresented items at about the rate of studied items presented in the middle of the lists. Subjects recalled items in Positions 4–11 an average of 47% of the time, compared with 55% recall of nonpresented items. Therefore, recall of the critical missing word was actually greater than recall for studied words in the middle of the list; this difference was marginally significant, t (29) = 1.80, SEM = .042, p = .08, two-tailed.

Recognition

After subjects had heard all 16 lists, they received the recognition test and provided remember–know judgments for items that were called old on the test. We first consider results for studied words and then turn to the data for the critical nonpresented lures.

Table 5.2 presents the recognition results for items studied in the list. (Keep in mind that we tested only three items from each list [i.e., those in Positions 1, 8, and 10].) It is apparent that the hit rate in the study + recall condition (.79) was greater than in the study + arithmetic condition (.65), t (29) = 5.20, SEM = .027, p < .001, indicating that the act of recall enhanced later recognition. Further, the boost in recognition from prior recall was reflected in a greater proportion of remember responses, which differed reliably, t (29) = 4.87, SEM = .033, p < .001.

Table 5.2 Recognition Results for Studied Items and Critical Lures in Experiment 2

ITEM TYPE AND CONDITION	PROPORTION OF OLD RESPONSES		
	OVERALL	R	K
Studied			
Study + recall	.79	.57	.22
Study + arithmetic	.65	.41	.24
Nonstudied	.11	.02	.09
Critical lure			
Study + recall	.81	.58	.23
Study + arithmetic	.72	.38	.34
Nonstudied	.16	.03	.13

Note. R = remember judgment; K = know judgment.

Know responses did not differ between conditions, t (29) < 1. The false-alarm rate for items from the nonstudied lists was .11, with most false positives judged as know responses.

Recognition results for the critical nonpresented lures are also shown in Table 5.2. The first striking impression is that the results for false-alarm rates appear practically identical to the results for hit rates. Therefore, to an even greater extent than in Experiment 1, subjects were unable to distinguish items actually presented from the critical lures that were not presented. Table 5.2 also shows that the act of (false) recall in the study + recall condition enhanced later false recognition relative to the study + arithmetic condition, in which the lists were not recalled. In addition, after recalling the lists subjects were much more likely to say that they remembered the items from the list, with remember judgments being made 72% of the time (i.e., .58 ÷ .81 × 100) for words that had never been presented. When the lists were presented but not recalled, the rate of remember judgments dropped to 53%, although this figure is still quite high. Interestingly, the corresponding percentages for items actually studied were about the same: 72% for remember judgments for lists that were recalled and 63% for lists that were not recalled.

One point that vitiates the correspondence between the results for studied and nonstudied items in Table 5.2 is that the false-alarm rates for the types of items differed when the relevant lists had not been studied. The rate for the regular list words was .11, whereas the rate for the critical lures (when the relevant prior list had not been studied) was .16, t (29) = 2.27, SEM = .022, p = .03, two-tailed. However, the difference was not great, and in both cases false alarms gave rise to more know responses than remember responses.

One further analysis is of interest. In the study + recall condition, we can consider recognition results for items that were produced in the recall phase (whether representing correct responding or false recall) relative to those that were not produced. Although correlational, such results provide an interesting pattern in comparing the effects of prior correct recall to prior false recall on later recognition. Table 5.3 shows the results of this analysis, including the means for studied items and for the critical items. For the studied items, recognition of items that had been correctly recalled was essentially perfect, and most old responses were judged to be remembered. Items not produced on the recall test were recognized half the time, and responses were evenly divided between remember and know judgments. These effects could have been due to the act of recall, to item selection effects, or to some combination. Nonetheless, they provide a useful point of comparison for the more interesting results about the fate of falsely recalled items, as shown in Table 5.3.

Table 5.3 Proportion of Items Judged to be Old on the Recognition Test in the Study + Recall Condition of Experiment 2 As a Function of Whether the Items Were Produced on the Immediate Free Recall Test

CONDITION	PRODUCTION RATE OF FREE RECALL	RECOGNITION		
		OVERALL	R	K
Studied				
Produced	.62	.98	.79	.19
Not produced	.38	.50	.26	.24
Critical lure				
Produced	.55	.93	.73	.20
Not produced	.45	.65	.38	.27

Note. R = remember judgment; K = know judgment.

The recognition results for the falsely recalled critical items closely resemble those for correctly recalled studied items. The probability of recognizing falsely recalled items was quite high (.93), and most of these items were judged to be remembered (.73) rather than known (.20). More remarkably, the critical items that were not produced were later (falsely) recognized at a higher rate (.65) than were items actually studied but not produced (.50); this difference was marginally significant, $t(29) = 1.81$, $SEM = .083$, $p = .08$, two-tailed. In addition, these falsely recognized items were judged to be remembered in 58% of the cases (i.e., $.38 \div .65 \times 100$), or at about the same rate as for words that were studied but not produced (52%). These analyses reveal again the powerful false memory effects at work in this paradigm, with people falsely remembering the critical nonstudied words at about the same levels (or even greater levels) as presented words.

GENERAL DISCUSSION

The primary results from our experiments can be summarized as follows: First, the paradigm we developed from Deese's (1959) work produced high levels of false recall in single-trial free recall. In Experiment 1, with 12-word lists, subjects recalled the critical nonstudied word after 40% of the lists. In Experiment 2, with 15-word lists, false recall increased, occurring on 55% of the occasions. Second, this paradigm also produced remarkably high levels of false recognition for the critical items; the rate of false recognition actually approached the hit rate. Third, the false recognition responses were frequently made with high confidence (Experiment 1) or were frequently accompanied by remember judgments (Experiment 2). Fourth, the act of recall increased both accurate recognition of studied items and the false recognition of the critical nonstudied items. The highest rates of false recognition and the highest proportion of remember responses to the critical nonstudied items occurred for those items that had been falsely recalled.

We discuss our results (a) in relation to prior work and (b) in terms of theories that might explain the basic effects. We then discuss (c) how the phenomenological experience of remembering events that never happened might occur, and (d) what implications our findings might have for the wider debates on false memories.

Relation to Prior Work

Prior work by Underwood (1965) has shown false recognition for lures semantically related to studied words, but as we noted in the introduction, these effects were often rather small in magnitude. In our experiments, we found very high levels of false recall and false recognition. Our recognition results are similar to those obtained by investigators in the 1960s and 1970s who used prose materials and found erroneous recognition of related material. For example, Bransford and Franks (1971) presented subjects with sentences that were related and created a coherent scene (e.g., The rock rolled down the mountain and crushed the hut. The hut was tiny). Later, they confidently recognized sentences that were congruent with the meaning of the complex idea, although the sentences had not actually been presented (e.g., The rock rolled down the mountain and crushed the tiny hut). Similarly, Posner and Keele (1970) showed subjects dot patterns that were distortions from a prototypic pattern. Later, they recognized the prototype (that had never been presented) at a high rate, and forgetting of the prototype showed less decline over a week than did dot patterns actually presented. Jenkins, Wald, and Pittenger (1986) reported similar observations with pictorial stimuli.

In each of the experiments just described, and in other related experiments (see Alba & Hasher, 1983, for a review), subjects recognized events that never happened if the events fit some general schema derived from the study experiences. A similar interpretation is possible for our results, too, although most researchers have assumed that schema-driven processes occur only in prose materials. Yet the lists for our experiments were generated as associates to a single word and therefore had a coherent form (e.g., words related to sleep or to other similar concepts). The word *sleep*, for example, may never have been presented in the list, but was the "prototype" from which the list was generated, and therefore our lists arguably encouraged schematic processing.

Although our results are similar to those of other research revealing errors in memory, several features distinguish our findings. First, we showed powerful false-memory effects in both recall and recognition within the same paradigm. The findings just cited, and others described below, all used recognition paradigms. Although some prior studies have reported false recall (e.g., Brewer, 1977; Hasher & Griffin, 1979; Spiro, 1980), these researchers used prose materials. Second, we showed that subjects actually claimed to remember most of the falsely recognized events as having occurred on the list. The items did not just evoke a feeling of familiarity but were consciously recollected as having occurred. Third, we showed that the effect of prior recall increased both accurate and false memories and that this effect of recall was reflected in remember responses.

Explanations of False Recall and False Recognition

How might false recall and false recognition arise in our paradigm? Actually, the earliest idea about false recognition—the implicit associative response—still seems workable in helping to understand these phenomena, although today we can elaborate on the idea with new models now available. Underwood (1965) proposed that false recognition responses originated during encoding when subjects, seeing a word such as *hot*, might think of an associate (*cold*). Later, if *cold* were presented as a lure, they might claim to recognize its occurrence in the list because of the earlier implicit associative response.

Some writers at the time assumed that the associative response had to occur consciously to the subject during study, so it was implicit only in the sense that it was not overtly produced. Another possible interpretation is that the subject never even becomes aware of the associative response during study of the lists, so that its activation may be implicit in this additional sense, too. Activation may spread through an associative network (e.g., Anderson & Bower, 1973; Collins & Loftus, 1975), with false-recognition errors arising through residual activation. That is, it may not be necessary for subjects to consciously think of the associate while studying the list for false recall and false recognition to occur. On the other hand, the predominance of remember responses for the critical lures on the later recognition test may indicate that the critical nonpresented words do occur to subjects during study of the list. That may be why subjects claim to remember them, through a failure of reality monitoring (Johnson & Raye, 1981).

In further support of the idea that associative processes are critically important in producing false recall, Deese (1959) showed that the likelihood of false recall in this paradigm was predicted well by the probability that items presented in the list elicited the critical nonpresented word in free association tests. In other words, the greater the likelihood that list members produced the critical nonpresented target word as an associate, the greater the level of false recall (see also Nelson, Bajo, McEvoy, & Schreiber, 1989). It is worth noting that some of Deese's lists that contained strong forward associations—including the famous "butterfly" list used in later research—did not lead to false recall. The particular characteristics of the lists that lead to false memories await systematic experimental study, but in general Deese reported that the lists that did not lead to false recall contained words that did not produce the critical targets as associates. The butterfly list did not elicit even one false recall in Deese's experiment.

If false recall and false recognition are produced by means of activation of implicit associative responses, then the reason our false-recognition results were more robust than those usually reported may be that we used lists of related words rather than single related words. Underwood (1965) and others had subjects study single words related to later lures on some dimension, and they showed only modest levels of false recognition, or in some cases none at all (Gillund & Shiffrin, 1984). In the present experiments, subjects studied lists of 12–15 items and the false-recognition effect was quite large. Hall and Kozloff (1973), Hintzman (1988), and Shiffrin, Huber, and Marinelli (1995) have shown that false recognition is directly related to the number of related words in a list. For example, Hintzman (1988, Experiment 1) presented from 0 to 5 items from a category in a list and showed that both accurate recognition of studied category members, as well as false recognition of lures from that category, increased as a function of category size. False recognition increased from about 8% when no category members were included in the list to around 35% when five category members occurred in the list. (These percentages were estimated from Hintzman's Figure 11.) Our lists were not categorized, strictly speaking, but the words were generally related. For our 15-item lists in Experiment 2 that did not receive recall tests, false recognition was 72%; the corresponding figure for recalled lists was 81%. It will be interesting to see if longer versions of standard categorized lists will produce false recognition at the same levels as the lists we have used and whether the average probability that items in the list evoke the lure as an associate will predict the level of false recognition. We are now conducting experiments to evaluate these hypotheses.

If the errors in memory occurring on both recall and recognition tests arise from associative processes, then formal models of associative processing might be expected to predict them. At least at a general level, they would seem to do so. For example, the search of associative memory (SAM) model, first proposed by Raaijmakers and

Shiffrin (1980) and later extended to recognition by Gillund and Shiffrin (1984), provides for the opportunity of false recognition (and presumably recall) by means of associative processes. Although it was not the main thrust of their paper, Shiffrin et al. (1995) demonstrated that the SAM model did fit their observation of an increased tendency to produce false alarms to category members with increases in the number of category exemplars presented.

Recently, McClelland (in press) has extended the parallel distributed processing (PDP) approach to explaining constructive memory processes and memory distortions. This model assumes that encoding and retrieval occur in a parallel distributed processing system in which there are many simple but massively interconnected processing units. Encoding an event involves the activation of selected units within the system. Retrieval entails patterns of reactivation of the same processing units. However, because activation in the model can arise from many sources, a great difficulty (for the model and for humans) lies in the failure to differentiate between possible sources of prior activation (McClelland, in press). Therefore, because what is encoded and stored is a particular pattern of activity, subjects may not be able to reconstruct the actual event that gave rise to this activity. For example, if presenting the words associated with *sleep* mimics the activity in the system as occurs during actual presentation of the word *sleep,* then the PDP system will be unable to distinguish whether or not the word actually occurred. Consequently, the PDP system would give rise to false memory phenomena, as McClelland (in press) describes.

As the examples above show, associative models can account for false-recall and false-recognition results, although we have not tried fitting specific models to our data. To mention two other models based on different assumptions, Hintzman's (1988) MINERVA 2 model, which assumes independent traces of events, modeled well the effect of increasing category size on the probability of identifying an item from the category as old; this was true both for correct recognition and false recognition. In addition, Reyna and Brainerd (1995) have also applied their fuzzy-trace theory to the problem of false memories.

Although most theorists have assumed that the false memory effects arise during encoding, all remembering is a product of information both from encoding and storage processes (the memory trace) and from information in the retrieval environment (Tulving, 1974). Indeed, false remembering may arise from repeated attempts at retrieval, as shown in Experiment 2 and elsewhere (e.g., Ceci, Huffman, Smith, & Loftus, 1994; Hyman, Husband, & Billings, 1995; Roediger et al., 1993). Retrieval processes may contribute significantly to the false recall and false recognition phenomena we have observed. Subjects usually recalled the critical word toward the end of the set of recalled items, so prior recall may trigger false recall, in part. Also, in the recognition test, presentation of words related to a critical lure often occurred prior to its appearance on the test; therefore, activation from these related words on the test may have enhanced the false recognition effect by priming the lure (Neely, Schmidt, & Roediger, 1983). The illusion of memory produced by this mechanism, if it exists, may be similar to illusions of recognition produced by enhanced perceptual fluency (Whittlesea, 1993; Whittlesea, Jacoby, & Girard, 1990). Indeed, one aspect of our results on which the theories outlined above remain mute is the phenomenological experience of the subjects: They did not just claim that the nonpresented items were familiar; rather, they claimed to remember their occurrence. We turn next to this aspect of the data.

Phenomenological Experience

In virtually all previous experiments using the remember–know procedure, false alarms have been predominantly labeled as know experiences (e.g., Gardiner & Java, 1993; Jones & Roediger, 1995; Rajaram, 1993). The typical assumption is that know responses arise through fluent processing, when information comes to mind easily, but the source of the information is not readily apparent (Rajaram, 1993). In addition, Johnson and Raye (1981) have noted that memories for events that actually occurred typically provide more spatial and temporal details than do memories for events that were only imagined. For these reasons, when we conducted Experiment 2 we expected that the false alarms in our recognition tests would, like other recognition errors, be judged by subjects to be known but not remembered. Yet our results showed that, in our paradigm, this was not so. Subjects frequently reported remembering events that never happened. Clearly, false memories can be the result of conscious recollection and not only of general familiarity.

Furthermore, in our current experiments we found that the act of recall increased both overall recognition and remembering of presented items and of the critical nonpresented items. We assume that generation of an item during a free recall test solidifies the subject's belief that memory for that item is accurate and increases the likelihood of later recognition of the item; why, however, should recall enhance the phenomenological experience of remembering the item's presentation? The enhanced remember responses may be due to subjects' actually remembering the experience of recalling the item, rather than studying it, and confusing the source of their remembrance; similarly, it could be that subjects remember thinking about the item during the study phase and confuse this with having heard it. Each of these mistakes would represent a source monitoring error (Johnson, Hashtroudi, & Lindsay, 1993). Note that our instructions to subjects about their remember–know responses specified that they were to provide remember judgments only when they remembered the item's actual presentation in the list (i.e., not simply when they remembered producing it on the recall test). Nonetheless, despite this instruction, subjects provided more remember responses for items from lists that had been recalled in Experiment 2.

The most promising approach to explaining such false remembering comes from an attributional analysis of memory, as advocated by Jacoby, Kelley, and Dywan (1989). They considered cases in which the aftereffects of past events were misattributed to other sources, but more importantly for present concerns, they considered cases in which subjects falsely attributed current cognitive experience to a concrete past event when that event did not occur. They hypothesized that the ease with which a person is able to bring events to mind increases the probability that the person will attribute the experience to being a memory. They also argued that the greater the vividness and distinctiveness of the generated event, the greater the likelihood of believing that it represents a memory (Johnson & Raye, 1981). Thus, in our paradigm, if subjects fluently generate (in recall) or process (in recognition) the word *sleep* (on the basis of recent activation of the concept) and if this fluency allows them to construct a clear mental image of how the word would have sounded if presented in the speaker's voice, then they would likely claim to remember the word's presentation. The act of recall increases the ease of producing an event and may thereby increase the experience of remembering. Jacoby et al.'s (1989) analysis offers promising leads for further research.

Implications

The results reported in this article identify a striking memory illusion. Just as perceptual illusions can be compelling even when people are aware of the factors giving rise to the illusion, we suspect that the same is true in our case of remembering events that never happened. Indeed, informal demonstration experiments with groups of sophisticated subjects, such as wily graduate students who knew we were trying to induce false memories, also showed the effect quite strongly.

Bartlett (1932) proposed a distinction between reproductive and reconstructive memory processes. Since then, the common assumption has been that list learning paradigms encourage rote reproduction of material with relatively few errors, whereas paradigms using more coherent (schematic) material (e.g., sentences, paragraphs, stories, or scenes) are necessary to observe constructive processes in memory retrieval. Yet we obtained robust false memory effects with word lists, albeit with ones that contain related words. We conclude that any contrast between reproductive and reconstructive memory is ill-founded; all remembering is constructive in nature. Materials may differ in how readily they lead to error and false memories, but these are differences of a quantitative, not qualitative, nature.

Do our results have any bearing on the current controversies raging over the issue of allegedly false memories induced in therapy? Not directly, of course. However, we do show that the illusion of remembering events that never happened can occur quite readily. Therefore, as others have also pointed out, the fact that people may say they vividly remember details surrounding an event cannot, by itself, be taken as convincing evidence that the event actually occurred (Johnson & Suengas, 1989; Schooler, Gerhard, & Loftus, 1986; Zaragoza & Lane, 1994). Our subjects confidently recalled and recognized words that were not presented and also reported that they remembered the occurrence of these events. A critic might contend that because these experiments occurred in a laboratory setting, using word lists, with college student subjects, they hold questionable relevance to issues surrounding more spectacular occurrences of false memories outside the lab. However, we believe that these are all reasons to be more impressed with the relevance of our results to these issues. After all, we tested people under conditions of intentional learning, with very short retention intervals, in a standard laboratory procedure that usually produces few errors, and we used college students—professional memorizers—as subjects. In short, despite conditions much more conducive to veridical remembering than those that typically exist outside the lab, we found dramatic evidence of false memories. When less of a premium is placed on accurate remembering, and when people know that their accuracy in recollecting cannot be verified, they may even be more easily led to remember events that never happened than they are in the lab.

REFERENCES

Alba, J. W., & Hasher, L. (1983). Is memory schematic? *Psychological Bulletin, 93,* 203–231.

Anderson, J. R., & Bower, G. H. (1973). *Human associative memory.* Washington, DC: V. H. Winston.

Anisfeld, M., & Knapp, M. (1968). Association, synonymity, and directionality in false recognition. *Journal of Experimental Psychology, 77,* 171–179.

Appleby, D. (1986). Déjà vu in the classroom. *Network, 4,* 8.

Bartlett, F. C. (1932). *Remembering: A study in experimental and social psychology.* Cambridge, England: Cambridge University Press.

Bransford, J. D., & Franks, J. J. (1971). The abstraction of linguistic ideas. *Cognitive Psychology, 2,* 331–350.

Brewer, W. F. (1977). Memory for the pragmatic implications of sentences. *Memory & Cognition, 5,* 673–678.

Ceci, S. J., Huffman, M. L. C., Smith, E., & Loftus, E. F. (1994). Repeatedly thinking about non-events. *Consciousness and Cognition, 3,* 388–407.

Cofer, C. N. (1967). Does conceptual organization influence the amount retained in free recall?. In B. Kleinmuntz (Ed.), *Concepts and the structure of memory* (pp. 181–214). New York: Wiley.

Collins, A. M., & Loftus, E. F. (1975). A spreading-activation theory of semantic processing. *Psychological Review, 82,* 407–428.

Cramer, P. (1965). Recovery of a discrete memory. *Journal of Personality and Social Psychology, 1,* 326–332.

Deese, J. (1959). On the prediction of occurrence of particular verbal intrusions in immediate recall. *Journal of Experimental Psychology, 58,* 17–22.

Gardiner, J. M. (1988). Functional aspects of recollective experience. *Memory & Cognition, 16,* 309–313.

Gardiner, J. M., & Java, R. I. (1993). Recognizing and remembering. In A. Collins, S. Gathercole, & P. Morris (Eds.), *Theories of memory* (pp. 168–188). Hillsdale, NJ: Erlbaum.

Gauld, A., & Stephenson, G. M. (1967). Some experiments related to Bartlett's theory of remembering. *British Journal of Psychology, 58,* 39–49.

Gillund, G., & Shiffrin, R. M. (1984). A retrieval model for both recognition and recall. *Psychological Review, 91,* 1–67.

Hall, J. F., & Kozloff, E. E. (1973). False recognitions of associates of converging versus repeated words. *American Journal of Psychology, 86,* 133–139.

Hasher, L., & Griffin, M. (1979). Reconstructive and reproductive processes in memory. *Journal of Experimental Psychology: Human Learning and Memory, 4,* 318–330.

Hintzman, D. L. (1988). Judgments of frequency and recognition memory in a multiple-trace memory model. *Psychological Review, 95,* 528–551.

Hyman, I. E., Husband, T. H., & Billings, F. J. (1995). False memories of childhood experiences. *Applied Cognitive Psychology, 9,* 181–197.

Jacoby, L. L., Kelley, C. M., & Dywan, J. (1989). Memory attributions. In H. L. RoedigerIII & F. I. M.Craik (Eds.), *Varieties of memory and consciousness: Essays in honour of Endel Tulving* (pp. 391–422). Hillsdale, NJ: Erlbaum.

Jenkins, J. J., Wald, J., & Pittenger, J. B. (1986). Apprehending pictorial events: An instance of psychological cohesion. In V.McCabe & G. J.Balzano (Eds.), *Event cognition: An ecological perspective* (pp. 117–133). Hillsdale, NJ: Erlbaum.

Johnson, M. K., Hashtroudi, S., & Lindsay, D. S. (1993). Source monitoring. *Psychological Bulletin, 114,* 3–28.

Johnson, M. K., & Raye, C. L. (1981). Reality monitoring. *Psychological Review, 88,* 67–85.

Johnson, M. K., & Suengas, A. G. (1989). Reality monitoring judgments of other people's memories. *Bulletin of the Psychonomic Society, 27,* 107–110.

Jones, T. C., & Roediger, H. L., III. (1995). The experiential basis of serial position effects. *European Journal of Cognitive Psychology, 7,* 65–80.

Lindsay, D. S., & Read, J. D. (1994). Psychotherapy and memories of childhood sexual abuse: A cognitive perspective. *Applied Cognitive Psychology, 8,* 281–338.

Loftus, E. F. (1993). The reality of repressed memories. *American Psychologist, 48,* 518–537.

Loftus, E. F., Miller, D. G., & Burns, H. J. (1978). Semantic integration of verbal information into a visual memory. *Journal of Experimental Psychology: Human Learning and Memory, 4,* 19–31.

Loftus, E. F., & Palmer, J. C. (1974). Reconstruction of automobile destruction: An example of the interaction between language and memory. *Journal of Verbal Learning and Verbal Behavior, 13,* 585–589.

McClelland, J. L. (in press). Constructive memory and memory distortions: A parallel-distributed processing approach. In D. L. Schacter, J. T. Coyle, G. D. Fischbach, M. M. Mesulam, & L. E. Sullivan (Eds.), *Memory distortion* Cambridge, MA: Harvard University Press.

McCloskey, M., & Zaragoza, M. (1985). Misleading postevent information and memory for events: Arguments and evidence against memory impairment hypotheses. *Journal of Experimental Psychology: General, 114,* 1–16.

Neely, J. H., Schmidt, S. R., & Roediger, H. L., III. (1983). Inhibition from related primes in recognition memory. *Journal of Experimental Psychology: Learning, Memory, and Cognition, 9,* 196–211.

Nelson, D. L., Bajo, M., McEvoy, C. L., & Schreiber, T. A. (1989). Prior knowledge: The effects of natural category size on memory for implicitly encoded concepts. *Journal of Experimental Psychology: Learning, Memory, and Cognition, 15,* 957–967.

Paul, I. H. (1959). Studies in remembering: The reproduction of connected and extended verbal material. *Psychological Issues, 1* (Monograph 2) 1–152.

Paul, L. M. (1979). Two models of recognition memory: A test. *Journal of Experimental Psychology: Human Learning and Memory, 5*, 45–51.

Payne, D. G., Toglia, M. P., & Anastasi, J. S. (1994). Recognition performance level and the magnitude of the misinformation effect in eyewitness memory. *Psychonomic Bulletin & Review, 1*, 376–382.

Posner, M. I., & Keele, S. W. (1970). Retention of abstract ideas. *Journal of Experimental Psychology, 83*, 304–308.

Raaijmakers, J. G. W., & Shiffrin, R. M. (1980). SAM: A theory of probabilistic search of associative memory. In G. H.Bower (Ed.), *The psychology of learning and motivation* (Vol. 14, pp. 207–262). New York: Academic Press.

Rajaram, S. (1993). Remembering and knowing: Two means of access to the personal past. *Memory & Cognition, 21*, 89–102.

Rajaram, S., & Roediger, H. L., III. (in press). Remembering and knowing as states of consciousness during recollection. In J. D.Cohen & J. W.Schooler (Eds.), *Scientific approaches to the question of consciousness* Hillsdale, NJ: Erlbaum.

Reyna, V. F., & Brainerd, C. J. (1995). Fuzzy-trace theory: An interim synthesis. *Learning and Individual Differences, 7*, 1–75.

Roediger, H. L., III, & Payne, D. G. (1985). Recall criterion does not affect recall level or hypermnesia: A puzzle for generate/recognize theories. *Memory & Cognition, 13*, 1–7.

Roediger, H. L., III, Wheeler, M. A., & Rajaram, S. (1993). Remembering, knowing, and reconstructing the past. In D. L. Medin (Ed.), *The psychology of learning and motivation: Advances in research and theory* (pp. 97–134). San Diego, CA: Academic Press.

Russell, W. A., & Jenkins, J. J. (1954). *The complete Minnesota norms for responses to 100 words from the Kent-Rosanoff Word Association Test.*(Tech. Rep. No. 11, Contract N8 ONR 66216, Office of Naval Research). University of Minnesota.

Schacter, D. L. (in press). Memory distortion: History and current status. In D. L. Schacter, J. T. Coyle, G. D. Fischbach, M. M. Mesulam, & L. E. Sullivan (Eds.) (in press). *Memory distortion* Cambridge, MA: Harvard University Press.

Schooler, J. W., Gerhard, D., & Loftus, E. F. (1986). Qualities of the unreal. *Journal of Experimental Psychology: Learning, Memory, and Cognition, 12*, 171–181.

Shiffrin, R. M., Huber, D. E., & Marinelli, K. (1995). Effects of category length and strength on familiarity in recognition. *Journal of Experimental Psychology: Learning, Memory, and Cognition, 21*, 267–287.

Spiro, R. J. (1980). Accommodative reconstruction in prose recall. *Journal of Verbal Learning and Verbal Behavior, 19*, 84–95.

Sulin, R. A., & Dooling, D. J. (1974). Intrusion of a thematic idea in retention of prose. *Journal of Experimental Psychology, 103*, 255–262.

Tulving, E. (1974). Cue-dependent forgetting. *American Scientist, 62*, 74–82.

Tulving, E. (1985). Memory and consciousness. *Canadian Psychologist, 26*, 1–12.

Underwood, B. J. (1965). False recognition produced by implicit verbal responses. *Journal of Experimental Psychology, 70*, 122–129.

Wheeler, M. A., & Roediger, H. L., III. (1992). Disparate effects of repeated testing: Reconciling Ballard's (1913) and Bartlett's (1932) results. *Psychological Science, 3*, 240–245.

Whittlesea, B. W. A. (1993). Illusions of familiarity. *Journal of Experimental Psychology: Learning, Memory, and Cognition, 19*, 1235–1253.

Whittlesea, B. W. A., Jacoby, L. L., & Girard, K. (1990). Illusions of immediate memory: Evidence of an attributional basis for feelings of familiarity and perceptual quality. *Journal of Memory and Language, 29*, 716–732.

Zaragoza, M. S., & Lane, S. M. (1994). Source misattributions and the suggestibility of eyewitness memory. *Journal of Experimental Psychology: Learning, Memory, and Cognition, 20*, 934–945.

APPENDIX

APPENDIX A: The Twenty-Four-Word Lists used in Experiment 2

Within-lists words were presented in this order, which generally follows the association norms. (We replaced two words here for reasons described in the Method section of Experiment 2.)

ANGER	BLACK	BREAD	CHAIR	COLD	DOCTOR	FOOT	FRUIT
mad	white	butter	table	hot	nurse	shoe	apple
fear	dark	food	sit	snow	sick	hand	vegetable
hate	cat	eat	legs	warm	lawyer	toe	orange
rage	charred	sandwich	seat	winter	medicine	kick	kiwi
temper	night	rye	couch	ice	health	sandals	citrus
fury	funeral	jam	desk	wet	hospital	soccer	ripe
ire	color	milk	recliner	frigid	dentist	yard	pear
wrath	grief	flour	sofa	chilly	physician	walk	banana
happy	blue	jelly	wood	heal	ill	ankle	berry
fight	death	dough	cushion	weather	patient	arm	cherry
hatred	ink	crust	swivel	freeze	office	boot	basket
mean	bottom	slice	stool	air	stethoscope	inch	juke
calm	coal	wine	sitting	shiver	surgeon	sock	salad
emotion	brown	loaf	rocking	Arctic	clinic	smell	bowl
enrage	gray	toast	bench	frost	cure	mouth	cocktail
GIRL	HIGH	KING	MAN	MOUNTAIN	MUSIC	NEEDLE	RIVER
boy	low	queen	woman	hill	note	thread	water
dolls	clouds	England	husband	valley	sound	pin	stream
female	up	crown	uncle	climb	piano	eye	lake
young	tall	prince	lady	summit	sing	sewing	Mississippi
dress	tower	George	mouse	top	radio	sharp	boat
pretty	jump	dictator	male	molehill	band	point	tide
hair	above	palace	father	peak	melody	prick	swim
niece	building	throne	strong	plain	horn	thimble	flow
dance	noon	chess	friend	glacier	concert	haystack	run
beautiful	cliff	rule	beard	goat	instrument	(horn	barge
cute	sky	subjects	person	bike	symphony	hurt	creek
date	over	monarch	handsome	climber	jazz	injection	brook
aunt	airplane	royal	muscle	range	orchestra	Syringe	fish
daughter	dive	leader	suit	steep	art	cloth	bridge
sister	elevate	reign	old	ski	rhythm	knitting	winding
ROUGH	SLEEP	SLOW	SOFT	SPIDER	SWEET	THIEF	WINDOW
smooth	bed	fast	hard	web	sour	steal	door
bumpy	rest	lethargic	light	insect	candy	robber	glass
road	awake	stop	pillow	bug	sugar	crook	pane
tough	tired	listless	plush	fright	bitter	burglar	shade
sandpaper	dream	snail	loud	fly	good	money	ledge
jagged	wake	cautious	cotton	arachnid	taste	cop	sill
ready	snooze	delay	fur	crawl	tooth	bad	house
coarse	blanket	traffic	touch	tarantula	nice	rob	open
uneven	doze	turtle	fluffy	poison	honey	jail	curtain
riders	slumber	hesitant	feather	bite	soda	gun	frame
rugged	snore	speed	furry	creepy	chocolate	villain	view
sand	nap	quick	downy	animal	heart	crime	breeze
boards	peace	sluggish	kitten	ugly	cake	bank	sash
ground	yawn	wait	skin	feelers	tart	bandit	screen
gravel	drowsy	molasses	tender	small	pie	criminal	shutter

ANGER	BLACK	BREAD	CHAIR	COLD	DOCTOR	FOOT	FRUIT
mad	white	butter	table	hot	nurse	shoe	apple
fear	dark	food	sit	snow	sick	hand	vegetable
hate	cat	eat	legs	warm	lawyer	toe	orange
rage	charred	sandwich	seat	winter	medicine	kick	kiwi
temper	night	rye	couch	ice	health	sandals	citrus
fury	funeral	jam	desk	wet	hospital	soccer	ripe
ire	color	milk	recliner	frigid	dentist	yard	pear
wrath	grief	flour	sofa	chilly	physician	walk	banana
happy	blue	jelly	wood	heat	ill	ankle	berry
fight	death	dough	cushion	weather	patient	arm	cherry
hatred	ink	crust	swivel	freeze	office	boot	basket
mean	bottom	slice	stool	air	stethoscope	inch	juice
calm	coal	wine	sitting	shiver	surgeon	sock	salad
emotion	brown	loaf	rocking	Arctic	clinic	smell	bowl
enrage	gray	toast	bench	frost	cure	mouth	cocktail

GIRL	HIGH	KING	MAN	MOUNTAIN	MUSIC	NEEDLE	RIVER
boy	low	queen	woman	hill	note	thread	water
dolls	clouds	England	husband	valley	sound	pin	stream
female	up	crown	uncle	climb	piano	eye	lake
young	tall	prince	lady	summit	sing	sewing	Mississippi
dress	tower	George	mouse	top	radio	sharp	boat
pretty	jump	dictator	male	molehill	band	point	tide
hair	above	palace	father	peak	melody	prick	swim
niece	building	throne	strong	plain	bora	thimble	flow
dance	noon	chess	friend	glacier	concert	haystack	run
beautiful	cliff	rule	beard	goat	instrument	thorn	barge
cute	sky	subjects	person	bike	symphony	hurt	creek
date	over	monarch	handsome	climber	jazz	injection	brook
aunt	airplane	royal	muscle	range	orchestra	syringe	fish
daughter	dive	leader	suit	steep	art	cloth	bridge
sister	elevate	reign	old	ski	rhythm	knitting	winding

ROUGH	SLEEP	SLOW	SOFT	SPIDER	SWEET	THIEF	WINDOW
smooth	bed	fast	hard	web	sour	steal	door
bumpy	rest	lethargic	light	insect	candy	robber	glass
road	awake	stop	pillow	bug	sugar	crook	pane
tough	tired	listless	plush	fright	bitter	burglar	shade
sandpaper	dream	snail	loud	fly	good	money	ledge
jagged	wake	cautious	cotton	arachnid	taste	cop	sill
ready	snooze	delay	fur	crawl	tooth	bad	house
coarse	blanket	traffic	touch	tarantula	nice	rob	open
uneven	doze	turtle	fluffy	poison	honey	jail	curtain
riders	slumber	hesitant	feather	bite	soda	gun	frame
rugged	snore	speed	furry	creepy	chocolate	villain	view
sand	nap	quick	downy	animal	heart	crime	breeze
boards	peace	sluggish	kitten	ugly	cake	bank	sash
ground	yawn	wait	skin	feelers	tart	bandit	screen
gravel	drowsy	molasses	tender	small	pie	criminal	shutter

Name:_____

READING COMPREHENSION QUESTIONS

Refer to the information you have just read to find the answers to these questions. Be sure that you do not simply copy what is already written in the article. Think about your answer and write it in your own words.

1. Write any words that you had to look up here, along with their definitions. If you did not need to look up any words, list and define several of the words you think the average college student may have found difficult. All students should have at least three words and definitions for this question.

2. Write the full reference for this article in APA style. For advice on APA style, consult www.apastyle.org.

3. Explain what is novel about this study that made it publishable. Be sure to describe exactly what previous studies lacked that this study offers. Simply describing this study, or simply describing previous studies, is insufficient.

Name:_____

4. Generally describe the methods used in the paper.

- How many subjects were there? If there was more than one experiment, list the number of subjects in each experiment.

- Who were the subjects (e.g., older adults, schizophrenic patients, college students)?

- What was it like to be a subject (i.e., what were the subjects required to do)? Provide enough detail that the reader can truly imagine what it was like to be a subject.

5. What were the main findings of this paper?

Name:_____

COMPREHENSION CHECK QUESTIONS

Refer to the information you have just read to find the answers to these questions. Be sure that you do not simply copy what is already written in the article. Think about your answer and write it in your own words.

1. Experiment Proposal

Pretend that you are an author on this paper and are tasked with determining future directions. Taking into account what has already been done in the field (i.e., the information presented in the Introduction) and the present study, what is a novel next step in this research? If you were one of the authors of this study, what would you do next and why? Be sure to explain why you would perform this next step. For example, proposing to replicate the study sampling from a different subject population is not sufficient, unless you explain why it is a reasonable next step.

Name:_____

2. Writing Critique

Pretend that you are a reviewer on this paper and are required to make a substantial suggestion on how to improve the writing. For example, you could offer an alternative explanation of how to describe the importance of the work, explain why the real-world application is insufficient, or suggest how the authors could describe their work in a more interesting way. If you were a reviewer, what would you say to improve the writing (not the methods) of this paper? Be sure to provide concrete suggestions. For example, do not simply say that an aspect of the paper was confusing. Demonstrate that you took the time to understand the material and offer a better way to explain the portion you found confusing.

Name:_____

3. Application Question

Think about how the work in this paper applies to the real world. Describe a scenario (either real or imagined) under which this work applies to your life. Do not use the real-world application mentioned in the paper. Rather, consider how this work is relevant to you (again, it could be imagined). Be sure to demonstrate that you understand the results of the paper through your real-world application.

Name:_____

TRUE OR FALSE STATEMENTS

Write three *true* statements here, noting the page number where the answer can be located.

1. _____
   _____
   _____
   _____
   _____

   • Page number where answer can be located: _____

2. _____
   _____
   _____
   _____
   _____

   • Page number where answer can be located: _____

3. _____
   _____
   _____
   _____
   _____

   • Page number where answer can be located: _____

Name:_____

Write three *false* statements here, noting the page number where the answer can be located. Then rewrite each statement to make it true.

1. _____
   _____
   _____

   • Rewritten to be true:
     _____
     _____

   • Page number where answer can be located: _____

2. _____
   _____
   _____

   • Rewritten to be true:
     _____
     _____

   • Page number where answer can be located: _____

3. _____
   _____
   _____

   • Rewritten to be true:
     _____
     _____

   • Page number where answer can be located: _____

Role of Schemata in Memory for Places

William F. Brewer and James C. Treyens

Abstract

A study of memory for places was carried out to examine five hypotheses about the use of schemata in memory performance: (a) that schemata determine what objects are encoded into memory; (b) that schemata act as frameworks for episodic information; (c) that schema-based information is integrated with episodic information; (d) that schemata facilitate retrieval; and (e) that schemata influence what is communicated at recall. Subjects were taken into what they thought was a graduate student's office and later were tested for memory of the room with either drawing recall, written recall, or verbal recognition. Memory scores for the objects were inferred in recall, supporting the integration hypothesis. Comparison of recall and recognition data supported the retrieval hypothesis. Analysis of the written descriptions supported the communication hypothesis. Saliency was positively correlated with recall and recognition for present objects, but was unrelated to retrieval. Saliency was negatively correlated with recognition for nonpresent objects, suggesting a metacognitive strategy in recognition of high-salient objects.

Brewer, W. F., & Treyens, J. C. (1981). Role Of Schemata In Memory For Places. *Cognitive Psychology*, 13(2), 207-230. Copyright © by Elsevier B.V. Reprinted with permission.

Much current research on human memory deals with the intentional learning of linguistic materials such as words, sentences, or stories. These experiments tend to be analogs of school tasks such as remembering the names of the states or the content of a paragraph in a textbook. The present paper uses an experimental task that is intended to be more analogous to the types of incidental memory that occur in everyday life. In particular, we have chosen to focus on memory for places. We are interested in investigating the memory processes that are involved when telling someone where a particular book is on a shelf or describing someone's office after your first visit.

Recent attempts to deal with memory for stories and with perception of real-world scenes have led to the development of theories in which existing knowledge plays a crucial role (Anderson & Pichert, 1978; Bobrow & Norman, 1975; Bower, Black, & Turner, 1979; Minsky, 1975; Neisser, 1976; Piaget & Inhelder, 1973; Rumelhart, 1980; Rumelhart & Ortony, 1977; Schank & Abelson, 1977; Spiro, 1977). It seems to us that the study of memory for real-world places requires theories of a similar nature.

The representational structures in these theories (schemata, frames, scripts, plans, prototypes) will be referred to here as schemata. Schemata are knowledge structures or sets of expectations based on past experience. They exist at various levels of abstraction and vary in their structural complexity (cf. Rumelhart, 1980).

Schema theories propose that perception, language comprehension, and memory are processes which involve the interaction of new (episodic) information with old, schema-based information. The basic assumption of schema theories is that an individual's prior experience will influence how he or she perceives, comprehends, and remembers new information.

Minsky (1975) suggests that perception is a schema-based process occurring over time which involves filling in details, collecting evidence, testing, deducing, and interpreting, on the basis of knowledge, expectations, and goals. Minsky hypothesizes that this complex process can take place rapidly because schemata already exist in memory which correspond to common environments, such as rooms. Information slots or variables in the internal structure of the schema which have not been filled with perceptual information are filled by default assignments based on stereotypic expectations derived from past experience. Kuipers' (1975) hypothetical example of room perception illustrates default assignments: if a quick perceptual scan of a room indicates that there is a clock on the wall, hands may be assigned to the internal representation by default, even though this particular clock does not have hands.

A number of schema theorists have focused directly on memory and have shown that memory performance is frequently influenced by schema-based expectations. Bartlett (1932) found that subjects' expectations and experiences distorted their recall of an unusual North American Indian folktale. Spiro (1977) found that recall of passages can be influenced by expectations based on information presented after reading the passage. Piaget and Inhelder (1973) showed that memories can be modified by schema development occurring between learning and recall. Anderson and Pichert (1978) have shown that an activated schema can aid retrieval of information in a recall task. While these studies have clearly demonstrated that schemata influence memory performance, the details of the process have not been worked out.

It appears to us that there are five fundamentally different ways in which schemata might influence memory performance: (a) they can determine what objects are looked at and encoded into memory; (b) they can act as a framework for new information; (c) they can provide schema-based information which becomes integrated with episodic information; (d) they can guide the retrieval process; and (e) they can determine what information is to be communicated at output.

Encoding. Minsky (1975) and Neisser (1976) have suggested that perception is guided by schemata. However, two different memory predictions are derivable from these theories. On the one hand, it might be hypothesized that subjects will spend more time looking at schema-relevant information and ignore information which does not fit into the currently active schemata. On the other hand, it might be hypothesized that subjects will only briefly glance at expected objects and spend more time looking at novel, unexpected objects. If it is assumed that looking time is directly related to how well an object is represented in memory, then the first encoding hypothesis predicts that schema-relevant information will be better remembered than unexpected information, while the second encoding hypothesis predicts that the unexpected information will be better remembered.

Framework. Schemata may serve as a framework in memory, so that schema-relevant episodic information is retained better than nonrelevant episodic information.

Integration. The episodic information and the schema-based information may be integrated in memory. In this case memory performance for schema-relevant information will be superior to that for nonschema information, since the memory performance for schema-relevant information is based on a mixture of new episodic information and old schema-based information. Inferences are said to occur when memory performance contains information from the schema that was not given in the episodic input. This general form of the integration model makes no claim about the degree of integration; the integration may be so complete that the subject cannot distinguish the episodic information from the schema-based information, or the two types of information may remain distinct.

Retrieval. Schema-based information may also be used in the process of retrieving information from memory. When individuals have been exposed to large amounts of information, they frequently retain more information than they can actually produce in a recall task. Several schema theorists (Anderson & Pichert, 1978; Lichtenstein & Brewer, 1980) have suggested that schemata are used to guide the search for information in memory; thus, information which is not related to the schema being used in retrieval will be harder to recall than information which is schema related.

Communication. When a subject is asked by an experimenter to recall previously presented information, the task is a form of communication between the two. If the subject's response mode is fairly open, as in a written description or narrative, then schemata can influence what information the subject gives in response. For example, Norman (1973) has pointed out that answers to questions are determined by schema-based assumptions of the answerer.

In developing an experimental paradigm to study place memory, we have chosen to study memory for rooms. This choice was based on a number of considerations. There has already been some interesting research on long-term memory for places by researchers from urban planning and geography (Downs & Stea, 1977; Lynch, 1960). These researchers have asked individuals to draw maps of towns and cities and have found a number of phenomena which appear to be the result of schema-based knowledge interacting with the information from the environment (e.g., the Boston Common is typically drawn as a rectangle, rather than as the five-sided figure it actually is). It is difficult to go beyond such observations in the study of long-term memory for public locations, since the experimenter does not have control over the characteristics of the locations involved. However, by choosing to study memory for rooms we can study place memory and yet have control over the input information. Even though rooms can easily be manipulated, they appear to be complex and meaningful enough to allow the results to be generalized to other types of real-life place memory. Finally, we wanted to study place memory in a naturalistic incidental learning situation, and using rooms made this very easy.

Given these considerations, the basic experimental paradigm used in the present research was quite simple. We designed a room to look like a graduate student's office. The subjects were taken into this room and were asked to wait there for a few minutes before the experiment began. Then, after a short time they were taken out of the experimental room and tested to determine their memory for various aspects of the room.

EXPERIMENTAL ROOM: DEVELOPMENT AND RATING

The experimental location studied in this paper was a room (2.73 × 1.82 × 2.08 m) which was designed to look like a graduate student's office. It contained a table with a typewriter and standard desk items. In another part of the room there was a table with a coffeepot and materials for making coffee. A third table held a Skinner box, tools, and electronic parts. There were shelves along one wall, and the other walls contained posters, a bulletin board, and a calendar. ... Most of the items in the room were placed there in order to make the room seem like a typical graduate-student office. However, for experimental purposes a few items not consistent with the office schema were included (e.g., a skull, a toy top) and a few items which would almost certainly be expected in such an office were deliberately omitted (e.g., books).

In order to provide objective measures of some characteristics of the experimental room, 61 objects in the room were rated on two dimensions: saliency and schema expectancy. The saliency rating was designed to indicate how noticeable an object was in the context of the room. Objects such as the skull and the Skinner box were high on this scale, while objects such as staples and an eraser were low. The schema-expectancy rating was intended to provide an index of subjects' graduate-student office schema by asking how likely the object was in the context of the room. Objects such as the desk and ceiling lights were high on this scale, while objects such as a model brain and a piece of bark were low.

Minsky's (1975) paper on the structure of everyday knowledge proposes that knowledge about rooms is organized into a "room frame." The room frame contains the information about rooms that one can be nearly certain about before encountering a particular room. Since Minsky has pointed out the theoretical importance of this type of knowledge, we were careful to include in the rating task items to test the room frame. We designated seven items to be room-frame items: walls, floor, ceiling, door, doorknob, light switch, and lights. These were chosen on a priori grounds as items that any room would almost certainly contain.

In addition to the objects actually in the room, a sample of 70 objects not in the room was chosen for rating on the same two scales. These objects were selected to vary along the full range of both scales. These items served as foils in a verbal recognition test.

The saliency rating task was carried out by 14 subjects, and the schema-expectancy rating task was carried out by 14 different subjects. Subjects were taken into the experimental office in groups of two or three and were given booklets containing the 131 objects to be rated.

The subjects in the saliency rating task were asked to rate the items on a 6-point scale with the following instructions: "Rate each object for *how noticeable the object is (or would be) in this room.* . . . Remember that some of the objects are actually in this room and some are not. If the object *is* in the room, base your rating on how noticeable that object *actually is.* If the object *is not* in the room, base your rating on how noticeable that object *would be* if it were in this room, given the general characteristics of the room." A response of 1 was defined as, "It would be *extremely unlikely* that I would notice the object," and a response of 6 was defined as, "It would be *extremely likely* that I would notice the object."

The subjects carrying out the schema-expectancy ratings were given the following instructions: "On the following pages are lists of objects (some actually in the room and some not actually in the room). Following each object is a scale from 1 to 6.

We would like you to use this scale to rate each object for *how likely the objects would be to appear in a room like this*. ... As an example, if you were in a kitchen carrying out this task, you would probably give an object such as a refrigerator a high number and an object such as a bed a low number. When making your rating *ignore whether or not the object is actually present in the room*. Simply base your rating on the likelihood that the object would occur in this room, given the general characteristics of the room." A response of 1 was defined as *"extremely unlikely* that the object would be found in a room like this," and a response of 6 was defined as *"extremely likely* that the object would be found in a room like this."

The mean saliency rating and the mean schema-expectancy rating were calculated for each of the 131 objects. The two scales are not independent. For the 61 objects present in the room, the correlation between saliency and schema expectancy is –.41; for the 70 objects not in the room, the correlation is –.69. It appears that saliency is based on two factors: a saliency intrinsic to the object and a saliency derived from its schema context. For example, a .45-caliber pistol is intrinsically more salient than a paper clip. However, an item also increases in saliency if it does not fit into the schema-based context. A spare tire is probably of intermediate intrinsic saliency, but in the context of a graduate-student office it becomes highly salient. This context effect appears to produce a portion of the negative correlation of saliency with schema expectancy. In addition, some of the negative correlation may be due to item sampling (especially for the nonpresent items). When nonpresent items of high salience are selected, few will be likely to occur in a graduate-student office, and so this intrinsic item bias will also lead to a negative correlation of saliency with schema expectancy.

Examination of the schema-expectancy scores provided considerable support for the existence of a common room schema. The subjects were in strong agreement that a room such as our experimental room is highly likely to contain a floor, a desk, a calendar, an eraser, and pencils, but is highly unlikely to contain a sewing machine or a .45-caliber pistol. The schema-extectancy data also support the a priori selection of room-frame items (items almost certain to be in a room). The six objects with the highest schema-expectancy scores were all room-frame items (door, floor, light switch, ceiling lights, walls, ceiling). The other a priori room-frame item, doorknob, was rated slightly below two strong office-frame items, desk and eraser.

The data also suggest that place schemata are not rigid preformed structures, but instead are much more flexible, utilizing the full extent of the subject's knowledge. In the present task the subjects were taken to a room in a psychology building and were asked to rate the objects in "this graduate student's office." In this context they gave high schema-expectancy ratings for experimental apparatus, worktable, and textbooks, even though it seems quite unlikely that these items would receive high expectancy scores in a rating of a generic "office" or of a different type of office, such as the office of a bank president.

The saliency ratings also showed considerable lawfulness. Subjects gave high saliency ratings to large visible objects (walls, desk), to attention-attracting objects (Playboy centerfold, skull), and to objects not fitting the graduate-student office schema (spare tire, rolling pin). Subjects gave low saliency ratings to small ordinary objects (eraser, paper clips). Overall, it appears that the rating tasks gave lawful data reflecting psychologically meaningful processes. The following experiment was designed to study the effects of schema expectancy and saliency on memory for places.

MEMORY EXPERIMENT

This experiment used the experimental room described above. The general procedure was designed to allow us to examine the episodic place information retained after a brief exposure to the experimental room in an unintentional setting. In order to examine different aspects of memory for the room, three groups of subjects performed different memory tasks.

Subjects

The subjects were undergraduates fulfilling a course requirement. There was a total of 86 subjects: 30 subjects carried out written recall and then verbal recognition; 29 subjects carried out drawing recall; and 27 subjects carried out verbal recognition only. Subjects were exposed to the experimental room individually and carried out the memory tests in groups of one or two.

Procedure for Room Exposure

The experimenter took the subject into the experimental wing of the Psychology Building and said, "I have to check to make sure that the previous hour's subject has completed the experiment." The experimenter then told the subject that he or she could "wait in my office." At this point the experimenter opened the door to the experimental office, turned on the lights, started a hidden stopwatch, and asked the subject to have a seat (all chairs but one had objects on top of them). The experimenter assured the subject that he would return shortly and then left the room, closing the door behind him. After 35 sec the experimenter reentered the office and asked the subject to follow him. The subject was immediately taken to a nearby seminar room where the subject was told that the real purpose of the experiment was to test his or her memory for the experimental office and then the memory task was given. Approximately 1 min elapsed between the time the subject left the experimental room and the time the subject began the memory task. The seminar room in which the memory tasks were given was quite different from the experimental office. It was a long rectangular room with two doors, a single long table, and 24 chairs.

A questionnaire given after the memory task showed that most subjects spent their time in the experimental room seated in the chair, looking around the room in order to guess what kind of person the graduate student was or to see if there were any indications as to what the experiment was going to be about. The deception appears to have been quite successful. The crucial item on the questionnaire was, "Did you think you would be asked to remember the objects in the office?" On this item, 93% of the 86 subjects responded "no."

Recall

Procedure. After being taken to the conference room, the subjects given the written recall task were asked to write down what they could remember about the experimental room. The instructions stated, "We would like you to describe for us everything you can remember about the room you were just in. . . . For each object please try to give its location and as complete a description as you can provide (shape, size, color, etc.). Write your description as if you were describing the room for someone who had never seen it." Immediately after the written recall task the subjects were given a verbal recognition test. Discussion of the data from this task will be deferred until later in the paper.

Subjects given the drawing recall task were provided with an outline of the experimental office and were asked to draw in the objects they could remember from the room. The instructions stated, "We would like you to draw everything you can remember about the room on the provided floor plan. . . . Represent each object in the location you remember it, and try to draw each object's size to scale. Label each object which you draw with its name." Subjects in both recall tasks were asked to work for a minimum of 15 min and could take up to 30 min.

Results and discussion. Criteria were developed to classify objects mentioned in the recall protocols as present objects, frame objects, or inferred objects. For the written recall task, present objects were objects described in enough detail so that someone could take the written protocol into the room and locate the indicated object. Frame objects were the same seven frame objects included in the rating tasks (door, floor, light switch, ceiling lights, walls, ceiling, doorknob). Inferred objects were objects given in enough detail so that they could have been identified if they had been present, but were not actually in the room. The scoring criteria were essentially the same for drawing recall. A number of items in the recall protocols did not fit into these three categories and were eliminated from the analysis: (a) objects that were not in the room, but might have resulted from misidentification (birds on mobile for fish on mobile); (b) vague responses ("the other chair had something lying on it"). In addition objects that were parts of a present object (keys on typewriter) were eliminated to simplify the scoring.

In written recall, a total of 88 different objects were recalled by one or more subjects. Of these, 7 were room-frame objects, 62 were present objects, and 19 were inferred objects. The recall data for each object are given in Table 6.1. The mean number of frame objects recalled per subject was 3.37, the median was 3, and the range was 1 to 6. The mean number of present objects was 13.50, the median 14.5, and the range was 5 to 20. The mean number of inferred objects was 1.13, the median was 1, and the range was 0 to 4. A correlational analysis was carried out to investigate the effects of object saliency and schema expectancy on written recall. Saliency and schema-expectancy scores were available for 43 of the objects given in recall (room-frame objects and inferred objects were not included). The correlation of saliency with recall frequency and the correlation of schema expectancy with recall frequency were calculated; since saliency and schema expectancy were negatively correlated, partial correlations were also calculated. All of these correlations are given in Table 6.2. Examination of these correlations shows that there are clearly independent effects of saliency and schema expectancy.

The data from drawing recall essentially replicated the findings from written recall. The correlation of the number of subjects recalling an object in drawing recall with the number recalling it in written recall is .94. Apparently, at this global level of analysis, drawing recall and written recall are roughly equivalent methods of measuring what information the subjects have picked up in their brief exposure to the room. In drawing recall a total of 77 different objects were recalled by one or more subjects. Of these, 61 were present in the office and 16 were inferred. Table 6.2 gives the correlations between schema expectancy, saliency, and drawing recall. The pattern of these correlations is very similar to that obtained with written recall.

Table 6.1 Number of Subjects Recalling Objects in Written Recall

OBJECT	NO. SUBJECTS[a]	OBJECT	NO. SUBJECTS[a]
Chair (next to desk)	29	Clown light switch	8
Desk	29	Coffee pot	8
#Wall	29	Skull	8
Chair (in front of desk)	24	Mobile	7
Poster (of chimp)	23	Road sign	7
#Door	22	Calendar	6

Continued

Table 6.1 Number of Subjects Recalling Objects in Written Recall *Continued*

OBJECT	NO. SUBJECTS[a]	OBJECT	NO. SUBJECTS[a]
Table (worktable)	22	Wine bottle	6
Shelves	21	Football-player doll	5
#Ceiling	16	Jar of creamer	5
Table (with coffee)	15	Pipe (cord)	5
Skinner box	14	Postcards	5
Child's chair	12	Tennis racket	5
#Floor	12	Blower fan	4
#Light switch	12		
Toy top	12	Colored patterns on	4
Brain	11	ceiling lights	
Parts, gadgets (on worktable)		Piece of bark	4
	11	*Filing cabinet	
Swivel chair	11	Frisbee Jar of coffee	3
Poster on ceiling	10	*Poster (in addition to	3
*Books	9	those in room)	
#Ceiling lights	9	Screwdriver	3
Poster (of food)	9	Snoopy picture	3
Typewriter	9	Rotary switches	3
Bulletin board	8	Cactus	2
Cardboard boxes	2	Hole in wall (for pipe)	1
*Coffee cup	2	Homecoming button	1
Computer cards	2	*Lamp	1
Papers on bulletin board	2	Magazines	1
*Pens	2	*Nails	1
Pot (for cactus)	2	Packets of sugar	1
Solder	2	Paper (on desk chair)	1
Vacuum tube	2	Papers on shelf	1
*Window	2	*Pencil holder	1
Wires	2	*Pencils	1
*Ball	1	Picnic basket	1
*Brain (in addition to	1	*Pliers	1
that in room)		Saucer	1
Brick	1	Scissors	1
Computer surveys	1	*Screws	1
(on floor)		Teaspoon	1
*Curtains	1	*Telephone	1
*Decals on walls	1	Umbrella	1

Table 6.1 Number of Subjects Recalling Objects in Written Recall   *Continued*

OBJECT	NO. SUBJECTS[a]	OBJECT	NO. SUBJECTS[a]
*Desk (in addition to those in room)	1	Wrench	1
#Doorknob	1		
Eraser	1		
Fan	1		
*Glass plate (covering desk)	1		
Globe	1		

Note. "#" indicates a frame object; "*" indicates an inferred object (i.e., an object not in the office).
[a]Maximum number of subjects = 30.

Overall, the results in the recall tasks give strong support for the action of schemata in memory for places. The evidence for the integration of episodic information with schema-based knowledge was very clear. There were a number of inferred objects in recall, and the inferred objects for which ratings were available received high schema-expectancy scores. The power of the schema-based information on subjects' recall of the room is evident when a subject draws in a window or set of shelves that are not present. The consistency and strength of the book inference is also impressive. Of the 81 different nonframe objects given in written recall, books, which were not there, were the 16th most frequently recalled objects. Of the 77 different objects given in drawing recall, books were the 12th most frequently recalled objects. It is interesting to look at inference items that were only given once in written recall. It might seem that responses at this low frequency are sporadic or random. However, several of these low-frequency inference items (pencil holder, telephone, window) were also given in drawing recall, demonstrating lawfulness in the inferences produced by the underlying office schema.

Table 6.2 Correlations Between Schema Expectancy, Saliency, and Recall for Written Recall and Drawing Recall

	RECALL FREQUENCY	SCHEMA EXPECTANCY	SALIENCY
Written recall[a]			
Recall frequency	1.00		
Schema expectancy	.27 (.55*)[b]	1.00	
Saliency	.47* (.64*)[c]	−.37*	1.00
Drawing recall[d]			
Recall frequency	1.00		
Schema expectancy	.42* (.68*)[b]	1.00	
Saliency	.36* (.66*)[c]	−.43*	1.00

[a] n = 43 objects.
[b] Saliency partialled out.
[c] Schema expectancy partialled out.
[d] n = 41 objects.
*$p < .05$.

The strong positive correlation between schema expectancy and recall also shows the effect of schema information on place memory. However, the recall data taken by themselves do not distinguish between schemata operating in encoding information, as a framework for information, by integration, or in the retrieval of information. There is, however, other evidence to suggest that an encoding hypothesis cannot account for this correlation. Loftus and Mackworth (1978) and Friedman (1979) have shown that subjects examining pictures tend to spend more time looking at *nonschema* objects than at schema-related objects. This suggests that schemata do influence looking time. However, if their findings can be generalized to our more naturalistic situation, then the encoding hypothesis cannot account for our positive correlation, since as applied to the looking-time data it would predict better recall for nonschema objects than schema-related objects, i.e., a negative correlation of recall frequency and schema expectancy.

The positive correlation between saliency and recall probably reflects the amount of attention devoted to the salient objects, but given the present findings, one could also hypothesize that saliency leads to a stronger memory representation or to more efficient retrieval.

Overall, the inferences in the recall data provide clear-cut evidence for the integration of episodic information and schema-based information. Furthermore, if it is assumed that on some occasions present objects with high schema-expectancy ratings are recalled on the basis of schematic information rather than on the basis of episodic information, integration would also contribute to the positive correlation between schema-expectancy ratings and recall. However, this correlation might also be due to the office schema acting as a framework or as a retrieval mechanism.

The data from the verbal recognition condition were designed to distinguish between some of the hypotheses about the use of schema-based information that were not distinguished by the recall data.

Verbal Recognition

Procedure. Subjects in this condition received only a verbal recognition test. After being taken out of the experimental room to the seminar room, they were given a booklet containing a list of object names. They were asked to rate each item for how certain they were that they had seen the named object in the experimental room. The instructions stated, "We would like you to indicate how certain you are that you remember seeing each object by circling one of the numbers from 1 to 6. Use 1 to indicate that you are absolutely certain that you did *not* see the object. Use 6 to indicate that you are absolutely certain that you *did* see the object. Use the numbers between 1 and 6 to indicate intermediate degrees of memory." The verbal recognition test consisted of 131 object names; 61 of the named objects had been in the experimental office and 70 had not.

Results and discussion. There was a strong effect of schema-based inferences in the verbal recognition data, as there had been in the recall data. Of the 51 nonframe items on the verbal recognition test with the highest recognition scores, 13 were not actually present in the room. It is clear that these 13 inferences reflect the influence of the office schema—all but one are in the top one-third of absent objects when ranked in terms of schema-expectancy scores.

Table 6.3 Correlations between Mean Recognition Scores, Schema Expectancy Ratings, and Saliency Ratings

	RECOGNITION	SCHEMA EXPECTANCY	SALIENCY
Present objects (without frame objects)[a]			
Recognition	1.00		
Schema expectancy	.21 (.58*)[b]	1.00	
Saliency	.48* (.69*)[c]	− .49*	1.00
Absent objects[d]			
Recognition	1.00		
Schema expectancy	.75* (.52*)[b]	1.00	
Saliency	−.69* (−.36*)[c]	− .69*	1.00

[a] $n = 54$ objects.
[b] Saliency partialled out.
[c] Schema expectancy partialled out.
[d] $n = 70$ objects.
*$p < .05$.

In order to examine the effects of schema expectancy and saliency on verbal recognition, a series of correlational analyses was carried out. Table 6.3 gives the correlations of saliency and schema expectancy with verbal recognition scores for present objects (not including the room-frame objects) and for absent objects. First we will discuss the positive correlations of schema expectancy and verbal recognition for present objects. On the basis of the previous recall data, we concluded that the positive correlations of schema expectancy with drawing recall and written recall could be the result of schema-based information operating as a framework in memory, operating as a retrieval mechanism, or becoming integrated with the episodic information. In the present recognition data, the verbal recognition items themselves should serve as retrieval cues and so should eliminate any effect due to retrieval processes. Thus, it appears that we can eliminate the schema-based retrieval account of the recognition data. Therefore the positive correlation between schema expectancy and verbal recognition should be due either to schema-based information operating as a framework in memory or to schema-based information becoming integrated with episodic information from the room.

The positive correlation of schema expectancy and verbal recognition for absent objects can apparently be accounted for by only one schema-based explanation. The positive correlation indicates that the subjects were more likely to state that they had seen a nonpresent object if the object was a strong member of the office schema. Since these decisions were being made for objects for which no episodic information was available, the responses must have been due totally to old schema-based knowledge, and therefore reflect the operation of the schema in integration, not as a framework or as a retrieval mechanism.

Next we will examine the correlations between saliency and verbal recognition. The positive correlation between saliency and recognition for *present objects* is probably due to increased looking time allocated to the more salient objects resulting in better memory. However, it is possible that the memory representation for salient objects is somehow simply stronger than that for nonsalient objects.

The correlation of saliency and verbal recognition scores for *absent objects* shows a qualitatively different pattern of results from that obtained for objects in the room. The correlation for objects not present in the room is negative. This suggests that when dealing with more ecologically valid memory tasks, a "simple" recognition task is not so simple. The negative correlation apparently results from the following process during the recognition task. When the subject is asked if some very salient object (e.g., a rat in a cage, or a Playboy centerfold) was in the room, the subject reasons: (a) if the object had been in the experimental room when I was there, I would have noticed it; (b) if I had noticed such a salient object, I would have remembered it; (c) I do not remember such an object; (d) thus, the object must not have been in the room. If a subject follows this reasoning process, then the *higher* the saliency of an object, the *lower* the likelihood of a false recognition response.

This I-would-have-seen-it-if-it-had-been-there phenomenon appears to be a variant of a type of inference discussed by Collins (1978) in a paper on reasoning in answering everyday questions. Collins calls this type of inference a lack-of-knowledge inference and states that it is very common in his data on answering everyday factual questions. Overall, the verbal recognition results support the operation of schemata in integration and the operation of a metacognitive strategy which allows subjects to avoid making false recognition responses for absent items of high saliency.

Verbal Recognition after Written Recall

Procedure. The subjects who provided the written recall data were given a verbal recognition test immediately afterward. Of the present objects given in the recall protocols, 80% had been included on the verbal recognition test. Thus, for many items we had data on recall and recognition for the same objects from the same subject.

Results and discussion. When subjects recalled an item in written recall, they almost always (96%) gave it a rating of 6 ("absolutely certain I remember seeing the object") in verbal recognition. However, they also gave ratings of 6 to many of the present objects that they had not been able to recall. In order to examine the issue of retrieval from memory, a "retrieval ratio" was developed for each object. The retrieval ratio was defined as the number of times an object was given in the recall task divided by the number of times it was given a 6 in the verbal recognition task. Thus, if 12 subjects gave an item a 6 in verbal recognition, but only 6 subjects had recalled the item on the written recall test, the retrieval ratio for that item would be .50. A high ratio (near 1.0) indicates that most subjects who gave the object a 6 in recognition also recalled the object. A low ratio (near 0) indicates that most subjects who gave the object a 6 in recognition did not recall the object. Retrieval ratios were calculated for all recalled present objects which were given ratings of 6 on the verbal recognition test by at least three subjects. A correlational analysis was carried out on the 36 items that met this criterion. The correlation of saliency and the retrieval ratio was –.04, while the correlation of schema expectancy and retrieval ratio was .56 ($p < .01$). Since the correlation of schema expectancy and saliency for this set of items was only –.19, the partial correlations with retrieval ratio were not very different from the simple correlations (.56 for expectancy and retrieval ratio with saliency partialled out, and .08 for saliency and retrieval ratio with expectancy partialled out).

The significant correlation of retrieval ratio and schema expectancy suggests that the office schema is used in the retrieval process. The near zero correlation between retrieval ratio and saliency suggests that the retrieval process is unaffected by an object's saliency. Given that an object is in memory (as indicated by the recognition task), it is more likely to be written down in the recall task if it is related to the office schema than if it is not. A concrete example of this effect is as follows: The typewriter was ranked high in the graduate-student office schema (rank of 12.5 among present, nonframe objects) and was given in written recall by 9 of the 10 subjects who gave it a rating of 6 in verbal recognition. In contrast, the skull was ranked low in the graduate-student office schema (rank 48 for present, nonframe objects on schema expectancy) and was recalled by only 8 of the 16 subjects who gave it a rating of 6 in recognition, despite its high saliency (rank 2 for present objects). Thus, the retrieval ratio analysis provides strong evidence that the room schema is being used as a retrieval mechanism in the recall task. In all of the analyses involving verbal recognition after recall the seven room-frame items have been omitted. Comparison of recall and recognition scores for these items suggests that the recall scores were influenced by the operation of the room schema in communication, as discussed below.

Written Recall: Qualitative Analysis

In addition to the quantitative findings already reported, the recall protocols from the subjects in the written recall condition provided qualitative information that allowed further examination of the use of schemata in integration and in communication.

Schemata—canonical location. Analysis of the recall protocols suggests that the office schema contains some information about the canonical location of objects. When books are inferred, they are almost always recalled as being on the shelves, while inferred objects such as pencils and pens are almost always recalled as being on the desk. Objects that were present in the room, but not in canonical locations, tended to shift to more canonical locations in recall. For example, there was a yellow pad on the seat of the desk chair. In the written recall condition, the only subject who recalled the yellow pad recalled it as being on the desk.

Schemata—color and shape. The use of schema-based information could also be seen in the recall of colors. The desk in the experimental room was brown. In written recall two subjects recalled the color correctly, but four subjects recalled it as gray. There were similar effects for shape. For example, the trapezoidal worktable was recalled as being square by one of the subjects in written recall. Thus, the qualitative analysis of the recall data provides additional support for the effects of the integration of episodic information and schema-based information.

Communication. The qualitative analysis of the recall data provided important data on the use of schemata in determining how information about the room was communicated to their audience. In the recall instructions the subjects were asked to give each object's location "and as complete a description as you can provide (shape, size, color, etc.)." Yet, in practice, there were enormous differences across objects as to how much auxiliary information was given. Much of the variation here appears to be attributable to the subjects' use of Grice's (1975) maxim of Quantity. Grice has argued that in carrying on conversations speakers obey a maxim of Quantity, by which a speaker attempts to make the contribution as informative as required, but not more informative than required. The subject's decision to report auxiliary information in the recall protocols appears to be based on the subject's assumptions about their audience's schema-based knowledge of the room and its contents and on the application of Grice's maxim of Quantity.

Communication—size. There were two objects in the room that were not of canonical size (the child's chair and the worktable). Size information was given for these two objects much more frequently than for any other objects in the room. For the child's chair 67% of the 12 subjects who recalled it used a size qualifier, whereas for the normal-size chair that the subjects sat in, not one of the 29 individuals who recalled it used a size qualifier. For the worktable 82% of the responses contained a size qualifier, whereas for the desk only 17% used a size qualifier. It appears that the subjects were obeying Grice's maxim. They omitted size information for objects of usual size, since they could assume that this information was already available in their audience's office-object schemata; however, for the objects of atypical size they added the size information.

Communication—material. There was a similar effect for information about the materials out of which objects were constructed. The subjects never gave auxiliary information about the materials for objects such as posters, postcards, the frisbee, or the wine bottle, since they could assume schema-based knowledge concerning what materials these objects were made from. The one object in the room that was slightly deviant with respect to material was the chair the subjects sat in—it was constructed of plastic. Auxiliary information about the material was given by 55% of the subjects who recalled this chair. Auxiliary information about materials was also given fairly frequently for the other pieces of furniture. Here, it was not that the material was unusual, but that it was indeterminant (i.e., most office furniture could be constructed of either metal or wood). The rates of material qualifiers in these cases were: 24% for the desk, 25% for the desk chair, 33% for the coffee table, and 18% for the worktable.

Communication—shape, orientation, and location. The results were similar for the other categories of auxiliary information. Shape information was rarely given, and when it was given it was for slightly noncanonical or indeterminant objects (e.g., the chair the subjects sat in had a curved back and 14% of the subjects included that information in their recalls). Orientation information (as distinct from location) was rarely given except for the one object in the room in a highly unusual orientation—a large metal detour sign on the worktable pointing toward the ceiling. In recall, 86% of the subjects gave orientation information when recalling the sign, whereas the next highest rate of orientation information was only 22%. Location information (for present nonframe objects) was almost always given in the recall protocols (93%), presumably because the exact location of most objects is not given by the office schema.

In general, the differential rates of recall of auxiliary information appear to reflect the use of schema information in conjunction with the maxim of Quantity. Even though the instructions said to report auxiliary information, the subjects systematically omitted information that was derivable from the room and object schemata, and reported auxiliary information when it deviated from the schemata or when it was indeterminant with respect to the schemata. The subjects were asked to recall the room as if they were describing it to someone who had never seen it. The data suggest that they were able to do this quite successfully. If they had been describing the room to the experimenter, there would have been no need to tell the experimenter that the worktable was small or that the chair they had been sitting in was made of plastic, since clearly the experimenter already knew this. Instead, the schema information and maxim of Quantity were used as if the audience was an idealized average individual who knows about graduate-student offices in general, but not about this particular graduate-student office.

Communication—negative statements. There were 11 sentences about objects in the room which contained negatives: 3 subjects stated that the room was not large, 2 stated that there were no windows, and 6 statements occurred once—that there were no rugs, that the chair was not against the wall, that the desk was not covered with knickknacks, that the coffee table was not made of wood, that the Skinner box had no top, and that the worktable was not square. Without a theoretical construct such as the room schema, the occurrence of these negative sentences is bizarre. The subjects were instructed to write down what they had seen in the room, and thus had no apparent reason to produce any negations. However, the explanation in terms of schemata seems quite straightforward. When communicating the information about the room, the subjects were considering their audience's office schema and pointing out the nonexistence of things that the subjects thought their audience might mistakenly infer on the basis of that schema. Thus, the list of negated sentences is, in effect, an explicit list from the subjects of those aspects of the experimental room that the subjects found to deviate from their schema.

Communication—article usage. Another example of room and office schema information determining aspects of the recall protocols is in article usage. In traditional grammatical accounts of English (e.g., Stockwell, Schacter, & Partee, 1973), the article *a* is said to be used to introduce new information into a discourse, while *the* is used anaphorically to refer to something that has already been mentioned in the discourse. For example, "I saw *a* platypus. *The* platypus was running along the river bank." More recent discussions of article usage (Linde, 1975; Norman & Rumelhart, 1975) have pointed out that *a* is used to introduce something into the current shared knowledge of the speaker and hearer, while *the* is used for things that are already in the shared knowledge of the speaker and hearer. Thus, "John moved into *a* new house last year. *The* kitchen is beautiful." In this case, the speaker introduces the concept of John's house into the shared knowledge of the speaker and hearer, and then can refer to *the kitchen,* since kitchens have been introduced by the house schema.

Since English article usage is sensitive to shared knowledge, we examined the article usage in the written recall data to see if it reflected schema-based knowledge. For each present object in the written protocols, the percent usage of *the* on first mention was calculated. The results showed a clear trimodal distribution: The high-usage set consisted of 7 objects (door, 100%; doorknob, 100%; floor, 100%; ceiling, 94%; light switch, 83%; walls, 81%; lights, 44%). The low-usage set consisted of 6 objects (bulletin board, 13%; typewriter, 11%; desk, 10%; shelves, 9%; chair, 7%; coffee table, 7%). The remaining 56 objects were never introduced with *the* on first mention. These results show remarkable sensitivity to shared schema knowledge on the part of the subjects. If one were describing the experimental room to someone who has been in it, then it would be quite natural to use an introductory *the* for unexpected and highly salient objects (e.g., the skull, the road sign), since one can assume that the other individual saw them and (since there was only one object of that type in the room) there could be no confusion about what was being referred to. The recall protocols show not a single example of introductory *the* for this type of object; clearly the subjects were (as instructed) directing their recall protocols to an audience whose schemata contained no specific information about the particular experimental room the subjects had been exposed to.

Examination of the objects that fell into the high article usage set shows that once it has been established that a room is being recalled, the subjects assume that the room-frame objects are in their audience's room schema. It should be noted that the seven objects selected by the empirical criterion of high introductory *the* usage are identical with the seven a priori room-frame objects selected by the experimenters when the room was being organized and scaled. Examination of the objects that fell into the low-usage group suggests another subtle use of schema knowledge. All of these items are instances of an office schema (as distinct from a room schema). It appears that a subset of subjects makes the assumption that it is possible to assume shared knowledge about objects in the office schema when communicating about an office. Overall, the article-usage data from the written recall protocols suggest that the subjects almost always assumed in their audience the presence of a room schema, sometimes assumed the presence of an office schema, and never assumed the presence of a schema for the particular experimental room.

Communication—omissions. Another aspect of the use of schema information in communication is in determining what information can be omitted. Very strong schema-related information such as room-frame information appears to be frequently omitted in the written protocols. This reduced production of room-frame objects in the written recall task was shown by subtracting an object's rank in recall (for present and room-frame objects) from its rank in verbal recognition (for present and room-frame objects; data from the verbal recognition only condition). These scores were calculated for the 15 objects with the highest recognition scores. There were 9 objects with negative scores (i.e., rank in recall below that expected from rank in recognition), and 7 of these 9 were the room-frame items. This analysis indicates that the room-frame objects are written down in recall less frequently than would be expected on the basis of their recognition scores, presumably because the subjects assume the room-frame information is already known to their audience.

Overall results. The qualitative analysis of the written recall protocols showed the integration of episodic information and schema-based information in the production of location, color, and shape inferences. In addition, the qualitative analysis found strong effects of schema-based knowledge determining what the subjects chose to communicate to the experimenter: They reported auxiliary information that was unusual or indeterminant with respect to room and object schemata; they omitted auxiliary information given by the schemata; they explicitly denied the existence of information they thought might be mistakenly inferred on the basis of the schemata; and finally, they adjusted their article usage in accordance with the schema information they assumed was available to their audience, using the definite article to introduce objects that they assumed were shared knowledge.

GENERAL DISCUSSION

This experiment shows that it is possible to bring the study of real-world place memory into the laboratory. The choice of an ecologically valid situation, such as the unintentional memory for rooms, has been important in theory development. Many recent discussions of schema theory have been relatively global and nonspecific. However, the complex and meaningful nature of the information available in the room led to an intricate set of empirical relations in our experiment and allowed us to be somewhat more specific in our theorizing and to show the operation of schemata on a number of different aspects of memory for places.

Our initial scaling of the office for schema expectancy and saliency uncovered a number of interesting characteristics of our subjects' perceptions of real-world places. The subjects' use of the schema-expectancy scale made it quite evident that they were relating our experimental room to their long-term knowledge of offices, e.g., they thought that pencils belonged in our office, but that a .45-caliber pistol did not. The fact that the subjects gave high schema-expectancy ratings to objects such as the experimental apparatus when they thought they were dealing with a psychology graduate-student office suggests that place schemata cannot be considered to be rigid frames, but are capable of rather subtle readjustments.

The negative correlation we found between schema expectancy and saliency suggests that both of these dimensions must be considered in an analysis of real-world places. Comparison of the ratings suggested that some objects have an intrinsic saliency, but that objects without a high intrinsic saliency are made salient if they deviate from the overall place schema.

The results of the memory experiment provided support for the operation of schemata in several quite specific aspects of place memory:

Encoding. Our experimental procedures provided no data on looking time per object, and so we have no evidence on the use of schemata in encoding. The work of Loftus and Mackworth (1978) and Friedman (1979) on looking at meaningful pictures suggests that schemata are involved in determining looking time. Both of these studies have found that looking time is longer for nonschema objects. The encoding hypothesis states that memory is a direct function of looking time. Therefore the looking-time data as applied to the encoding hypothesis predict that memory for low-schema objects should be better, but our basic findings are that high-schema objects show better memory performance. If the looking-time data can be generalized to our experimental paradigm of unintentional exposure to an actual room, then the use of schemata to determine looking time cannot be used to account for our memory results.

Framework. The results of this experiment allowed no unique test of the hypothesis that schemata can serve as a framework which preserves schema-relevant episodic information. It is possible that the positive correlations of schema expectancy with recall and with verbal recognition could result from the room schema serving as a framework to improve recall of schema-related objects from the experimental room. However, these positive correlations could also be explained by the integration of episodic information from the experimental room with old room-schema knowledge, or, for the recall data, by the use of the room schema as a retrieval mechanism. Thus, there are several findings that could support the framework hypothesis, but in each case, there is at least one other plausible hypothesis that can give an equivalent account of the data.

Integration. The hypothesis that memory for places is often a result of the integration of new episodic information with old schema-based information was given strong support in this experiment. In both drawing recall and written recall, the subjects recalled a number of objects that were not in the experimental room. The inferred objects were invariably high-schema-relevant objects. Thus, the recall of these items must have been due to schema-based knowledge about offices becoming integrated with the actual episodic information about the experimental room. The high positive correlation of schema expectancy and verbal recognition scores for objects that were not present in the room is also strong support for the integration hypothesis, since for objects not present, there could be no episodic information, and all of the effect must be due to old-schema knowledge. The finding that a number of items with high verbal-recognition scores were not actually in the experimental room and that these items were high-office-schema items shows the power of schema information in influencing place memory.

Retrieval. The hypothesis that schema information can serve as a retrieval mechanism was supported by the analysis of recall and verbal recognition data for the same objects from the same subjects. Given that an item was strongly recognized in verbal recognition, it was more likely to have been written down in the recall task if it was a high-office-schema object. Thus, the office schema apparently enabled subjects to retrieve objects from memory that otherwise would have been inaccessible. Given this finding, it seems very likely that at least part of the general positive correlation of schema expectancy and recall was due to office-schema information serving as a retrieval mechanism in recall.

Communication. The analysis of the written recall data shows powerful effects of schemata on the communication of responses. The subjects report auxiliary information that is unusual with respect to the room schema, and tend not to write down information that they can assume is known by their audience. They adjust their article usage in accordance with the place-schema information they assume in their audience, using the definite article to introduce objects that they feel are given by the room schema.

The finding that the communication effect in our experiment is to emphasize recall of nonschema information and deemphasize the recall of information given by the schema, avoids a problem that has frequently occurred in other research. In studies of the effect of schemata on recall of narratives (Anderson & Pichert, 1978; Rumelhart, 1977; Thorndyke, 1977), the general finding is better recall of schema-relevant information. Most of these investigators have wanted to show an effect of schemata on memory, and yet with this type of material it is always possible that the schemata are operating in the communication of the recalls (i.e., the subjects choose to omit the nonschema information at recall, because they assume it is not important). Thus, in studies of the recall of narratives, the potential effects of schemata in memory are confounded with the effects of schemata in communication. In the present experimental paradigm, the subjects adopted the strategy of communicating the nonschema information and not communicating the information given by the schema. The adoption of this communication strategy by the subjects in our written recall task avoided the usual confounding of an effect of schemata in communication with the other uses of schemata and allowed us to provide more precise tests of other hypotheses.

Saliency. The initial scaling of the experimental office demonstrated that saliency must be distinguished from schema expectancy. It seems likely that the positive correlation between saliency and memory performance found in all three experimental conditions reflects the amount of attention devoted to the salient objects; however, other hypotheses are possible. The negative correlation of saliency with verbal recognition of absent objects suggests the operation of a powerful metacognitive strategy in recognition memory. The subjects use an I-would-have-seen-it-if-it-had-been-there strategy to avoid making false recognition responses for items of high saliency.

Overall, the results of this experiment suggest that place schemata play an important and complex role in place memory. The interaction of the schemata in various aspects of the recall process produces an interesting inverted U-shaped function of the relationship of schema expectancy and recall of objects, given that the objects are shown to be in memory by a recognition test. Objects of very high schema expectancy (e.g., room-frame objects) are not given in recall as much as might be expected, since the subjects assume that they are known to their audience. The objects of high to medium-high schema expectancy are typically recalled. The objects of low schema expectancy are not recalled as much as might be expected from their recognition scores because there are no schemata to facilitate their retrieval.

REFERENCES

Anderson, R. C., & Pichert, J. W. Recall of previously unrecallable information following a shift in perspective. *Journal of Verbal Learning and Verbal Behavior,* 1978, 17, 1–12.

Bartlett, F. C. *Remembering.* Cambridge, England: Cambridge Univ. Press, 1932.

Bobrow, D. G., & Norman, D. A. Some principles of memory schemata. In D. G. Bobrow & A. Collins (Eds.), *Representation and understanding: Studies in cognitive science.* New York: Academic Press, 1975.

Bower, G. H., Black, J. B., & Turner, T. J. Scripts in memory for text. *Cognitive Psychology,* 1979, 11, 177–220.

Collins, A. Fragments of a theory of human plausible reasoning. In D. L. Waltz (Ed.), *Theoretical issues in natural language processing—2.* New York: Association for Computing Machinery, 1978.

Downs, R. M., & Stea, D. *Maps in minds: Reflections on cognitive mapping.* New York: Harper & Row, 1977.

Friedman, A. Framing pictures: The role of knowledge in automatized encoding and memory for gist. *Journal of Experimental Psychology : General,* 1979, 108, 316–355.

Grice, H. P. Logic and conversation. In P. Cole & J. L. Morgan (Eds.), *Syntax and semantics,* Vol. 3, *Speech acts.* New York: Seminar Press, 1975.

Kuipers, B. J. A frame for frames: Representing knowledge for recognition. In D. G. Bobrow & A. Collins (Eds.), *Representation and understanding: Studies in cognitive science.* New York: Academic Press, 1975.

Lichtenstein, E. H., & Brewer, W. F. Memory for goal-directed events. *Cognitive Psychology*, 1980, 12, 412–445.

Linde, C. The linguistic encoding of spatial information (Doctoral dissertation, Columbia University, 1974). *Dissertation Abstracts International*, 1975, 35, 4483A. (University Microfilms No. 74-28, 512)

Loftus, G. R., & Mackworth, N. H. Cognitive determinants of fixation location during picture viewing. *Journal of Experimental Psychology: Human Perception and Performance*, 1978, 4, 565–572.

Lynch, K. *The image of the city.* Cambridge, MA: MIT Press, 1960.

Minsky, M. A framework for representing knowledge. In P. H. Winston (Ed.), *The psychology of computer vision.* New York: McGraw-Hill, 1975.

Neisser, U. *Cognition and reality.* San Francisco: Freeman, 1976.

Norman, D. A. Memory, knowledge, and the answering of questions. In R. L. Solso (Ed.), *Contemporary issues in cognitive psychology: The Loyola symposium.* New York: Wiley, 1973.

Norman, D. A., & Rumelhart, D. E. Reference and comprehension. In D. A. Norman, D. E. Rumelhart, & LNR Research Group, *Explorations in cognition.* San Francisco: Freeman, 1975.

Piaget, J., & Inhelder, B. *Memory and intelligence.* New York: Basic Books, 1973.

Rumelhart, D. E. Understanding and summarizing brief stories. In D. LaBefge & S. J. Samuels (Eds.), *Basic processes in reading: Perception and comprehension.* Hillsdale, NJ: Lawrence Erlbaum, 1977.

Rumelhart, D. E. Schemata: The building blocks of cognition. In R. J. Spiro, B. C. Bruce, & W. F. Brewer (Eds.), *Theoretical issues in reading comprehension: Perspectives from cognitive psychology, linguistics, artificial intelligence, and education.* Hillsdale, NJ: Lawrence Erlbaum, 1980.

Rumelhart, D. E., & Ortony, A. The representation of knowledge in memory. In R. C. Anderson, R. J. Spiro, & W. E. Montague (Eds.), *Schooling and the acquisition of knowledge.* Hillsdale, NJ: Lawrence Erlbaum, 1977.

Schank, R. C., & Abelson, R. P. *Scripts, plans, goals, and understanding.* Hillsdale, NJ: Lawrence Erlbaum, 1977.

Spiro, R. J. Remembering information from text: The "state of schema" approach. In R. C. Anderson, R. J. Spiro, & W. E. Montague (Eds.), *Schooling and the acquisition of knowledge.* Hillsdale, NJ: Lawrence Erlbaum, 1977.

Stockwell, R. P., Schacter, P., & Partee, B. H. *The major syntactic structures of English.* New York: Holt, Rinehart, & Winston, 1973.

Thorndyke, P. W. Cognitive structures in comprehension and memory of narrative discourse. *Cognitive Psychology*, 1977, 9, 77–110.

Name:_____

READING COMPREHENSION QUESTIONS

Refer to the information you have just read to find the answers to these questions. Be sure that you do not simply copy what is already written in the article. Think about your answer and write it in your own words.

1. Write any words that you had to look up here, along with their definitions. If you did not need to look up any words, list and define several of the words you think the average college student may have found difficult. All students should have at least three words and definitions for this question.

2. Write the full reference for this article in APA style. For advice on APA style, consult www.apastyle.org.

3. Explain what is novel about this study that made it publishable. Be sure to describe exactly what previous studies lacked that this study offers. Simply describing this study, or simply describing previous studies, is insufficient.

Name:_____

4. Generally describe the methods used in the paper.

    • How many subjects were there? If there was more than one experiment, list the number of subjects in each experiment.

    • Who were the subjects (e.g., older adults, schizophrenic patients, college students)?

    • What was it like to be a subject (i.e., what were the subjects required to do)? Provide enough detail that the reader can truly imagine what it was like to be a subject.

5. What were the main findings of this paper?

Name:_____

COMPREHENSION CHECK QUESTIONS

Refer to the information you have just read to find the answers to these questions. Be sure that you do not simply copy what is already written in the article. Think about your answer and write it in your own words.

1. Experiment Proposal

Pretend that you are an author on this paper and are tasked with determining future directions. Taking into account what has already been done in the field (i.e., the information presented in the Introduction) and the present study, what is a novel next step in this research? If you were one of the authors of this study, what would you do next and why? Be sure to explain why you would perform this next step. For example, proposing to replicate the study sampling from a different subject population is not sufficient, unless you explain why it is a reasonable next step.

Name:_____

2. Writing Critique

Pretend that you are a reviewer on this paper and are required to make a substantial suggestion on how to improve the writing. For example, you could offer an alternative explanation of how to describe the importance of the work, explain why the real-world application is insufficient, or suggest how the authors could describe their work in a more interesting way. If you were a reviewer, what would you say to improve the writing (not the methods) of this paper? Be sure to provide concrete suggestions. For example, do not simply say that an aspect of the paper was confusing. Demonstrate that you took the time to understand the material and offer a better way to explain the portion you found confusing.

Name:_____

3. Application Question

Think about how the work in this paper applies to the real world. Describe a scenario (either real or imagined) under which this work applies to your life. Do not use the real-world application mentioned in the paper. Rather, consider how this work is relevant to you (again, it could be imagined). Be sure to demonstrate that you understand the results of the paper through your real-world application.

Name:_____

TRUE OR FALSE STATEMENTS

Write three *true* statements here, noting the page number where the answer can be located.

1. _____
   _____
   _____

   - Page number where answer can be located: _____

2. _____
   _____
   _____

   - Page number where answer can be located: _____

3. _____
   _____
   _____

   - Page number where answer can be located: _____

Name:_____

Write three *false* statements here, noting the page number where the answer can be located. Then rewrite each statement to make it true.

1. _____
   _____
   _____

   - Rewritten to be true:
   _____
   _____

   - Page number where answer can be located: _____

2. _____
   _____
   _____

   - Rewritten to be true:
   _____
   _____

   - Page number where answer can be located: _____

3. _____
   _____
   _____

   - Rewritten to be true:
   _____
   _____

   - Page number where answer can be located: _____

Incubation and the Persistence of Fixation in Problem Solving

Steven M. Smith and Steven E. Blankenship

Abstract

Extra work on unsolved problems may lead to more improvement if the new work is delayed rather than undertaken immediately after initial solution attempts. Such a result constitutes incubation in problem solving. "Unconscious work" on a problem, commonly assumed to be responsible for incubation effects, may not be necessary to observe the phenomenon. We hypothesize that fixation, a block to successful problem solving, may develop during initial solution attempts and persist, interfering with immediate extra work more than with delayed extra work. Five experiments are reported in which fixation was induced to prevent optimal performance on the initial test of Remote Associates Test (RAT) problems (e.g., Mednick, 1962). After the fixation manipulation in three of the experiments, the effects of incubation intervals were examined by retesting the fixated problems. Both fixation (poorer initial problem-solving performance) and incubation (more improvement after a delayed retest than an immediate retest) were found in all the experiments which tested for the effects. In Experiments 1, 2, and 3, misleading distractors were presented alongside the RAT problems during the initial test of the problems to cause fixation. In Experiment 4, a block of paired

Smith, S. M., & Blankenship, S. E. (1991). Incubation And The Persistence Of Fixation In Problem Solving. *The American Journal of Psychology*, 104(1), 61-87. Copyright © by University of Illinois Press. Reprinted with permission.

associates—pairing the RAT words with the misleading distractors prior to problem solving—successfully induced fixation, indicating that the distractors affected memory retrieval. In Experiment 5, a trial-by-trial technique allowed fixation and incubation to be induced and tested separately for each item. All of our findings of incubation effects appear to have depended upon the initial induction of fixation. Although the experiments may not be representative of all naturally occurring cases of incubation, they provide a methodology for the study of fixation and incubation effects in problem solving in the laboratory.

When initial attempts at solving a problem fail, the problem may be temporarily put aside, during which time a little-understood stage of problem solving known as *incubation* may occur. A period of incubation may result in insight, in which the problem solver becomes suddenly and unpredictably aware of the solution to a problem. The time in which the unsolved problem has been put aside refers to the *incubation period* or *incubation time*; if insight occurs during this time, the result is referred to as an *incubation effect*. Although the idea of incubation effects has appeal to common personal experience, it has not enjoyed great empirical support in controlled laboratory studies of problem solving. Commonly cited discussions of incubation effects often appear in the literature not as reports of empirical studies, but rather as textbook discussions (Anderson, 1975; Posner, 1973; Woodworth & Schlosberg, 1954).

Several empirical studies have tested incubation effects in problem solving (Dominowski & Jenrick, 1972; Driestadt, 1969; Fulgosi & Guilford, 1968; Gall & Mendelsohn, 1967; Gick & Holyoak, 1980; Murray & Denny, 1969; Olton & Johnson, 1976; Patrick, 1986; Smith & Blankenship, 1989). A few of these experiments found incubation effects (Dreistadt, 1969, one experiment; Fulgosi & Guilford, 1968, one experiment; Murray & Denny, 1969, one experiment; Patrick, 1986, one experiment; Smith & Blankenship, 1989, four experiments). Of these studies, the only replicated findings of incubation effects are those reported by Smith and Blankenship, which employed a paradigm similar to that used in the present experiments. Of the remaining experiments, findings of incubation have been unreliable. Neither Dominowski and Jenrick (1972), Olton and Johnson (1976), Gall and Mendelsohn (1967), nor Gick and Holyoak (1980) found any incubation effects. Fulgosi and Guilford (1968) found an incubation effect after a 20-min but not after a 10-min interruption. Olton and Johnson (1976) reported failures to replicate effects by Fulgosi and Guilford (1968), Dreistadt (1969), and Silveira (1971, cited in Olton &Johnson, 1976). Murray and Denny (1969) reported a single effect, restricted to high ability subjects, and Patrick's (1986) one finding of an effect occurred only for low ability subjects. In sum, these studies provide neither a strong base of empirical support for the putative phenomenon of incubation nor a reliable means of observing the phenomenon in the laboratory. Clearly, a reliable method for observing and studying incubation effects in the laboratory is needed if we are to extend our knowledge beyond anecdotal accounts and speculation.

Perhaps one of the greatest obstacles to research on incubation effects is an adherence to the common assumption that incubation must be the result of unconscious problem solving. Authors writing about incubation routinely cite the introspections of the French mathematician Henri Poincare. Poincare's self-described insights into the nature of a set of mathematical functions claimed that "the role of this unconscious work in mathematical invention appears to me incontestable" (quoted in Perkins, 1981, p. 49). Unfortunately, consensual ways of observing and inducing such putative unconscious processes are not known. Even if such processes could be studied empirically, it is not clear that all incubation effects result from the same causes. Furthermore, there are several alternative explanations to the unconscious work hypothesis, many of which are at least as plausible, and which have some empirical basis. These alternatives will be treated in greater depth in the general discussion of the present paper. Although we hope eventually to discover the efficacy of the various alternative explanations, in the present study we have set as our goal the reliable induction and observation of incubation effects in a controlled setting.

The key to observing incubation effects in the laboratory, we believe, is to temporarily thwart solutions to otherwise tractable problems. Problems that are solved immediately require no incubation, and intractable problems which cannot be solved even with unlimited time will not be influenced by incubation time. A preliminary block to problem solving, which we will refer to as *fixation*, was described by Woodworth and Schlosberg (1954) in their discussion of incubation: "When the thinker makes a false start, he slides insensibly into a groove and may not be able to escape at the moment" (p. 841). The inescapability of fixated thinking in initial problem-solving attempts thus creates the possibility of an incubation effect, or successful problem solving following some time away from the problem. According to Woodworth and Schlosberg, "[T]he incubation period simply allows time for an erroneous set to die out and leave the thinker free to take a fresh look at his problem" (p. 841). This "set-breaking" view of incubation effects has also been noted by Posner (1973) and Anderson (1975).

One of the most creative and extensive treatments of fixation as mental set has been carried out by Luchins and Luchins (e.g., 1959, 1970). The paradigm induced *Einstellung*, or mental set, by presenting several problems in sequence, all of which could be solved using a specific algorithm. After this mental set induction, subjects received a critical problem which could be solved with a very simple and obvious solution, or with the *Einstellung* solution. Very few subjects saw the simple solution, relying instead on the previously encountered mental set. Such was often the case even when the critical problem could not be solved with the *Einstellung* solution. Thus, the immediately preceding experience with the set solution caused fixation, a block to successful problem solving.

Another approach to the issue of fixation has been studies of *functional fixedness* (e.g., Duncker, 1945; Maier, 1931), an inability that many subjects have in thinking of unusual uses for familiar objects. In the now famous two-string problem, subjects have difficulty in thinking of using pliers or an electronic device as a pendulum to solve a problem.

Because subjects' fixating experiences occurred prior to their participation in the experiment, functional fixedness may be seen as more long-lasting than the mental set induced after a few moments in the *Einstellung* studies. On the other hand, functional fixedness has been shown to be manipulable within an experimental session (e.g., Adamson, 1952; Adamson & Taylor, 1954). After performing a task in which either a switch or a relay was used in completing an electric circuit, subjects were given the choice of using one of the two objects as the pendulum in the two-string problem. Subjects have been found to avoid using the object recently involved in the circuitry problem, whether it was the switch or the relay (e.g., Birch & Rabinowitz, 1951). Subjects apparently had difficulty thinking of an object as a pendulum if it had just been used as a piece of electronic equipment, indicating that functional fixedness can be situationally induced. Furthermore, Adamson and Taylor (1954) found that the likelihood that the fixation procedure caused this effect to be observed was a negative function of the time between the circuit problem (the fixation procedure) and the two-string problem, observing performance after a delay of 30 min, 1 hr, 1 day, or 1 week.

A more recent approach to fixation has been taken by Jones (1989) and Jones and Langford (1987), working with the tip-of-the-tongue (TOT) phenomenon. They found that cases of TOT experiences increased if interlopers (words which sound or mean something like the target word) were read to subjects along with the definitions of rare words used to induce TOT states. The interlopers apparently blocked access to the correct targets, thus inducing a kind of fixation in memory retrieval. This accessibility approach to fixation will be considered more extensively in a later discussion.

The present set of experiments was partly intended to study and control fixation, the first part of this hypothetical pattern of cognition which leads to incubation. Inducing fixation during initial problem solving might more consistently provide the opportunity to observe incubation, which should occur as the initial induced fixation dissipates. The present studies were concerned with finding materials and techniques for inducing both fixation and incubation in problem solving.

The problems used in the present experiments were Remote Associate Test (RAT) items (e.g., Mednick, 1962). Each problem consisted of three words (e.g., ARM COAL PEACH). The solution is a single word which forms a common word or phrase with each of the three RAT test words. For example, the solution "Pit" makes the common word or phrase armpit, COAL PIT, and PEACH PIT. In the present experiments, problem solving was fixated by priming information inappropriate to correct solutions of problems. For example, associating ARM with LEG, COAL with FURNACE, and PEACH with PEAR should have primed inappropriate information. The primed inappropriate information should have been more accessible than the correct target information, thus making each problem more difficult to solve.

The present experiments were also concerned with incubation effects. Incubation effects were tested in the present experiments by retesting unsolved RAT problems either immediately or after a period of incubation. Demanding tasks were inserted in the incubation intervals so that subjects would not continue to work on unsolved problems during the period of incubation. An incubation effect is herein defined as greater improvement in solving initially unsolved problems when retesting occurs after a delay rather than immediately following the initial test.

In a study by Patrick (1986), RAT problems were used to examine the role of ability in incubation effects. A prior study by Murray and Denny (1969) had found incubation effects only for "low ability" subjects, ability being measured by a Gestalt Transformation Test. Patrick used subjects' performance on an initial test of the RAT problems to assess ability more directly. He found that incubation effects were limited to high ability subjects (i.e., those scoring above the median on the initial test), in contrast to Murray and Denny's finding. Therefore, the importance of subjects' ability in findings of incubation effects was assessed in the present experiments.

EXPERIMENT 1

In Experiment 1, fixation was induced by presenting misleading associates in italics on the page alongside each of the three RAT words. Subjects were told that the words in italics were examples of associates of the RAT words. No associates were presented in the nonfixation control group. It was hypothesized that performance on fixation problems (i.e., problems with inappropriate priming) would be worse than performance on nonfixation problems. This method is conceptually similar to color-word and picture-word (Stroop) interference paradigms (e.g., Klein, 1964; Lupker, 1979). In both cases, performance may be thwarted or delayed by accompanying stimuli which tend to elicit retrieval of responses which are similar to the correct response, but which are also incorrect.

Incubation periods were manipulated by inserting demanding interpolated activities between an initial and later attempt at solving an RAT problem. All groups should show overall improvement in problem solving at the retest, because extra work should provide extra solutions. The experimental finding of incubation concerns the amount of improvement seen in an immediate retest compared with a delayed (incubated) retest. An incubation effect is observed when incubation time yields greater problem-solving improvements at the retest relative to improvements in the no-incubation condition.

It was predicted that incubation effects would be found for fixation groups. Although induced fixation may persist through an immediate retest, continuing to thwart solutions, it should be more likely to dissipate before a delayed retest, allowing greater improvements. Without induced fixation, the nonfixation group should have less of a block from which to recover at retest. Thus, it was predicted that retest improvements for the nonfixation group would not significantly differ for incubation versus no-incubation conditions.

Method

Subjects

Participants were 39 students who volunteered to fulfill part of an introductory psychology course requirement. Subjects were randomly assigned to treatment groups: 10 in the fixation/incubation group; 11 in the fixation/ no-incubation group; 10 in the nonfixation/incubation group; and 8 in the nonfixation/no-incubation group.

Materials

The 20 Remote Associates Test (RAT) items used as experimental problems are shown in the Appendix. Each RAT item contains three words. The solution to a RAT problem is a word which is an associate of each of the three test words on a given item. The example explained to subjects was washer, shopping, picture (correct answer is "window").

A related associate (not a correct solution) was printed in parentheses in italics next to each RAT word. The misleading associates are also shown in the Appendix. Subjects were told that the distractors were examples of the kind of associates that are correct solutions.

Design

Half of the treatment groups (fixation) were given simultaneous fixation with the RAT items and half were not (nonfixation). The RAT retest was given after no interval for half of the groups (no incubation), and after a 5-min incubation period for the other half (incubation). Thus, a 2 (Fixation) × 2 (Incubation) between-subjects design was used.

Procedure

The 20 RAT items were each given twice (RAT-1 and retest). In the fixation conditions, incorrect associates were presented simultaneously with RAT items. Four RAT problems (with or without misleading associates) appeared on each of five pages in the experimental test booklets, and subjects were allowed 2 min/page.

For the groups given a period of incubation, a science fiction short story was given to subjects to study for 5 min (ostensibly, for a later test) following RAT-1. The incubation groups were not informed of the subsequent retest. The no-incubation groups were given the retest immediately after the last page of RAT-1.

Booklets with the same 20 RAT problems in the original order were issued to subjects for the retest, either after no interval, or after the 5-min short story. No associates were presented at the retest. Subjects were allowed 4 min for each page of 4 problems on the retest.

Results

Fixation

Nonfixation subjects solved more than twice as many problems as fixation subjects on the initial test (Table 7.1). A t test was computed comparing fixation and nonfixation groups, using proportion correct on the first test (RAT-1) as the dependent measure. Fixation significantly[1] decreased performance on RAT-1, $t(37) = 3.69$.

Incubation

The proportion of problems not solved on the initial test that were solved at retest defined the improvement score. An incubation effect was found for the fixation groups. At retest, incubation subjects who had been fixated solved .41 of the initially unsolved problems, whereas the fixated no-incubation subjects solved only .19 of the unsolved items (Table 7.2). The effect of incubation was significant for the fixated group, $t(19) = 3.88$.

No incubation effect was found for nonfixation subjects. Incubation subjects in the nonfixation condition solved .32 of the unsolved problems, compared with .22 improvement for the nonfixation/no-incubation condition (Table 7.2). The effect of incubation was not significant for the nonfixation group, $t(16) = 1.23$.

Table 7.1. Mean proportions correct on RAT-1 in Experiment 1 for fixation and nonfixation groups

GROUP		
FIXATION	NONFIXATION	FIXATION EFFECT
.10	.25	.15

Note. There were 20 problems on RAT-1. Fixation effect = (nonfixation RAT-1 proportion correct) – (fixation RAT-1 proportion correct).

Table 7.2. Mean improvement in Experiment 1 for incubation vs. no-incubation groups

CONDITION	GROUP		INCUBATION EFFECT
	INCUBATION	NO INCUBATION	
Fixation	.41	.19	.22
Nonfixation	.32	.22	.10

Note. Improvement = (no. newly solved at retest)/(20 – no. solved on RAT-1). Incubation effect = (incubation improvement) – (no-incubation improvement).

An ANOVA tested incubation effects as a function of ability, as defined by RAT-1 performance. Subjects were divided into three groups according to the number correctly solved on the initial RAT: above the median, at the median, and below the median. Because there was a main effect of fixation, the medians for the fixation and nonfixation groups were computed independently such that, for example, high-scoring fixation subjects were classified with high-scoring nonfixation subjects in the high ability group.

The 2 × 3 (Incubation × Ability) anova used improvement (i.e., the proportion of initially unsolved problems that were solved at the retest) as the dependent measure. Ability was low, median, or high. There was a significant Ability × Incubation interaction, $F(2, 33) = 3.88$, $MS_e = .02$. Participants who scored low or at the median had greater incubation effects than those with high ability (findings for Experiments 1, 2, and 5 appear in Table 7.9).

Discussion

A clear, robust effect of fixation was observed as a result of the distractors presented with the RAT problems in Experiment 1. Subjects in the nonfixation condition solved more than twice the number of problems solved by the fixation subjects on the initial RAT. This fixation resulted not from the repeated use of an algorithm, as in the water-jar problem series of Luchins and Luchins (1959), nor was it caused by long-term preexperimentally induced fixation, as in Maier's (1931) 2-string (functional fixedness) problem. Rather, the fixation effect appeared to be caused by presenting misleading distractors that were related to the target solution.

Incubation effects were also observed in Experiment 1. The effect of incubation was significant in the condition in which subjects were first given a fixation treatment, but not in the nonfixation condition. Thus, support was evidenced for the idea that incubation may result from the dissipation of fixation, a problem-solving block. This is not to say that there are no other possible causes of incubation effects. Rather, we claim to have demonstrated one way to observe incubation in the laboratory.

Ability, as measured by performance on the initial RAT, was related to incubation effects in Experiment 1. The finding of greater incubation for low ability subjects contradicts the findings of Patrick (1986), whose incubation effects with RAT problems were limited to high ability subjects.

EXPERIMENT 2

Experiment 1 showed that problem solving can be diverted away from appropriate solutions. In Experiment 2 we tried to maximize the effects of fixation using a method of presenting the misleading associates in a way that made them essentially unavoidable. The RAT problems were presented individually on a computer screen while misleading associates were flashed on the screen and a voice synthesizer spoke the misleading associates aloud.

Experiment 2 also tested the usefulness of a solution time metric in measuring fixation. It was hypothesized that even when a problem is solved, fixation might prolong the problem-solving process. Therefore, solutions as well as solution times were recorded in Experiment 2. In some treatment conditions, the first two letters of the correct answer were provided for the subject, making the problems very easy. It was expected that the problems with hints would be easy to solve, but that it would require more time to find solutions in the fixation condition. Because the two-letter hints were expected to keep performance near the ceiling for the initial RAT, we expected that incubation would be observed only in the no-hints condition. As in Experiment 1, it was predicted that incubation effects would occur following fixation, but not in the condition with no initial fixation.

Method

Subjects

Participants were 79 students who volunteered to fulfill part of an introductory psychology course requirement. Subjects were randomly assigned to treatment groups: 10 in seven of the eight experimental treatment groups, and 9 in the nonfixation/no hints/incubation group.

Materials

Of the 20 RAT problems listed in the Appendix, 10 were used in Experiment 2. The RAT words were presented in all uppercase letters with the three words arranged vertically on the screen of an Amiga 1000 computer. In the conditions in which hints were presented simultaneously with the three RAT words, 2-letter hints (the first two letters of the correct solution) were shown near the bottom of the screen. In the conditions in which fixation was induced, each distractor appeared on the screen next to its related RAT word. The misleading distractors, printed in lowercase letters, flashed on and off at a 1-s rate, and a voice synthesizer spoke aloud each RAT word-distractor pair. A message, which remained at the top of the screen during all of the RAT problems, stated that the solutions were for only the words printed in uppercase letters. On the retest, all problems appeared with 2-letter hints. The incubation material consisted of the same story used in the incubation task in Experiment 1. The story was printed on the screen such that subjects could page forward through the story using the return key on the Amiga keyboard.

Design

On the initial RAT (RAT-1), subjects received either hints or no hints, and fixation (i.e., misleading distractors) or no fixation. The retest occurred either immediately after the last problem of RAT-1 or after a period of incubation.

Procedure

Subjects participated individually. After being familiarized with the computer screen and keyboard, subjects were given instructions about the RAT problems and, if appropriate, the hints and distractors (referred to by the experimenter as "associates"). As in Experiment 1, subjects were told that the distractors were examples of the kind of associates that are the correct solution. Subjects were shown the example problem along with the solution; they were instructed to type the solution on the keyboard and then to press the return key. Subjects were requested to type their answers as quickly as possible because it was a timed test. The time from the presentation of a RAT problem until the first keystroke was recorded for each trial. The specific keystrokes were also recorded. The subject had 1 min to respond, after which the next problem appeared.

In the no-incubation condition, an instruction to press the return key appeared on the screen immediately after the 10th problem. The first problem, with a 2-letter hint, appeared on the screen 2 s after the key was pressed (the first retested item). The remaining RAT items were also retested in the same order and manner as the first presentations. In the incubation condition, an instruction to read a story carefully appeared after the 10th RAT problem. To advance through the story on the screen, subjects pressed the return key; 5 min was allowed to read the story. After 5 min, the 10 RAT problems were retested as in the no-incubation condition.

Results

Fixation

A 2 × 2 (Fixation × Hints) anova was computed using number correct on RAT-1 as the dependent measure. There was a significant effect of fixation, $F(1, 73) = 6.27$, $MS_e = 2.69$; nonfixation subjects solved more problems on RAT-1 than did fixation subjects (Table 7.3). There was also a significant effect of hints, $F(1, 73) = 159.36$, $MS_e = 2.69$, indicating that performance on RAT-1 was far superior when subjects were given the 2-letter hints.

Another 2 × 2 (Fixation × Hints) ANOVA was computed using solution response time (RT) on RAT-1 as the dependent measure. There was a significant effect of fixation, $F(1, 73) = 18.96$, $MS_e = 23.48$, indicating that the presentation of the distractors with the RAT problems considerably delayed solution times relative to the nonfixation condition (Table 7.3). The effect of hints was also significant, $F(1, 73) = 30.98$, $MS_e = 23.48$, again showing faster soluton times with hints.

Incubation

Two 2 × 2 (Incubation × Hints) anovas using improvement as the dependent measure were computed, one for the fixation condition, and one for the nonfixation condition.

For the fixation condition, there was a significant effect of incubation on improvement, $F(1, 34) = 4.63$, $MS_e = .09$, indicating greater improvement in the incubation than in the no-incubation condition (Table 7.4). There was also an effect of hints, $F(1, 34) = 7.93$, with superior performance in the condition in which hints were given. For the nonfixation condition, there was no effect either of incubation, $F < 1.0$, or of hints, $F(1, 30) = 2.63$, $MS_e = .12$.

A 2 × 2 (Incubation × Ability) ANOVA was computed using improvement as the dependent measure. Ability was low, median, or high for subjects scoring below, at, or above the median on RAT-1. Separate medians were used for the hints + fixation; hints + nonfixation; no hints + fixation; and no hints + nonfixation conditions. Although somewhat greater incubation effects were found for the low group than for the high and median groups (Table 7.9), the Incubation × Ability interaction did not approach significance, $F < 1.0$.

Table 7.3. Mean proportions correct and response times (RTs) on RAT-1 in Experiment 2 for fixation and nonfixation groups

CONDITION	GROUP		FIXATION EFFECT
	NONFIXATION	FIXATION	
Hints			
Proportion correct	.86	.75	.11
RT(s)	7.68	14.19	6.51
No hints			
Proportion correct	.37	.29	.08
RT(s)	15.53	18.67	3.14

Note. There were 10 problems on RAT-1. For the proportion correct score, fixation effect = [(nonfixation RAT-1 proportion correct) – (fixation RAT-1 proportion correct)] × 10. For the RT score, fixation effect = (fixation RAT-1 RT) – (nonfixation RAT-1 RT).

Table 7.4. Mean improvement scores in Experiment 2 as a function of hints and fixation

CONDITION	GROUP		INCUBATION EFFECT
	INCUBATION	NO INCUBATION	
Fixation			
Hints	.57	.27	.30
No hints	.21	.08	.13
Nonfixation			
Hints	.36	.38	–.02
No hints	.16	.20	–.04

Note. Improvement = (no. newly solved at retest)/(10 – no. solved on RAT-1). Incubation effect = incubation improvement – no incubation improvement.

Discussion

The fixation manipulation in Experiment 2, with flashing and spoken-aloud distractors, was clearly an effective detriment to problem solving. The solution time measure was even more sensitive to fixation manipulations than was the accuracy measure. This effect was particularly noteworthy in the condition in which 2-letter hints were provided on RAT-1; more than an additional 6 s of solution time was needed for the fixation group, compared with the nonfixation group, even though good hints were provided on RAT-1.

Incubation was found only in the group that was initially fixated on RAT-1. This finding of an incubation effect following fixation is similar to the incubation effect in Experiment 1, which was also found only in the fixation condition.

Incubation effects appeared to be somewhat greater for low ability subjects, although the interaction was not significant. As in Experiment 1, however, it is clear that high ability subjects did not show the greatest incubation effects, in contrast to Patrick's (1986) study.

EXPERIMENT 3

Misleading associates were presented simultaneously with RAT problems in Experiments 1 and 2. A potential limitation of this procedure is that it cannot be known how much of the observed fixation effects were caused by the presence of the distractors and how much was caused by the relatedness of the distractors to the target solutions. In Experiment 3, the fixation effect was examined as a function of the relatedness of the distractors to the RAT problems. Distractors were either related or unrelated to the RAT problems (see Appendix). In Experiment 3, as in Experiments 1 and 2, the distractors were presented simultaneously with RAT problems. If the physical presence of the distractors was a source of the observed fixation effects in Experiments 1 and 2, then problem solving with any distractors, related or unrelated, should be worse than with no distractors. If the relatedness of the distractors is a factor, then related distractors should cause worse performance on RAT problems than unrelated distractors. It is also possible that both factors may have an effect.

Method

Subjects

Participants were 120 students who volunteered to fulfill part of an introductory psychology course requirement. They were randomly assigned to treatment groups.

Design, procedure, and materials

The design, procedure, and materials used in Experiment 3 were identical to those used in Experiment 1, with the following exceptions: (a) Rather than two levels of fixation, as in Experiment 1, there were three levels—related (related associates printed next to RAT problems), unrelated (unrelated paired distractors), and none (no distractors); (b) the unrelated distractors were drawn from the related distractors of RAT problems which were not used in this experiment; and (c) participants were not retested. Thus, the experiment manipulated one between-subjects variable, fixation.

Results

A one-way ANOVA was computed examining the effect of fixation (related vs. unrelated vs. none) on number of problems solved. The analysis found a significant effect of fixation, $F(2, 117) = 31.41$, $MS_e = 6.40$. Subjects with no distractors solved the most RAT problems, those with related distractors solved the fewest, and those with unrelated distractors scored midway between the other two groups (Table 7.5). Newman-Keuls pairwise comparisons ($a = .05$) indicated that related distractors caused significantly worse performance than did unrelated distractors or no distractors, and that unrelated distractors caused worse performance than did no distractors (critical difference for $r = 2$ was .11; for $r = 3$, critical difference was .13).

Discussion

The results of Experiment 3 support both the hypothesis that the words presented alongside the RAT problems deterred problem-solving performance and the hypothesis that the relatedness of the distractors to the correct target solution caused fixation. That unrelated distractors caused worse performance than the condition with no distractors suggests that distraction from attention may have blocked performance. The finding that related distractors caused significantly worse performance than unrelated distractors, however, suggests a different cause of fixation, such as a memory retrieval block. These conclusions hold not only for Experiment 3, but for Experiments 1 and 2 as well.

This description of fixation in problem solving is analogous to output interference, that is, a retrieval block which accrues during free recall, or which is induced by part-list cuing (e.g., Rundus, 1973). According to this model, memory is searched using sampling-with-replacement (e.g., Shiffrin, 1970). During the recall process, each retrieved item, whether retrieved by the subject or provided by the experimenter, is incremented in strength and replaced within the current search set. Thus, after a number of retrievals from a search set have occurred, the set of already-retrieved items is more accessible than the not-yet-retrieved items, thus causing a temporary retrieval block. The part-list cues provided by the experimenter in these memory studies are analogous to the fixating distractors employed in the present experiments to block retrieval of the correct target information.

Table 7.5. Mean proportion correct in Experiment 3 for related vs. unrelated vs. no-distractor conditions

	TYPE OF DISTRACTOR		
	RELATED	UNRELATED	NONE
	.13	.24	.35

Note. There were 20 problems on the test.

The accessibility hypothesis suggested somewhat different techniques for inducing initial fixation in solving RAT problems. Rather than inducing fixation with simultaneously presented distractors, we primed misleading information prior to the initial RAT. These techniques were examined in Experiments 4 and 5.

EXPERIMENT 4

To avoid the interpretive problems of using simultaneous distractors, as in Experiments 1, 2, and 3, fixation in Experiments 4 and 5 was accomplished before the RAT items were presented. In the fixation condition in Experiment 4, subjects were first given a paired associates learning (PAL) task which used the 60 RAT-words as stimulus members of each pair and the 60 misleading associates as response members. This manipulation was expected to temporarily strengthen the associations of RAT-words to inappropriate responses, so that retrieval of the solution would be blocked on the subsequent Remote Associates Test. It was hypothesized, therefore, that solution rates on the RAT would be worse following PAL (fixation) than in the condition with no fixation task.

Method

Subjects

Participants were 38 students who volunteered to fulfill part of an introductory psychology course requirement. Subjects were randomly assigned to three treatment groups: two of the experimental treatment conditions had 10 subjects each, and the fixation/no-incubation group had 8.

Materials

The same RAT problems used in Experiment 1 were again used in Experiment 4, except that the 20 problems were arranged on a single page. The PAL task consisted of the 60 RAT words (3 words/problem), with an associate printed in italics next to each word. The associates were the same misleading associates used in Experiment 1. The PAL list was presented on a single page.

Design and procedure

For subjects given PAL (fixation), the experiment began with the PAL task. Subjects were given the PAL page, and they were told to study the pairs in anticipation of a subsequent test in which they would be given a stimulus member (i.e., a RAT word) and would be asked to recall the response (italicized) member of the pair. Study time was 5 min. For the PAL test, subjects were given the 60 words and were asked to write the correct associate next to each word, with 5 min allowed for this memory task. After the PAL test, subjects were given the original study list and were asked to write in any associates on their test that they had missed. This procedure was intended to strengthen all associations between the RAT words and the misleading associates.

The RAT problems followed the PAL task for fixation groups, or comprised the only task for nonfixation groups. The 20 RAT items were presented on a single page with instructions printed at the top. Subjects were given 5 min to complete as many of the RAT problems as they could.

Results

The fixation group scored 37% less than the nonfixation group on RAT-1 (Table 7.6). A t test comparing fixation and nonfixation conditions was computed using scores on RAT-1 as the dependent measure. Fixation significantly decreased performance on RAT-1, $t(36) = 3.12$.

Discussion

A robust effect of fixation was found, even though the fixating distractors were not presented at the same time as the initial RAT problems. Fixation was induced in the paired associates task, and the detrimental interfering effect apparently persisted into the problem-solving phase of the experiment. Thus, this fixation effect was not caused by distracted attention, as could have occurred in the previous experiments, but rather by temporary activation or priming of the incorrect solutions.

EXPERIMENT 5

Although the block of paired associates learned before the RAT problems caused fixation in Experiment 4, the fixating events and the initial attempts to solve the problems were somewhat remote, potentially allowing unknown processing to influence problem solving. Furthermore, Smith and Blankenship (1989), in observing incubation effects in problem solving, demonstrated the importance of immediate retesting of problems. To better observe the relationship between the fixating event, an initial problem-solving attempt, and a retest of a problem, we used a procedure that would allow item-by-item tests.

Table 7.6 Mean proportion correct in Experiment 4 for fixation vs. nonfixation groups

	GROUP		
FIXATION	NONFIXATION		FIXATION EFFECT
.24	.39		.15

Note. There were 20 problems on the test. Fixation effect = (nonfixation proportion correct) – (fixation proportion correct).

In Experiment 5, fixation was induced immediately before each RAT problem via a paired associates trial. A set of three paired associates was presented and tested immediately before each RT problem. The paired associates were either the three subsequent RAT words, each paired with its related distractor, or three paired associates unrelated to the subsequent RAT problem. The procedure used in Experiment 5 included an initial test and a retest of each RAT problem. The retest of a problem occurred either immediately after the initial test of a RAT problem, or after 30 s or 2 min of a free association task. Thus, each trial consisted of three paired associates (related or unrelated to the subsequent RAT problem) which were presented and then tested, then a RAT problem, then a free association task (0, 0.5, or 2 min), and finally a retest of the RAT problem.

It was predicted that improvement following fixation would be greater for more delayed retests than for an immediate retest, but that improvement following non-fixation would not vary as a function of the delay of retest. That is, incubation was predicted for the fixated items, but not for the nonfixated problems.

Method

Subjects

Participants were 69 students who volunteered to fulfill part of an introductory psychology course requirement.

Design and materials

A subset of 12 of the RAT problems used in Experiment 1 was used in Experiment 5. Half of the problems were in the fixation condition and half were in the nonfixation condition. One-third of the fixation items and one-third of the nonfixation items were retested after no delay, one-third were retested after 0.5 min of free associations, and one-third were retested after 2 min of free associations. Thus, Experiment 5 used a 2 × 3 (Fixation × Incubation) within-subjects design.

The paired associates consisted of RAT words with an associate printed next to each word. The associates were the same misleading associates used in Experiment 1, and were presented in sets of three paired associates. Half of the paired associates were related to the critical RAT test words, and half were not related. There were 12 sets of paired associates, one set preceding each initial RAT problem.

The free association stimuli were one-syllable common English nouns, none of which appeared as a test word or solution to a RAT problem. They were presented as a single word on each slide.

The two response pages consisted of rows of blanks for the subjects' responses. For each trial there were three spaces for the paired associates, a space for the initial solution to a RAT problem, six spaces for each free associate, and another single space for the retest of the same RAT item.

Procedure

Subjects were told to memorize the paired associates in pairs for the immediate paired associates test. For free association slides, they were asked to use the 15 s to generate six free associates to each free association stimulus word. Subjects were instructed on the RAT as in the previous experiments. After subjects had been told what to do on the paired associates test, the Remote Associates Test, and the free association tests, they were shown the test slides at a rate of 15 s/slide. Subjects wrote their responses in the appropriate spaces on the response page as the slides appeared.

Results

Fixation

Performance for nonfixation items was better than for fixation problems on RAT-1 (Table 7.7). A t test was computed to compare performance on fixation items versus nonfixation items on the initial test of each RAT problem. The effect of fixation was significant, $t(68) = 2.38$.

Incubation

As in Experiments 1 and 2, incubation effects were computed independently for the fixation and nonfixation conditions. Improvement, again defined as the proportion of initially unsolved items that were solved at the retest, was used as the dependent measure. Cases in which subjects solved all the initial problems in a condition allowed for no improvement; data from those subjects were deleted from the incubation analyses.

Table 7.7 Mean proportion correct on RAT-1 in Experiment 5 for fixation vs. nonfixation conditions

CONDITION		
FIXATION	NONFIXATION	FIXATION EFFECT
.15	.19	.04

Note. There were 6 fixation and 6 nonfixation items on RAT-1. Fixation effect = (nonfixation RAT-1 proportion correct) – (fixation RAT-1 proportion correct).

An incubation effect was found for the fixation condition; improvement in the immediate retest condition averaged only 2%, compared with 13% in the condition in which the retest was most delayed (Table 7.8). The effect of incubation was significant for the fixation items, $F(2, 92) = 6.99$, $MS_e = .03$. There was no effect of incubation for the nonfixation items, $F < 1.0$.

A 3×3 (Incubation x Ability) anova was computed using improvement scores as the dependent measure. Ability was low, median, or high for those scoring below, at, and above the median, respectively, on the initial tests of the RAT problems. The Incubation x Ability interaction was significant, $F(2, 66) = 2.81$, $MS_e = .10$; incubation effects were smaller for the low ability subjects than for the median or high ability subjects.

Discussion

The item-by-item test procedure for testing fixation and incubation effects was successful in revealing both phenomena. As in Experiment 4, the fixation manipulation operated by diverting memory rather than by distracting attention, because each fixation manipulation occurred prior to the initial test of a RAT item. Furthermore, it cannot be concluded that simply preceding the RAT problems with a memory test serves to fixate problem solving; in Experiment 5 all problems were preceded by a paired associates task, regardless of the fixation condition. A fixation effect was observed by comparing problem-solving performance following related paired associates with performance following unrelated paired associates.

Incubation effects appeared only for the fixation condition, a result consistent with the findings of Experiments 1 and 2. The fine control over the presentation orders and times for the RAT problems in Experiment 5 may have been important for observing this relationship between fixation and incubation.

Table 7.8 Mean improvement and incubation effects in Experiment 5 for 0-min, 0.5-min, and 2-min incubation conditions

| | INCUBATION TIME | | | |
CONDITION	0 MIN	0.5 MIN	2 MIN	INCUBATION EFFECT
Fixation	.02	.00	.13	.11
Nonfixation	.14	.13	.20	.06

Note. Improvement = (no. newly solved at retest)/(2 − no. solved on RAT-1). Incubation effect = (2-min improvement) − (0-min improvement).

Even though improvement scores were worse for the fixated items, incubation effects (i.e., greater improvement at retest following a delay compared with an immediate retest) were greater following fixated trials (Table 7.8). Thus, it appears that the fixation effect was strong enough to carry over to the retest of the RAT problems, and that relief from this persistent fixation did not occur except perhaps for the longest incubation periods.

Ability was related to incubation effects in Experiment 5, with the greatest effect seen in the high ability subjects. This differs from the effect of ability on incubation in Experiment 1 in which low ability subjects showed the greatest incubation effect, and in Experiment 2 in which ability was not related to incubation effects.

GENERAL DISCUSSION

The five experiments demonstrate very clearly that performance on RAT problems can be made to suffer by introducing misleading information either prior to or during the test of RAT problems. All fixation manipulations were effective at decreasing initial RAT scores.

Incubation effects were found in all three experiments which tested incubation, and occurred only following fixation manipulations. Although the results do not demonstrate that fixation is necessary or sufficient for producing the type of incubation effects observed in common everyday experience, they do show a way that reliable incubation effects can be observed in the laboratory. Furthermore, the pattern of incubation following a problem-solving block is consistent with anecdotal accounts of incubation in which the problem solver first "slides insensibly into a groove and may not be able to escape at the moment [after which] the incubation period simply allows time for an erroneous set to die out and leave the thinker free to take a fresh look at his problem" (Woodworth & Schlosberg, 1954, p. 841).

The present experiments demonstrated a variety of techniques, all of which were effective at inducing fixation (i.e., decreased initial problem-solving performance). The Stroop-like effects of the simultaneous distractors may suggest a methodology for observing interference in problem solving, similar to color-word or picture-word interference effects observed in relatively simple naming tasks. The manipulations that may affect attention (Experiments 1, 2, and 3), however, may not be as methodologically clean for inducing a memory retrieval block as techniques that prime memory but cannot cause perceptual distraction at the time of the problem-solving task (Experiments 4 and 5).

Several hypotheses about the cause(s) of incubation have been advanced in the literature on the subject. The set-breaking hypothesis discussed earlier (e.g., Woodworth & Schlosberg, 1954) is a commonly offered explanation, but certainly not the only one. The fatigue hypothesis (e.g., Woodward & Schlosberg, 1954, p. 838) states that mental fatigue thwarts initial problem solving, and that after a rest more energy can be given to an unsolved problem. Another hypothesis has it that intermittent conscious work on the problem continues during the incubation period; thus, incubation results from extra work on problems. Both the fatigue hypothesis and the extra work hypothesis assume that the subject is not busily engaged in work during the incubation period, allowing either a rest or extra work during the unfilled time. Although the present set of experiments did not critically test these hypotheses, it should be noted that the incubation filler tasks used in Experiments 1,2, and 5 were very difficult and demanding, and they were stressed to the subjects as being no less important than the problem-solving tasks.

Another hypothesis was offered by Yaniv and Meyer (1987), who used a modified tip-of-the-tongue (TOT) paradigm (e.g., Brown & McNeill, 1966) to investigate a type of incubation effect. After reading subjects a definition of a rare word which induced the TOT state (i.e., subjects felt that they knew the word but could not name it), Yaniv and Meyer collected a feeling-of-knowing judgment for the word. The unretrieved word was then inserted among other words and nonwords in a lexical decision task (e.g., Meyer & Schvaneveldt, 1971). Priming of initially unretrieved words was found, as evidenced by performance on the lexical decision task. Yaniv and Meyer interpreted this as evidence in support of the memory sensitization hypothesis, which states that the partial activation resulting from the initial unsuccessful retrieval attempt makes the activated target more accessible to subsequent attempts. Yaniv and Meyer explained incubation by hypothesizing (a) that targets for initially unsolved problems are sensitized via the initial retrieval attempts (as evidenced by their data), and (b) that with increased incubation times there are more opportunities for encounters with the relevant target. Thus, according to this explanation, as time goes by it is more likely that the problem solver will "stumble across" the correct target, and will be exceptionally sensitive to recognizing the target as a solution.

Another explanation of incubation effects is that the relevant target information for a problem increases in accessibility over time such that at one point it emerges into consciousness, thus providing the solution to a problem. This type of explanation is consistent with the idea that retrieval or problem solving continues to occur at some unconscious or tacit level after the initial failed attempts. Perkins (1981) referred to this as the "still-waters theory," which states that "thinking runs deep even though quiet on the surface, or quiet at least as far as the problem of interest is concerned. Active thinking, much as a person might do consciously, proceeds unconsciously for a considerable period while the person rests or attends to other matters" (p. 50). Perkins also listed a number of alternative explanations of incubation experiences, including "physical refreshment, forgetting details, finding new approaches, or noticing clues in unexpected circumstances" (p. 52). After reviewing a number of anecdotal cases of incubation effects ranging from personal experiences to the insights of Charles Darwin, Perkins concluded that "deferring a troublesome problem and returning to it later occasionally helps for reasons that have nothing to do with extended unconscious thinking" (p. 57).

We offer an alternative mechanism by which the accessibility of a target might increase over time after the initial failed attempts at a problem. This mechanism does not depend upon the occurrence of unconscious problem solving. Our hypothesis is based upon the possibility that initial unsuccessful attempts at solving a problem result in a memory retrieval block, similar to output interference (e.g., Rundus, 1973). Given a problem or a memory probe for which a possible (but incorrect) response is a blocking piece of information (i.e., one whose accessibility has been temporarily increased), it should be the case that other possible responses, including the correct target, are at least temporarily decreased in accessibility.[2] This situation operationally defines a retrieval block (e.g., Roediger & Neely, 1982), in which retrieval of the desired target is prevented. As more time elapses after the initial failed attempts, the retrieval block may "wear off"; that is, the blocking material may decrease in accessibility, making the correct target relatively more accessible. Thus, this explanation provides a mechanism for the hypothesized progressive increase in accessibility of an initially unretrieved target.

Evidence in support of an accessibility approach to incubation effects was reported in four experiments by Smith and Blankenship (1989). They used a test-retest procedure similar to that used in the present experiments, with misleading information presented at the initial test. In those studies, although the fixating effects of the misleading information were not examined, it was found that memory of the misleading information was inversely related to incubation effects. That is, with longer incubation intervals, there was greater problem-solving improvement, and poorer recall of the misleading distractors.

That the momentary accessibility of the target solution was decreased by retrieval blocks was indicated in at least two of the present experiments (4 & 5). Factors other than retrieval blocks, however, are also likely to affect target accessibility and, therefore, fixation and incubation. For example, increased sensitivity to a solution may also affect target accessibility, as suggested by Yaniv and Meyer (1987). Encountering the target solution or associates of the target during the incubation period will probably increase the accessibility of the solution. Variations in the way that memory is probed may affect target accessibility. Temporary mental fatigue might also result in a momentary block to problem solving. A retrieval block is, however, a reasonable hypothetical cause of failures in initial problem solving, especially because early incorrect retrievals can induce such a block.

Ability, as measured by performance on the initial problem-solving tasks, was not obviously or reliably related to incubation effects in the present experiments (Table 7.9). Numerically, the largest incubation effects occurred for the group scoring high on the initial RAT in one experiment (5), for the median group in one experiment (2), and for the low scoring group in one experiment (1). Thus, the present results dispute both the conclusion of Murray and Denny (1969) that incubation is restricted to low ability subjects, and of Patrick (1986) that incubation occurs only in high scoring subjects. Instead, we propose that incubation may be most likely to occur when easy-to-solve problems are initially thwarted by fixation. What makes a problem easy in a control (nonfixated) condition may relate, for example, to the subject's problem-solving ability, practice, the presence of useful hints, or the normative difficulty of the problem. In terms of accessibility, this means that when problems with highly accessible solutions (under control conditions) are fixated during or prior to initial problem-solving attempts, the increase over time in accessibility of the temporarily blocked solutions will be great, thus causing incubation.

Table 7.9 Incubation effects as a function of ability

EXPERIMENT	ABILITY		
	HIGH	MEDIAN	LOW
1	.02 (15)	.13(3)	.29 (18)
2	.00 (23)	.19 (29)	.02 (27)
5	.70 (5)	.18(14)	.06 (17)

Note. Ability was determined by scores on RAT-1, above, at, or below the median for the high, median, and low ability groups. Numbers in parentheses indicate the number of subjects in each group. For Experiments 1 and 2, incubation = (incubated improvement) – (nonincubated improvement). For Experiment 5, incubation effect = (2-min improvement) – (0-min improvement).

Because incubation effects have not enjoyed much support in past laboratory studies, finding incubation effects in three of the present experiments adds considerably to the empirical foundation of incubation effects in the laboratory. In all three of those findings, incubation was detected only following the fixation manipulation. In no comparison was a reliable incubation effect found without a prior fixation manipulation. These results support the contention that incubation in problem solving can be observed as fixation loses its potency.

Appendix: RAT test items shown in uppercase, distractors in lowercase (related associate/unrelated associate), and solutions in boldface

	PROBLEMS		SOLUTIONS
1. LICK	SPRINKLE	MINES	**salt**
tongue/pupil	rain/square	gold/plaza	
2. WIDOW	BITE	MONKEY	**spider**
woman/pail	chew/page	wrench/church	
3. TYPE	GHOST	STORY	**writer**
style/world	goblin/school	tale/ankle	
4. SURPRISE	LINE	BIRTHDAY	**party**
trick/town	angle/pond	cake/top	
5. WHEEL	ELECTRIC	HIGH	**chair**
tire/child	cord/coat	low/letter	
6. CAT	SLEEP	BOARD	**walk**
nap/mind	might/vegetable	wood/pump	
7. SHIP	OUTER	CRAWL	**space**
ocean/police	inner/soap	floor/money	
8. BALL	STORM	MAN	**snow**
soccer/tea	tornado/file	boy/carrot	
9. FAMILY	APPLE	HOUSE	**tree**
mother/step	pie/worship	home/errand	
10. ATTORNEY	SELF	SPENDING	**defense**
lawyer/nail	me/herd	shopping/scar	
11. WORM	SCOTCH	RED	**tape**
bug/diaper	whiskey/farm	green/empty	
12. WATER	PICK	SKATE	**ice**
bath/win	choose/milk	board/calf	
13. RIVER	NOTE	BLOOD	**bank**
lake/omen	music/April	wound/grouch	
14. ROUGH	RESISTOR	BEER	**draft**
smooth/holster	circuit/nude	bottle/sole	
15. FOOD	CATCHER	HOT	**dog**
eat/in-law	pitcher/pail	cold/harbor	
16. HEARTED	FEET	BITTER	**cold**
broken/bottle	inches/hem	sweet/rifle	
17. DARK	SHOT	SUN	**glasses**
light/seam	gun/desk	moon/crank	
18. SANDWICH	GOLF	CANADIAN	**club**
jelly/sentence	course/robin	Montreal/neon	
19. GRAVY	SHOW	TUG	**boat**

	PROBLEMS		SOLUTIONS	
potato/baseball	movie/stitches	pull/profit		
20. ARM	COAL	PEACH	**pit**	
leg/election	furnace/belly	pear/football		

NOTES

This research was supported by National Institute of Mental Health Grant 1 RO1 MH44730-01 to Steven M. Smith. The authors wish to express their gratitude to Edward Vela, whose help on the project was very valuable, and to Allison Cohen, Susan Costin, Michele Grossman, Jay Laengrich, Jesse Stakes, and John Williamson, who collected the reported data. The authors also thank Donelson Dulany and Janet Metcalfe, whose comments on an earlier form of this manuscript were very helpful.

Correspondence concerning this article should be addressed to Steven M. Smith, Department of Psychology, Texas A&M University, College Station, TX 77843. Received for publication July 19, 1989; revision received March 6, 1990.

1. Significance levels were fixed at $p < .05$ for all statistical tests reported. Two-tailed tests were used for all t tests reported.
2. Theoretically, this decrease in target accessibility could be accomplished in a number of ways, including lateral inhibition (i.e., activation of the incorrect target inhibits other related targets), or a probabilistic retrieval model (e.g., Rundus, 1973; Shiffrin, 1970). In the probabilistic model, the overall probability of retrieving an item remains at 1.0; therefore, increasing the probability of retrieving an item necessarily decreases the probability of retrieving other responses.

REFERENCES

Adamson, R. E. (1952). Functional fixedness as related to problem solving: A repetition of three experiments. *Journal of Experimental Psychology, 44*, 288–291.

Adamson, R. E., & Taylor, D. W. (1954). Functional fixedness as related to elapsed time and to set. *Journal of Experimental Psychology, 47*, 122–126.

Anderson, B. F. (1975). *Cognitive psychology.* New York: Academic Press.

Birch, H. G., & Rabinowitz, H. S. (1951). The negative effect of previous experience on productive thinking. *Journal of Experimental Psychology, 41*, 121–125.

Brown, R., & McNeill, D. (1966). The "tip of the tongue" phenomenon. *Journal of Verbal Learning and Verbal Behavior, 5*, 325–337.

Dominowski, R. L., &Jenrick, R. (1972). Effects of hints and interpolated activity on solution of an insight problem. *Psychonomic Science, 26*, 335–337.

Dreistadt, R. (1969). The use of analogies and incubation in obtaining insights in creative problem solving. *Journal of Psychology, 71*, 159–175.

Duncker, K. (1945). On problem solving. *Psychological Monographs, 55*(5, Whole No. 270).

Fulgosi, A., 8c Guilford, J. P. (1968). Short-term incubation in divergent production. *American Journal of Psychology, 81*, 241–246.

Gall, M., 8c Mendelsohn, G. A. (1967). Effects of facilitating techniques and subject/experimenter interactions on creative problem solving. *Journal of Personality and Social Psychology, 5*, 211–216.

Gick, M. L., 8c Holyoak, K. J. (1980). Analogical problem solving. *Cognitive Psychology, 12*, 306–355.

Jones, G. V. (1989). Back to Woodworth: The role of interlopers in the tip of the tongue phenomenon. *Memory Cognition, 17*, 69–76.

Jones, G. V., 8c Langford, S. (1987). Phonological blocking in the tip of the tongue state. *Cognition, 26*, 115–122.

Klein, G. S. (1964). Semantic power measured through the interference of words with color naming. *American Journal of Psychology, 77*, 576–588.

Luchins, A. S., 8c Luchins, E. H. (1959). *Rigidity of behavior.* Eugene: University of Oregon Press.

Luchins, A. S., 8c Luchins, E. H. (1970). *Wertheimer's seminars revisited: Problem solving and thinking* (Vol. 3). Albany: Faculty-Student Association, State University of New York.

Lupker, S. J. (1979). The semantic nature of response competition in the picture-word interference task. *Memory & Cognition, 7*, 485–495.

Maier, N. R. F. (1931). Reasoning in humans. II. The solution of a problem and its appearance in consciousness. *Journal of Comparative Psychology, 12*, 181–194.

Mednick, S. A. (1962). The associative basis of the creative process. *Psychological Review, 69*, 220–232.

Meyer, D. E., 8c Schvaneveldt, R. W. (1971). Facilitation in recognizing pairs of words: Evidence of a dependence between retrieval operations. *Journal of Experimental Psychology, 90*, 227–234.

Murray, H. G., 8c Denny, J. P. (1969). Interaction of ability level and interpolated activity (opportunity for incubation) in human problem solving. *Psychological Reports, 24*, 271–276.

Olton, R. M., 8c Johnson, D. M. (1976). Mechanisms of incubation in creative problem solving. *American Journal of Psychology, 89*, 617–630.

Patrick, A. S. (1986). The role of ability in creative "incubation." *Personality & Individual Differences, 7*, 169–174.

Perkins, D. N. (1981). *The mind's best work.* Cambridge, MA: Harvard University Press.

Posner, M. I. (1973). *Cognition: An introduction.* Glenview, IL: Scott, Foresman.

Roediger, H. L., Ill, & Neely, J. H. (1982). Retrieval blocks in episodic and semantic memory. *Canadian Journal of Psychology, 36*, 213–242.

Rundus, D. (1973). Negative effects of using list items as recall *cues. Journal of Verbal Learning and Verbal Behavior, 12*, 43–50.

Shiffrin, R. M. (1970). Memory search. In D. A. Norman (Ed.,), *Models of human memory* (pp. 375–447). New York: Academic Press.

Smith, S. M., & Blankenship, S. E. (1989). Incubation effects. *Bulletin of the Psychonomic Society, 27*, 311–314.

Woodworth, R. S., & Schlosberg, H. (1954). *Experimental psychology* (rev. ed.). New York: Holt, Rinehart 8c Winston.

Yaniv, I, 8c Meyer, D. E. (1987). Activation and metacognition of inaccessible stored information: Potential bases for incubation effects in problem solving. *Journal of Experimental Psychology: Learning, Memory, and Cognition, 13*, 187–205.

Name:_____

READING COMPREHENSION QUESTIONS

Refer to the information you have just read to find the answers to these questions. Be sure that you do not simply copy what is already written in the article. Think about your answer and write it in your own words.

1. Write any words that you had to look up here, along with their definitions. If you did not need to look up any words, list and define several of the words you think the average college student may have found difficult. All students should have at least three words and definitions for this question.

2. Write the full reference for this article in APA style. For advice on APA style, consult www.apastyle.org.

3. Explain what is novel about this study that made it publishable. Be sure to describe exactly what previous studies lacked that this study offers. Simply describing this study, or simply describing previous studies, is insufficient.

Name:_____

4. Generally describe the methods used in the paper.

- How many subjects were there? If there was more than one experiment, list the number of subjects in each experiment.

- Who were the subjects (e.g., ol4der adults, schizophrenic patients, college students)?

- What was it like to be a subject (i.e., what were the subjects required to do)? Provide enough detail that the reader can truly imagine what it was like to be a subject.

5. What were the main findings of this paper?

Name:_____

COMPREHENSION CHECK QUESTIONS

Refer to the information you have just read to find the answers to these questions. Be sure that you do not simply copy what is already written in the article. Think about your answer and write it in your own words.

1. Experiment Proposal

Pretend that you are an author on this paper and are tasked with determining future directions. Taking into account what has already been done in the field (i.e., the information presented in the Introduction) and the present study, what is a novel next step in this research? If you were one of the authors of this study, what would you do next and why? Be sure to explain why you would perform this next step. For example, proposing to replicate the study sampling from a different subject population is not sufficient, unless you explain why it is a reasonable next step.

Name:_____

2. Writing Critique

Pretend that you are a reviewer on this paper and are required to make a substantial suggestion on how to improve the writing. For example, you could offer an alternative explanation of how to describe the importance of the work, explain why the real-world application is insufficient, or suggest how the authors could describe their work in a more interesting way. If you were a reviewer, what would you say to improve the writing (not the methods) of this paper? Be sure to provide concrete suggestions. For example, do not simply say that an aspect of the paper was confusing. Demonstrate that you took the time to understand the material and offer a better way to explain the portion you found confusing.

Name:_____

3. Application Question

Think about how the work in this paper applies to the real world. Describe a scenario (either real or imagined) under which this work applies to your life. Do not use the real-world application mentioned in the paper. Rather, consider how this work is relevant to you (again, it could be imagined). Be sure to demonstrate that you understand the results of the paper through your real-world application.

Name:_____

TRUE OR FALSE STATEMENTS

Write three *true* statements here, noting the page number where the answer can be located.

1.   _____
   _____
   _____
   _____
   _____

   • Page number where answer can be located: _____

2.   _____
   _____
   _____
   _____
   _____

   • Page number where answer can be located: _____

3.   _____
   _____
   _____
   _____
   _____

   • Page number where answer can be located: _____

Name:_____

Write three *false* statements here, noting the page number where the answer can be located. Then rewrite each statement to make it true.

1. _____
   _____
   _____

   - Rewritten to be true:
     _____
     _____

   - Page number where answer can be located: _____

2. _____
   _____
   _____

   - Rewritten to be true:
     _____
     _____

   - Page number where answer can be located: _____

3. _____
   _____
   _____

   - Rewritten to be true:
     _____
     _____

   - Page number where answer can be located: _____

Skill in Chess

Experiments with Chess-Playing Tasks and Computer Simulation of Skilled Performance Throw Light on Some Human Perceptual and Memory Processes

Herbert A. Simon and William G. Chase

Abstract

As genetics needs its model organisms, its *Drosophila* and *Neurospora*, so psychology needs standard task environments around which knowledge and understanding can cumulate. Chess has proved to be an excellent model environment for this purpose. About a decade ago in the pages of this journal, one of us, with Allen Newell, described the progress that had been made up to that time in using information-processing models and the techniques of computer simulation to explain human problem-solving processes (1). A part of our article was devoted to a theory of the processes that expert chess players use in discovering checkmating combinations (2), a theory that was subsequently developed further, embodied in a running computer program, MATER, and subjected to additional empirical testing (3).

The MATER theory is an application to the chess environment of a more general theory of problem solving that employs heuristic search as its core element (4). The MATER theory postulates that problem solving in the chess environment, as in other well-structured task environments, involves a highly selective heuristic search through a vast maze of possibilities. Normally, when a chess player is trying

Simon, H. A., & Chase, W. G. (1973). Skill in Chess: Experiments With Chess-playing Tasks and Computer Simulation of Skilled Performance Throw Light on Some Human Perceptual and Memory Processes. *American Scientist*, 61(4), 394-403. Copyright © by Sigma XI. Reprinted with permission.

to select his next move, he is faced with an exponential explosion of alternatives. For example, suppose he considers only ten moves for the current position; each of these moves in turn breeds ten new moves, and so on. Searching to a depth of six plies (three moves by White and three by Black) will already have generated a search space with a million paths. Hence, if *every* legal move is considered (as would be the case in an exhaustive search), an enormous search space would be generated. Such a search is beyond the capacity of the human player, as well as present-day computers. Humans seldom search more than a hundred paths in choosing a move or finding a checkmate, and they seldom consider more than two or three possible moves per position.

The MATER theory postulates that humans don't consider moves at random. Rather, they use information from a position and apply some general rules (heuristics) to select a small subset of the legal moves for further consideration. For example, one powerful heuristic that MATER uses in finding checkmates is to examine first those moves that permit the opponent the fewest replies. A comparison of the MATER program with thinking-aloud protocols from human chess players confirms the importance of heuristic search as a basic underlying process.

While the MATER theory was successful in accounting for much of what was known about chess thinking in mating situations, some important empirical phenomena—some of them known when the theory was formulated, some of them discovered subsequently— eluded the theory's grasp. In this paper, after describing the phenomena, we should like to tell the story of a ten-year effort to account for the recalcitrant facts.

An important by-product of this effort has been to bring about a convergence of the theory of problem solving with theories that have been developed to explain quite different phenomena, which psychologists label "perception," "rote learning," and "memory." In the past, both theorizing and experimentation relating to these different kinds of tasks—problem solving, perceiving, learning by rote, and remembering—have tended to go their separate ways. In the course of our story we will see how these theories come together to explain chess skill; we will see the important constraint that a limited-capacity short-term memory imposes on problem solving in chess and how this limit can be bypassed by specific perceptual knowledge acquired through long experience, stored in long-term memory, and accessed by perceptual discrimination processes.

THE PHENOMENA

In Amsterdam, Adriaan de Groot, who was the first psychologist to carry out extensive experiments on problem solving using chess as the task, also initially formulated his theory in terms of heuristic search (5). His subjects ranged from quite ordinary players to some of the strongest chess grandmasters in the world, including several former world champions. He was puzzled by one thing: none of the statistics he computed to characterize his subjects' search processes—number of moves examined, depth of search, speed of search—distinguished the grandmasters from the ordinary players. He could only separate them by the fact that the grandmasters usually chose the strongest move in the position, while ordinary players often chose weaker moves. Why were the grandmasters able to do this? Wherein lay their chess skill?

The perceptual basis of chess mastery. One clue to this riddle came when de Groot repeated and extended an experiment that had been performed earlier in the USSR (6). He displayed a chess position to his subjects for a very brief period of time (2 to 10 seconds) and then asked them to reconstruct the position from memory. These positions were from actual master games, but games unknown to his subjects. The results were dramatic. Grandmasters and masters were able to reproduce, with almost perfect accuracy (about 93% correct), positions containing about 25 pieces. There was a quite sharp drop-off in performance somewhere near the boundary between players classified as masters, who did nearly as well as grandmasters, and players classified as experts, who did significantly worse (about 72%). Good amateurs (Class A players in the American rating scheme) could replace only about half the pieces in the same positions, and novice players (from our own experiments) could recall only about eight pieces (about 33%). There is a quite nice gradation on this perceptual task as a function of chess skill, and we have verified this in our own experiments (7).

We went one step further: we took the same pieces that were used in the previous experiment, but now constructed random positions with them. Under the same conditions, all players, from master to novice, recalled only about three or four pieces on the average—performing significantly more poorly here than the novice did on the real positions. (The same result was obtained by W. Lemmens and R. W. Jongman in the Amsterdam laboratory, but their data have never been published, 8.)

In sum, these experiments show that chess skill cannot be detected from the gross characteristics of the search processes of chess players but can be detected easily using a perceptual task with meaningful chess content. The experiment with random boards shows that the masters' superior performance in the meaningful task cannot be explained in terms of any general superiority in visual imagery. The perceptual skill is chess-specific. Moreover, a theory of problem solving in chess that does not include perceptual processes cannot be an adequate theory—cannot explain the superior ability of the strong player to choose the right moves.

Eye movements at the chess board. The second set of phenomena we must consider are also perceptual, but of a more recent discovery. Explanations in terms of heuristic search postulate that problem solving, and cognition generally, is a serial, one-thing-at-a-time process. (We are oversimplifying matters to make the issue clear, but the oversimplification will suffice for the present.) Many psychologists have found this postulate implausible and have sought for evidence that the human organism engages in extensive parallel processing (9). The intuitive feeling that much information can be "acquired at a glance" argues for a parallel processor. Of course, the correctness of the intuition depends both on the amount of information that can actually be acquired and upon what is meant by a "glance." If a glance means a single eye fixation (lasting anywhere from a fifth of a second to a half-second or longer), then we know that there are high-speed serial processes (e.g. short-term memory search, visual scanning) that operate within this time range (10). Thus, it is certainly interesting and relevant to find out how the human eye extracts information from a complex visual display like a chess position and to see whether this extraction process is compatible with the assumptions of the heuristic search theories.

A pair of Russian psychologists, Tichomirov and Poznyanskaya, placed an expert before a chess position with instructions to find the best move, and they observed his eye movements during the first 5 seconds of the task (11). The eye movements were inconsistent with the hypothesis that the subject, during these 5 seconds, was searching through a tree of possible moves and their replies.

To describe further what Tichomirov and Poznyanskaya found, we must say a word about how the eye operates. The eye has a central region of high resolution, the fovea (about 1° in radius), surrounded by a periphery of decreasingly lower resolution. Most information about visual patterns is acquired while the fovea is fixated on them; and the eye moves abruptly, in so-called saccadic movements, from one point of fixation to the next. There are at most about four or five saccadic movements per second.

In Tichomirov and Poznyanskaya's record of the first 5 seconds of their subject's eye movements, there were about 20 fixations. Most of these centered on squares of the board occupied by pieces that any chess player would consider to be of importance to the position. There were few fixations at the edges or corners of the board or on empty squares. Moreover, a large number of the saccades moved from one piece to another, where the former piece stood in a "chess" relation—that is, an attack or defense relation—to the latter. For example, the eye would move frequently from a pawn to a Knight that attacked it, or to a Knight that defended it, or from a Queen to a pawn it attacked.

It is important to note that the saccadic movements were not random—therefore, that some information must have been acquired peripherally about the target square before the saccade began. From other evidence, we know that a strong chess player can *recognize* a piece within a radius of 5° to 7° from his point of fixation; for

FIGURE 8.1

In this middle game position, used by Tichomirov and Poznyanskaya in their eye movement experiments, Black is to play.

eye-movement studies show that he can frequently replace such a piece correctly on a board when he has had no closer point of fixation to it (12).

The Russian experiments are of interest for two reasons. First, while the saccadic eye movements themselves are serial, some parallel visual capacity appears to be operating, for, since the saccade is not random, information about the target square must be acquired peripherally. From what we know about search and scanning rates, it can be concluded that the processes of scanning the periphery for the next target square and preparing the next saccade must overlap in time with the processes of searching memory for the identity and function of a piece (or square) presently occupying the fovea. Visual scanning experiments show that an eye fixation does not allow enough time both to recognize a pattern in the fovea and to scan the visual periphery for a likely target for the next fixation unless the two processes overlap in time (13, 14).

Even more important, the Russian experiments confirm the existence of an initial "perceptual phase," earlier hypothesized by de Groot, during which the players first learn the structural patterns of the pieces before they begin to look for a good move in the "search phase" of the problem-solving process. The experiments of Tichomirov and Poznyanskaya have been repeated and confirmed both in Amsterdam and in our own laboratory. How shall we extend the heuristic search theory or problem solving to accommodate them?

EXPLAINING THE EYE MOVEMENTS

Among the ground rules that ought to be followed in building theories, one of the most important is the rule of parsimony. If, in order to explain each new phenomenon, we must invent a new mechanism, then we have lost the game. Theories, gradually modified and improved over time, are convincing only if the range of phenomena they explain grows more rapidly than the set of mechanisms they postulate.

In the present instance, there are two ways in which we may seek to preserve parsimony as we extend the theory. First, we may examine our existing theory to see whether the mechanisms already incorporated in it might be adequate if they were reorganized. Second, if we need additional mechanisms to explain some of the phenomena, then, instead of inventing them ad hoc, we may draw upon mechanisms already postulated or known in other parts of psychology—mechanisms whose existence already has empirical support. We will explore both of these routes for improving the theory while preserving parsimony.

Perceptual processes in MATER. Let us return to the MATER theory and see how much we must add to, or subtract from, it in order to account for the eye movement data. MATER, as noted earlier, is a program for discovering mating combinations by selective search. What is the basis for the selectivity? A fundamental idea imbedded in MATER is that forceful moves should be explored first, where a forceful move is one that accomplishes some significant chess function, like attacking or capturing a piece or restricting the movements of the opponent. Discovering the opportunities for forceful moves in any chess position involves perceiving the attack, defense, and threat relations that hold among pairs and clusters of pieces on the chessboard—it is basically a perceptual process.

Hence, if we examine MATER a level or two below the executive routine that organizes its search, we see that the program is composed chiefly of a collection of processes for noticing significant chess relations among pieces or squares. In the program as originally organized, these processes were enlisted in the service of the

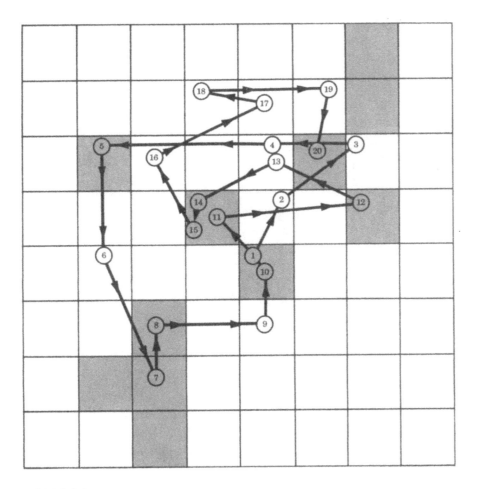

FIGURE 8.2

Eye movements of an expert player are recorded for the first 5 seconds, by Tichomirov and Poznyanskaya. The 10 squares occupied by the most active pieces (see Figure 8.1) are shaded.

heuristic search for a mating combination. Are these noticing processes a sufficient base on which to build a theory of the eye movements?

The PERCEIVER program. It proved surprisingly easy to simulate the eye movements. It was not difficult to replace MATER's executive program with a new program that used the same perceptual processes to guide the scanning of the board, and when this was done, a good correspondence was found between the squares fixated during the first 20 saccades by the human player and the squares fixated by the program (15).

The program, dubbed PERCEIVER, operates in a very simple manner. With the simulated fovea fixated on a square of the board, information is acquired peripherally about pieces standing on nearby squares that attack or defend the fixated square, or that are attacked or defended by the piece on that square. Attention is then assumed

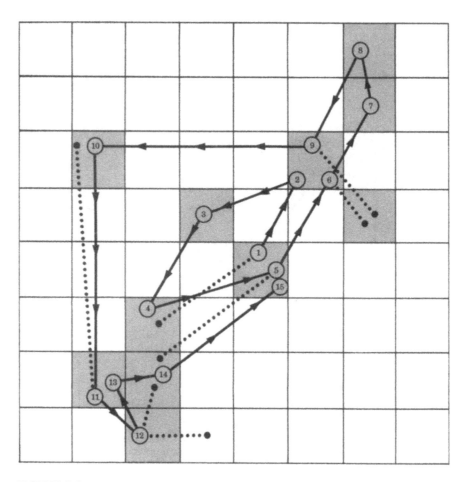

FIGURE 8.3

The solid line represents eye movements and the broken lines represent relations noticed peripherally in this record of simulated eye movements during the period of initial orientation from the PERCEIVER program. The 10 squares occupied by the most active pieces (see Figure 8.1) are shaded.

to switch to one of these nearby squares, and, unless it immediately returns to the square already fixated, causes a saccadic movement to the new square. With the fovea fixated on the new square, the process simply repeats. A moment's reflection will convince the reader that a process having this structure will cause a biased random walk of the fixation point around the board, returning most frequently to those regions where relations among pieces are densest and spending little time on the edges of the board.

Figure 8.1 is one of the positions used by Tichomirov and Poznyanskaya in their eye-movement experiments; Figure 8.2 is a record of the first 20 fixations of their expert in this position; and Figure 8.3 shows the first 15 fixations produced by PERCEIVER in the same position. Of interest is the fact that the PERCEIVER simulation, by means of its simple mechanism of attending to attack and defense relations, shows the same preoccupation with the important pieces as does the human expert.

There are three points we need to make about this simulation. First, no new mechanisms were invoked; it was sufficient to reorganize the lower-level perceptual mechanisms of MATER. The difference between the behavior of MATER and the behavior of PERCEIVER lies largely in a difference in goal or motivation at different stages in the problem solving process. The empirical data from human subjects indicate that initially the player sets himself (not necessarily consciously or deliberately, but perhaps habitually) the task of acquiring information about the chess-significant relations on the board (PERCEIVER). Having acquired this information, he turns to generating moves and exploring their consequences (MATER). There would be no great difficulty in revising MATER to conform to this pattern—with the perceptual, information-gathering phase preceding the cognitive, heuristic search phase. As a matter of fact, one earlier computer chess program, written by Newell, Shaw, and Simon in 1958, had much of this flavor (16), and another such program is now being constructed by Berliner (17).

Second, there is nothing a priori parallel about PERCEIVER; the simple rules that drive the simulated eye around the chessboard are, in fact, serially organized, and it is a simple matter to simulate them in real time on standard computers. Even if realistic time parameters, estimated from human performance, were assigned to the various processes of PERCEIVER, it is still not clear that anything resembling a parallel process would be necessary. This problem is related to the third point.

Third, there is one level of perceptual processing that is finessed and one level that is entirely missing in PERCEIVER. The part that is finessed is the mechanism that recognizes the chess pieces in the first place. What is more important, while PERCEIVER notices attacks and defenses, it has no processes for organizing and remembering this information once it is attended to. But, as we shall see, the organizing process itself drives the eye movements. It is quite plausible that these missing processes operate partly in parallel with the scanning processes of PERCEIVER.

THE BOARD RECONSTRUCTION EXPERIMENT

Nothing in the perceptual mechanisms we have described so far will allow us to account for the spectacular skill of chess masters in reconstructing positions that they have seen for only a few seconds. Both MATER and PERCEIVER gloss over details of the process for recognizing a chess piece—noticing that it is a Bishop, say, rather than a pawn. Each piece is represented by a little bundle of features—its color, for example, and its type (King, Queen, etc.). The programs do not undertake to explain or simulate the feature extraction process, but simply assume that it is performed and that previous learning has stored in long-term memory the requisite information about the capabilities of the different kinds of pieces. More important, neither program contains any mechanisms for the recognition of meaningful, familiar patterns of pieces—neither program has a mechanism for the extensive storage in long-term memory of familiar patterns, nor indeed do they have a long-term memory of any complexity. But it is precisely this kind of pattern-recognition process that lies at the heart of the master's reconstructive ability.

Elementary perceiver and memorizer. Still retaining our respect for parsimony, we note that there already exists in psychology an information processing theory to explain how feature-bundles can become familiarized, associated with other information in long-term memory, and used as components in larger organizations of structures. This theory, called EPAM (Elementary Perceiver and Memorizer), was initially developed by Feigenbaum to explain some of the principal empirical findings about the rote learning of nonsense syllables in the standard serial anticipation and paired-associate paradigms (18).

Among the striking phenomena that had been observed in rote learning are: (1) a characteristic shape of the serial position curve (in serial anticipation learning), (2) a three-to-one (approximately) time advantage in learning meaningful over meaningless and familiar over unfamiliar syllables, (3) certain characteristic differences in learning times between similar and dissimilar stimulus and response items, and (4) certain conditions that determine whether rote learning will have an incremental or an all-at-once appearance. EPAM has been successful in accounting for all of these phenomena (19).

The program of EPAM, and hence the theory it embodies, is quite simple. EPAM learns by growing a discrimination net—a tree-like structure whose nodes contain tests that may be applied to objects that have been described as bundles of perceptual features. When a familiar object is perceived, it is recognized by being sorted through the EPAM net. At the terminal branches of the EPAM net are stored partial "images"—also in the form of feature bundles—of the objects sorted to the respective terminals, together with other information about the objects.

The EPAM theory also plays an important role in explaining the eye movements. Recall that in the previous section, PERCEIVER was found inadequate because it contained no mechanism for recognizing pieces and patterns of pieces. A more complete theory of eye movements would require that PERCEIVER have access to EPAM.

The processes of EPAM influence the eye movements via the way the discrimination net is searched. Figure 8.4 illustrates a small section of the net with two terminal nodes. Observe that the nodes contain questions about the contents of specific squares; depending upon what is found at a square, a decision is made concerning which square to query next. In short, the EPAM net is organized as a set of instructions, albeit abstract, for scanning the board for familiar patterns. These

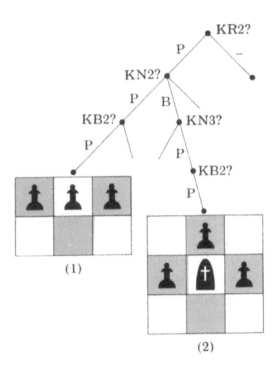

FIGURE 8.4

A portion of the EPAM net for chess shows the terminal nodes for two patterns: (1) three pawns on second rank, and (2) fianchettoed Bishop. At each node is shown the test executed there. For KR2?, for example, read: "What piece stands on the King's Rook Two Square?" The patterns at the terminal nodes are for illustrative purposes only: all the information needed to recognize the pattern is imbedded in the logic of the discrimination net. The terminal node has the internal name of the node, an abstract symbolic reference (internal address) that can be stored in short-term memory as a single chunk.

instructions must then be interpreted by the perceptual system (PERCEIVER) in order to extract the information, and eye movements may well be necessary to execute the instructions. For small clusters of pieces, some of these successive recognition steps may be executed in a single foveal fixation, without saccadic movement. Thus, eye movements may be of two kinds: (1) initial familiarization, in which simple chess functions (attack, defense) are noticed, and (2) recognition, in which complex patterns are scanned.

This explanation of the eye movements gains additional support from the work of Noton and Stark, who developed independently a similar theory (20). They proposed that people's memory of a picture will determine how that picture is subsequently scanned for recognition, and they presented evidence that, under the appropriate conditions, eye movements followed stereotypic "scanpaths" before the picture was recognized. EPAM makes this same strong assumption—that patterns are recognized by scanning the configuration for specific features in a particular order.

EPAM has a recursive structure. This means that any object, once familiarized and incorporated in the net, can itself serve as a perceptual feature of a more complex object. Thus, once the various types of chess pieces—Kings, pawns, Bishops—have become familiarized, these can become features of more complex configurations, say, a "fianchettoed castled Black King's position" (see Figure 8.1 for this pattern in the upper-right part of the board). Once familiarized (and this particular pattern is known to every strong player), such a complex can, in turn, serve as a perceptual feature of a still more complex pattern—e.g. an entire chess position.

We have now illustrated the recursive structure of EPAM with a chess example, but the EPAM program was not constructed with this application in mind. In the context of rote verbal learning, the lowest-level features in EPAM are the geometrical and topological properties of English letters. With familiarization, the EPAM net expands to encompass the letters themselves, which then can be used as components (test nodes) of nonsense syllables. Familiarization of the syllables, in turn, makes these available as components of syllable pairs or lists, and so on. Thus, EPAM postulates a single learning process, identical with what we have been calling familiarization, and a single kind of output of that process, a new unit or *chunk*.

The EPAM theory implies that the length of time required for a learning task will be proportional to the number of new chunks that have to be familiarized in order to perform the task. This implication also fits the empirical evidence very well, the basic learning time being about 5 seconds per chunk (21).

Chunks and short-term memory. Finally, an additional mechanism, short-term memory, is needed in order to understand the reproduction experiment—a mechanism for holding all that information for the short period of time before it is recalled. George Miller, in order to account for the observed invariances in memory-span experiments, first postulated such a memory system with a constant capacity of about seven chunks (22). Miller showed that the well-known limit on the amount of information that can be held in short-term memory is not to be measured in bits, but in chunks—the capacity is about "seven, plus or minus two" familiar units of any kind. By acquiring new familiar units (e.g. octal digits) and learning to recode information in terms of those units (e.g. recoding from binary to octal), holding a constant number of *chunks* in short-term memory allows one to hold an increased number of *bits* (in the example, a gain of three to one). The chunk of EPAM theory has these same characteristics.

Since Miller's influential article was published, there has been a tremendous amount of research on short-term memory, and virtually every present-day theory about cognitive processes incorporates such a memory system. Much research on thinking and problem solving has shown that, outside of strategies, the only other human characteristic that consistently limits performance in a wide variety of tasks is the small capacity of short-term memory. And without a short-term memory, EPAM theory by itself does not account for the verbal learning phenomena mentioned earlier. Short-term memory, then, is one of the basic cognitive capacities. For our purposes, we assume that what gets stored in short-term memory are the internal names of chunks (e.g. "fianchettoed castled Black King's position"), which serve as memory addresses or retrieval cues for information about the chunks in long-term memory.

Let us return now to the chessboard construction phenomena. From Miller's chunking hypothesis, EPAM theory, and the limited capacity of short-term memory, we would predict that a chessboard can be reconstructed from information held in short-term memory if, and only if, it can be encoded in not more than about seven familiar perceptual chunks. If a single piece on a particular square constitutes a chunk for a subject, then he should be able to recall only about seven pieces. If he can recall the positions of more than twenty pieces, then it must be that each chunk consists, on average, of a configuration of about three pieces.

We now have a proposed explanation for the remarkable ability of chess masters to reconstruct positions—an explanation that meets our requirements of parsimony. We have employed only mechanisms that are well rooted in other parts of psychological theory: (1) a limited-capacity short-term memory that can hold the names of only about seven chunks, (2) a vast repertoire of familiar patterns stored as chunks in long-term memory, and a recognition mechanism—the EPAM net—for getting at them, and (3) the related chunking process that builds these patterns and their retrieval mechanisms in the first place.

The next task is to find more direct ways to test the theory. Several routes are open: we can seek direct empirical evidence for the existence of these chunks and see if the memory span for chunks is of the order of seven; we can attempt to simulate the reproduction task using the mechanisms of the theory within a computer program; and we can calculate whether the hypothesis leads to reasonable estimates of the number of familiar chunks a chess master must have stored in long-term memory. We consider these in turn.

Empirical identification of chunks. The logic we used in isolating the chunks was to see if, during the reconstruction of a position, chunk boundaries could be identified by long pauses. Time measurements have been used for identifying chunks in other experimental tasks. McLean and Gregg, for example, had subjects memorize permutations of the alphabet (23). They then timed the intervals (latencies) between successive letters in the subjects' recitals of the lists. They obtained convincing evidence that the permuted alphabet was stored in memory, not as a single uniform list, but as a hierarchy of segments; the individual letter segments most frequently were three or four letters in length. Within-chunk latencies were much shorter than between-chunk latencies.

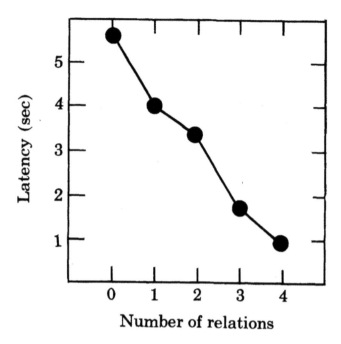

FIGURE 8.5

Mean latencies between successively placed pieces in the reconstruction task are plotted as a function of the number of chess relations between the pieces.

Adapting this technique to our task, we videotaped subjects reconstructing chess positions and measured the latencies in placing successive pieces. In order to estimate what interval would correspond to a chunk boundary, we performed a second experiment, in which the subject also reconstructed a chess position but with the original position in view. The two boards were so placed that the subject had to turn his head to look from the one to the other. We found that, when the subject placed two or more pieces on the board without turning his head, each latency was almost always under 2 seconds. We assumed that, under these speeded conditions, subjects load a single chunk into short-term memory when they view the board and then look directly over and recall that chunk. (It would be inefficient, under these conditions, to store more than one chunk, be-cause they would then have to store the chunk names—there isn't enough room in short-term memory to store the structural information comprising more than one chunk—and then at recall use each chunk name in succession to retrieve the chunk from long-term memory—a time-consuming procedure.) We therefore assumed that, in the reconstruction task, a pause longer than 2 seconds indicated the retrieval of a chunk from long-term memory via the chunk name in short-term memory.

To check the plausibility of this 2-second criterion, we counted the number of chess relations that held between pairs of successively placed pieces. The relations counted were attacks, defenses, proximity, identity of type (e.g. both Rooks or pawns), and color. There was a strong negative correlation between numbers of relations and latency (see Figure 8.5).

Next, we compared the pattern of frequencies of the between-chunk relations (greater than 2 seconds) with the pattern of the within-chunk relations (less than 2 seconds) and both of these with the pattern that would have been observed had the pieces been replaced in random order. We made this comparison for both forms of the reconstruction experiment—from memory and in sight of the board (see Table 8.1). For the two forms of the experiment, the within-chunk relational patterns were highly correlated (Pearson correlation coefficient of .89), but these patterns were only slightly correlated with the corresponding between-chunk patterns (coefficients of .12, .18, .10, and .23) and not at all correlated with the random pattern (−.04 and −.03). On the other hand, the two between-chunk patterns were strongly correlated with each other (.91) and with the random pattern (.87 and .81). Thus, there is strong evidence that the 2-second criterion in fact marks chunk boundaries.

What was the nature of the chunks thus delineated? Most of them were local clusters of pieces in arrangements that recur with high frequency in actual chess positions. (The fianchettoed castled King's position mentioned earlier actually occurs in about ten percent of all recent games between grandmasters.) In the case of a subject who is a chess master, we were able to classify 75% of his chunks as highly stereotyped. Of the 77 chunks observed in his performance of the memory experiment, 47 were pawn chains, sometimes with a nearby supporting or block-ading piece. Ten chunks were castled King's positions. Twenty-seven chunks were other clusters of pieces of the same color, and 19 of these were of common types: 9 consisted of pieces on their original squares in the back rank, and 9 of connected Rooks or connected Queen and Rook. These are configurations a chess master has seen thousands of times—as often as we have seen many of the familiar words in our reading vocabularies. There is as much reason to suppose in the one case as in the other that they are stored in his long-term memory and that he will usually recognize them when he sees them.

Table 8.1. Intercorrelation matrix for the Sight-of-Board Constructions (1 and 3), Memory Constructions (2 and 4), and Hypothetical Random Constructions (5).

	1	2	3	4	5
1. Within-chunk		.89	.12	.18	−.04
2. Less than 2 sec			.10	.23	−.03
3. Between-chunk				.91	.81
4. Greater than 2 sec					.87
5. Random					

Thus far the empirical data support our theory, but we must mention one piece of evidence that is equivocal. If we accept the 2-second criterion for chunk boundaries, then we can measure directly the number of chunks our subjects are holding in short-term memory when they attempt to reconstruct the board. Our theory predicts that the number of chunks will be the same for strong and weak players, but that the average chunk size will vary by a factor of two or three with chess skill.

This prediction is not borne out fully. When we compare, for example, the data from the memory experiment for a chess master with the data for a Class A player, we find that the master recalled about twice as many pieces as the Class A player, but the former's chunks averaged only about 50% larger than the latter's, while the average number of chunks he recalled also averaged about 50% more. The average sizes of the first chunks recalled by master and Class A player were 3.8 and 2.6, respectively; the average numbers of chunks per position were 7.7 and 5.7, respectively. Now the latter numbers are of the right order of magnitude—not far from the memory span of seven—but the difference between them is not predicted by the theory. At the moment, we have no good explanation for the discrepancy, but have simply placed it as an item high on the research agenda. Our hunch is that a less, simplistic model of the structure of chunks and their interrelations, or of the organization of chunks in short-term memory, will be needed to attain a better second approximation.

The MAPP simulation. A second approach to testing the theory of the chessboard reconstruction task was to build a computer program, MAPP, to simulate the observed phenomena (24). The general outlines of the program follow immediately from our description of the theory. The program contains a learning component

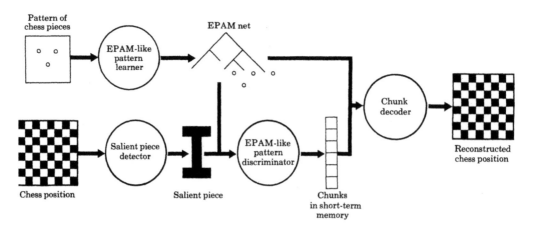

FIGURE 8.6

A schematic representation of the principal components of MAPP shows the learning and performance processes used to reconstruct a chess position.

to acquire and store in memory a large set of configurations of chess pieces and a performance component to carry out the board reconstruction task (Figure 8.6).

Consider first the performance component. When a chess position is presented, the program must scan the board in some way in order to notice the pieces and their relations. The scanning program is a simplified version of PERCEIVER, hence can be viewed as a simulation of the eye movements and control of attention. When a piece is fixated (salient piece), an EPAM-like discrimination process seeks to recognize the cluster of pieces surrounding the fixated piece as a familiar chunk. If it is successful, the symbol designating this chunk is stored in short-term memory. This process is repeated at successive points of fixation until no more pieces become salient or short-term memory capacity is reached, whichever occurs first. Finally, in the reconstruction phase, the terminal information in the EPAM net is used to decode the symbols held in short-term memory into locational information for each of the pieces in a chunk and thus to reconstruct the position.

The learning component of MAPP is a simplified version of the portion of EPAM that grows or elaborates the discrimination net and stores information at its terminal nodes. The input to the program consists of many different configurations of pieces (of two to seven pieces each) that occur frequently as components of chess positions. If such a pattern has been familiarized previously, the program will simply recognize it; if it has not, it will discriminate it from patterns previously learned, will add tests to the EPAM net to implement the discrimination, will create a new terminal node to designate the new pattern, and will store information about the pattern at that node.

Thus the MAPP program is a hybrid of a simplified PERCEIVER with a simplified EPAM; the finer details of those prior programs are not essential to demonstrating the phenomena. With a net of about 1,000 patterns, the performance of MAPP on the reconstruction task is about equal to that of a Class A player, twice as good as a beginner's, but only half as good as a master's. In a typical set of positions, MAPP recalled 51% of the pieces placed correctly by the master, but only 30% of the pieces missed by the master, indicating that its chunks were not dissimilar from the master's. Finally, the within-chunk chess relations of pieces recalled successively by MAPP were highly similar to those of the human subjects, while the between-chunk relations were close to the random pattern.

The chess master's vocabulary. We can extrapolate from the present performance of the MAPP program to estimate how large a vocabulary of chess patterns would have to be stored in the EPAM net to match the performance of the chess master. The distribution of different patterns by frequency is highly skewed, like the frequency distribution of words in natural language. Assuming that the patterns in the present MAPP net are those most frequently encountered in chess games, and assuming the same degree of skewness for chess patterns as for words, we can estimate that something of the order of 50,000 patterns would have to be stored to match the master's performance. Is this a plausible estimate from other viewpoints? We can check its plausibility in two ways.

First, there are no instant experts in chess—certainly no instant masters or grandmasters. There appears not to be on record any case (including Bobby Fischer) where a person has reached grandmaster level with less than about a decade's intense preoccupation with the game. We would estimate, very roughly, that a master has spent perhaps 10,000 to 50,000 hours staring at chess positions, and a Class A player 1,000 to 5,000 hours. For the master, these times are comparable to the times that highly literate people have spent in reading by the time they reach adulthood. Such people have reading vocabularies of 50,000 words or more. If a chunk is a chunk is a chunk as to learning time (as EPAM theory proposes), then we would expect the chess master to have a comparable chess vocabulary. Our estimate agrees well with that reached previously.

Finally, we may ask: given the variety of possible chess positions from well-played games, how big a vocabulary of patterns must we have so that each position could be represented by a distinct set of seven, or so, patterns? If N is the number of possible positions, while P is the number of patterns, then the requirement is $P^7 > N$. If $P = 50,000$, then P^7 is approximately 8×10^{32}. The latter number, in turn, is close to 6^{40}. Now if we played chess games to a depth of 20 moves for each player and at each choice an average of 6 reasonable moves were available, approximately 6^{40} different games could be played. Since there are probably not, on the average, six reasonable moves at each choice point, 50,000 patterns should be more than enough to accommodate the positions that could be reached in such games. It should be emphasized that this estimate is very crude, since it does not take into account that some patterns are much more frequent than others. Nevertheless, it is reassuring that it gives results that are not inconsistent with those arrived at by other routes. Until we can get better data—possibly by expanding the EPAM net—it seems reasonable to assume that a chess master can recognize at least 50,000 different configurations of pieces on sight, and a grandmaster even more.

FAMILIARITY BREEDS COMPETENCE

If the MAPP theory provides an explanation—at least a first approximation—of the chess master's superior skill in quickly perceiving chess positions and then reconstructing them from memory, it leaves unexplained the link between this superiority and his chessplaying prowess. How does the theory solve the riddle with which we began—that the statistics of the master's search appear indistinguishable from the statistics of the weaker player's search?

Two facts that have not been much studied in the laboratory, but which are well known in chess circles, need to be mentioned. First, the master and grandmaster not only select good moves but they often—much oftener than weak players—notice these moves in the first few seconds after they look at a new position. Having noticed such a move, the master may continue to analyze the position for some minutes before he is satisfied that it is the best move—and sometimes his analysis will show that his first impulse was wrong. Nevertheless, his ability to notice moves "at a glance" is always astonishing to lesser players.

Second, although the average time per move in serious tournament chess is 3 to 4 minutes (which means that some moves are made rapidly, while others are brooded over for as much as half an hour), a master or grandmaster can beat players of inferior skill while taking only a few seconds per move and playing simultaneously against many players. His play in these games is not of the same quality as in his more deliberate tournament games, but it is strong enough to beat most experts and almost all players of lower class.

The most likely explanation of these facts is that the chess master is not only acquainted with tens of thousands of familiar patterns of pieces, but that with many of these patterns are associated plausible moves that take advantage of the features represented by the pattern (25). Many of the basic heuristics that guide the search for good moves are based on the presence of a pattern on the board. For example, every chess player of even moderate skill is familiar with the advice: "If there's an open file, put a Rook on it." He knows that the advice is not meant quite literally, that what is really meant is *"consider* putting a Rook on it." The pattern of an open file will trigger the heuristic and initiate a move in the heuristic search. Some patterns (perhaps many hundreds) may actually be associated with an algorithmic solution—traps and combinations that lead to the guaranteed win of a piece, a checkmate, or whatnot—in which a series of moves may be played almost by rote.

Thus, we suggest that the key to understanding chess skill—and the solution to our riddle—lies in understanding these perceptual processes. The patterns that masters perceive will suggest good moves to them. The structure of the search process through possible moves will not be very different from that of weaker players; only the paths suggested by the patterns will be different.

Such a view of chess skill is quite amenable to theorizing in terms of production systems. By a *production* is meant a routine consisting of two parts: a *condition* part and an *action* part. The condition part tests the presence or absence of a specific (perceptual) feature (e.g. an open file); the action part, which is executed whenever the condition is satisfied (whenever the feature is recognized as being present), generates a chess move for consideration that is relevant to that specific feature (e.g. putting a Rook on the open file). A separate analysis routine can then carry out the tree search required for a final evaluation of proposed moves. The advantage of modeling human behavior with production systems is that such systems are very simple and rulelike, avoiding many of the inflexibilities of algorithmic programming languages. They can mimic learning by simply adding new productions (2d), and they have the perceptual flavor we need to simulate the pattern-recognition processes in chess.

While the evidence is not yet in, it becomes increasingly plausible that the cognitive processes underlying skilled chess performance have some such organization as this. Such a scheme would account for the association of chess-playing skill with the ability to recognize numerous perceptual patterns on the board.

There is another question which we haven't addressed directly, but whose answer is implicit in what we have been saying. The question is: how does one become a master in the first place? The answer is *practice*—thousands of hours of practice. This is implicit in the EPAM theory; what is needed is to build up in long-term memory a vast repertoire of patterns and associated plausible moves. Early in practice, these move sequences are arrived at by slow, conscious heuristic search —"If I take that piece, then he takes this piece ..."—but with practice, the initial condition is seen as a pattern, quickly and unconsciously, and the plausible move comes almost automatically. Such a learning process takes time— years—to build the thousands of familiar chunks needed for master-level chess.

Clearly, practice also interacts with talent, and certain combinations of basic cognitive capacities may have special relevance for chess. But there is no evidence that masters demonstrate more than above-average competence on basic intellectual factors; their talents are chess-specific (although World Champion caliber grandmasters may possess truly exceptional talents along certain dimensions). The acquisition of chess skill depends, in large part, on building up recognition memory for many familiar chess patterns.

We now have an account of perceptual skills in chess that is consistent with theories drawn from other parts of psychology. There is no lack of tasks for continuing research, and the environment of chess continues to be one of the most fruitful for cognitive studies.

REFERENCES

1. Simon, H. A., and A. Newell. 1964. Information processing in computer and man. *American Scientist* 52:281–300.
2. Simon, H. A., and P. A. Simon. 1962. Trial and error search in solving difficult problems: Evidence from the game of chess. *Behavioral Science* 7:425–29.
3. Baylor, G. W., Jr., and H. A. Simon. 1966. A chess mating combinations program. *AFIPS Conference Proceedings, 1966 Spring Joint Computer Conference* 28:431–47. Washington, D.C.: Spartan Books.

4. Newell, A., and H. A. Simon. 1972. *Human Problem Solving*. Englewood Cliffs, New Jersey: Prentice-Hall.

5. deGroot, A. D. 1965. *Het Denken van den Schaker*. Trans, as *Thought and Choice in Chess*. The Hague: Mouton & Company.

6. Djakow, I. N., N. W. Petrowski, and P. A. Rudik. 1927. *Psychologie des Schachspiel*. Berlin: Walter de Gruyter.

7. Chase, W. G., and H. A. Simon. 1973. Perception in chess. *Cognitive Psychology* 4:55–81.

8. Jongman, R. W. 1968. Het Oog van de Meester. (Doctoral dissertation, University of Amsterdam.) Assen: Van Gorcum & Company.

9. Neisser, U. 1963. The imitation of man by machine. *Science* 139:193–97.

10. Sternberg, S. 1969. Memory-scanning: Mental processes revealed by reaction-time experiments. *American Scientist* 57:421–57.

11. Tichomirov, O. K., and E. D. Poznyanskaya. 1966. An investigation of visual search as a means of analyzing heuristics. *Soviet Psychology* 5:2–15. (Trans, from *Voprosy Psikhologii* 2(4):39–53).

12. Noordzij, P. 1967. Registratie van oogbewegingen bij schakers. Unpublished working paper, Psychology Laboratory of the University of Amsterdam.

13. Williams, L. G. 1966. The effect of target specification on objects fixated during visual search. *Perception & Psychophysics* 1:315–18.

14. Ellis, S. H., and W. G. Chase. 1971. Parallel processing in item recognition. *Perception & Psychophysics* 10:379–84.

15. Simon, H. A., and M. Barenfeld. 1969. Information-processing analysis of perceptual processes in problem solving. *Psychological Review* 76:473–83.

16. Newell, A., J. C. Shaw, and H. A. Simon. 1958c. Chess-playing programs and the problem of complexity. *IBM Journal of Research and Development* 2:320–35.

17. Private communication.

18. Feigenbaum, E. A. 1961. The simulation of verbal learning behavior. *Proceedings of the Western Joint Computer Conference*, 121–32. (Reprinted in Feigenbaum & Feldman, eds. 1963. *Computers and Thought*. New York: McGraw-Hill.)

19. Simon, H. A., and E. A. Feigenbaum. 1964. An information-processing theory of some effects of similarity, familiarization, and meaningfulness in verbal learning. *Journal of Verbal Learning and Verbal Behavior* 3:385–96.

20. Noton, D. and L. Stark. 1971. Scanpaths in eye movements during pattern perception. *Science* 171:308–11.

21. Simon, H. A. 1969. *The Sciences of the Artificial*. Cambridge: M. I. T. Press, pp. 35–38.

22. Miller, G. A. 1956. The magical number seven, plus or minus two. *Psychological Review* 63:81–97.

23. McLean, R. S., and L. W. Gregg. 1967. Effects of induced chunking on temporal aspects of serial recitation. *Journal of Experimental Psychology* 74(4): 455–59.

24. Simon, H. A., and K. Gilmartin. 1973. A simulation of memory for chess positions. *Cognitive Psychology* (in press).

25. Chase, W. G., and H. A. Simon. 1973. The mind's eye in chess. In *Visual Information Processing*, ed. W. G. Chase. Proceedings of Eighth Annual Carnegie Psychology Symposium. New York: Academic Press.

26. Newell, A., and H. A. Simon. 1972. *Human Problem Solving*. Englewood Cliffs, New Jersey: Prentice-Hall.

Name:_____

READING COMPREHENSION QUESTIONS

Refer to the information you have just read to find the answers to these questions. Be sure that you do not simply copy what is already written in the article. Think about your answer and write it in your own words.

1. Write any words that you had to look up here, along with their definitions. If you did not need to look up any words, list and define several of the words you think the average college student may have found difficult. All students should have at least three words and definitions for this question.

2. Write the full reference for this article in APA style. For advice on APA style, consult www.apastyle.org.

3. Explain what is novel about this study that made it publishable. Be sure to describe exactly what previous studies lacked that this study offers. Simply describing this study, or simply describing previous studies, is insufficient.

Name:_____

4. Generally describe the methods used in the paper.

   • How many subjects were there? If there was more than one experiment, list the number of subjects in each experiment.

   • Who were the subjects (e.g., older adults, schizophrenic patients, college students)?

   • What was it like to be a subject (i.e., what were the subjects required to do)? Provide enough detail that the reader can truly imagine what it was like to be a subject.

5. What were the main findings of this paper?

Name:_____

COMPREHENSION CHECK QUESTIONS

Refer to the information you have just read to find the answers to these questions. Be sure that you do not simply copy what is already written in the article. Think about your answer and write it in your own words.

1. Experiment Proposal

Pretend that you are an author on this paper and are tasked with determining future directions. Taking into account what has already been done in the field (i.e., the information presented in the Introduction) and the present study, what is a novel next step in this research? If you were one of the authors of this study, what would you do next and why? Be sure to explain why you would perform this next step. For example, proposing to replicate the study sampling from a different subject population is not sufficient, unless you explain why it is a reasonable next step.

Name:_____

2. Writing Critique

Pretend that you are a reviewer on this paper and are required to make a substantial suggestion on how to improve the writing. For example, you could offer an alternative explanation of how to describe the importance of the work, explain why the real-world application is insufficient, or suggest how the authors could describe their work in a more interesting way. If you were a reviewer, what would you say to improve the writing (not the methods) of this paper? Be sure to provide concrete suggestions. For example, do not simply say that an aspect of the paper was confusing. Demonstrate that you took the time to understand the material and offer a better way to explain the portion you found confusing.

Name:_____

3. Application Question

Think about how the work in this paper applies to the real world. Describe a scenario (either real or imagined) under which this work applies to your life. Do not use the real-world application mentioned in the paper. Rather, consider how this work is relevant to you (again, it could be imagined). Be sure to demonstrate that you understand the results of the paper through your real-world application.

Name:_____

TRUE OR FALSE STATEMENTS

Write three *true* statements here, noting the page number where the answer can be located.

1. _____
   _____
   _____
   _____
   _____

   • Page number where answer can be located: _____

2. _____
   _____
   _____
   _____
   _____

   • Page number where answer can be located: _____

3. _____
   _____
   _____
   _____
   _____

   • Page number where answer can be located: _____

Name:_____

Write three *false* statements here, noting the page number where the answer can be located. Then rewrite each statement to make it true.

1. _____
   _____
   _____

   • Rewritten to be true:
     _____
     _____

   • Page number where answer can be located: _____

2. _____
   _____
   _____

   • Rewritten to be true:
     _____
     _____

   • Page number where answer can be located: _____

3. _____
   _____
   _____

   • Rewritten to be true:
     _____
     _____

   • Page number where answer can be located: _____

How to Exploit Diversity for Scientific Gain

Using Individual Differences to Constrain Cognitive Theory

Edward K. Vogel and Edward Awh

Abstract

People often show considerable systematic variability in their ability to perform many different cognitive tasks. In this article, we argue that by combining an individual-differences approach with an experimental-cognitive-neuroscience approach one can often further constrain potential theories of the underlying cognitive mechanisms. In support of this proposal, we outline three basic benefits of using an individual-differences approach: validating neurophysiological measures, demonstrating associations among constructs, and demonstrating dissociations among apparently similar constructs. To illustrate these points, we describe recent work by us and other researchers that utilizes each of these techniques to address specific questions within the domain of visual working memory. It is our hope that some of these techniques for utilizing individual variability may be applied to other domains within cognitive neuroscience.

People vary considerably across countless dimensions: physical characteristics and political and religious beliefs, as well as specific skills and aptitudes. This variability can also be observed at a finer level in terms of how individual brains work: Some people have crisp clear memories of long-ago events, while others

Vogel, E. K., & Awh, E. (2008). How to Exploit Diversity for Scientific Gain: Using Individual Differences to Constrain Cognitive Theory. *Current Directions In Psychological Science*, 17(2), 171-176. Copyright © by SAGE Publications. Reprinted with permission.

can't even recall what they did this morning; some can focus attention on an object or task for an extended period of time, while others are easily distracted by anything other than what they are trying to accomplish. This rich diversity in cognitive ability arises through a mix of genetic and environmental contributions and can be thought of as the results of "nature's experiments" (Cronbach, 1957). However, in the context of most standard cognitive neuroscience studies, this variability across individuals is typically treated as a nuisance or as error variance, potentially obscuring differences between levels of their independent variables. Treating individual differences in this way makes sense for cognitive neuroscientists attempting to understand how cognitive constructs such as perception, attention, and memory operate at the general level. Most cognitive neuroscientists are interested in understanding how everyone thinks, not trying to catalog and characterize the entire range of abilities across the population or understand how and why a given individual thinks differently from another. In this article, we argue that these are not mutually exclusive goals, and that by characterizing individual differences in ability within the context of a sound experimental design, one can often learn a great deal more about how a cognitive process operates at a basic level.

In the 50 years since Cronbach's (1957) classic article, there have been many studies that have successfully combined an individual-differences approach with a standard experimental one across several areas of psychology and many domains within the study of cognition (e.g., Kirchoff & Buckner, 2006; Thompson-Schill, Braver, & Jonides, 2005; Wilmer & Nakayama, 2007; Yovel & Kanwisher, 2005). Because the study of individual differences in cognition covers a very broad area, our more manageable goal for this article is to detail how we and others have recently used this combined approach to address specific questions within the subdomain of visual working memory. In particular, we focus on three primary virtues or benefits of the individual-differences approach, and how we have used each of these to gain traction on some specific issues within the visual-working-memory domain. We use specific issues in visual working memory as test cases for describing how the rich data on individual variability can be exploited to help constrain theory, with the hope that some of these tricks can be exported to other domains within cognitive neuroscience.

USING INDIVIDUAL DIFFERENCES TO VALIDATE NEUROPHYSIOLOGICAL MEASURES

In the mid-1990s, Luck and Vogel (1997) were interested in measuring how many visual objects a person could hold in working memory at the same time. To this end, they developed a task in which participants are shown a brief array of simple objects (e.g., colored squares; see Figure 9.1a) that they must remember over a blank gap of about 1 second. After this blank gap, the participants are present-ed either with a test array that is identical to the first array or with an array in which a single item has changed color, and they simply report whether the two arrays are the same or different. Using this change-detection procedure, Luck and Vogel estimated that visual-working-memory capacity is limited to approximately 3 to 4 items. Interestingly, although the average capacity in these initial studies consistently hovered around 3 to 4 items, there were actually large and consistent differences in performance across individuals, ranging from about 1.5 objects up to over 6 objects (see Figure 9.1b). At the time, these individual differences were essentially disregarded by the authors as noise, with the real interest being focused on the surprisingly low mean of 3 to 4 objects.

It is now clear that significant theoretical progress can be made by examining the neural activity that mediates performance in a cognitive measure. For example, while it is usually assumed that change-detection scores are determined by the num-ber of items that can be maintained during the memory period, performance might also be influenced by interference during the retrieval stage of the task. However, if task performance is directly associated with neural activity during the retention interval of the task, then behavioral performance can be more confidently attributed to the maintenance of information in working memory. Likewise, this convergence of behavioral and neural data can reinforce the interpretation of the neural data. A well-known difficulty in cognitive neuroscience is determining whether the neural activity of interest is causally related to the cognitive ability of interest or whether it is epiphenomenal. For example, if an increase in brain activation is found when more information is held in memory, this could be caused either by increased activity in brain regions that mediate the process of interest or by a generalized increase in neural activity when the task becomes more effortful. However, if these increases in neural activity are predicted by behavioral performance in the task, then one can more confidently conclude that the neural activity is a valid measure of the underly-ing cognitive construct.

Along these lines, Vogel and Machizawa (2004) developed an event-related potential (ERP; scalp-recorded electrical brain waves) measure of maintaining information in visual working memory by using a variation of the change-de-tection task. In this study, when they time-locked the ERPs to the onset of the memory array, they observed a large negative voltage wave beginning after 200 milliseconds that persists throughout the retention interval until presentation of the test array. They referred to this activity as the contralateral delay activity (CDA). An exciting attribute of the CDA was that its amplitude increased as a function of the number of items the participant was remembering on a given trial. However, while the CDA increased for arrays of 1, 2, or 3 objects, it reached a limit somewhere between 3 and 4 objects—showing no further increases for larger array sizes (see Figure 9.1c). These results on their own were highly informative, because they demonstrated that this novel neurophysiological data showed a similar characteristic to behavioral performance in this task—namely, that it is limited to representing approximately 3 items at a time. Moreover, the authors took the logic of a behavior–neurophysiology coupling one step further, by testing whether the exact point at which the CDA reached a limit was different for each subject depending upon his or her specific memory capacity. Indeed, they found a strong correlation ($r = .78$) between an individual's memory capacity and the point at which the CDA reached asymptote (see Figure 9.1d).

Without the individual-difference analysis, this study would still have made a solid case that the CDA likely reflected visual-working-memory representations. However, the argument would have rested primarily on the finding that the observed neural limit just happened to occur at approximately the same number of items as the typical behavioral limit. By contrast, the individual-difference analysis allowed the investigators to make a much stronger argument that was based upon the entire distribution of capacity scores, not just the mean score. Thus the consideration of individual variability in this study helped to validate the CDA as a neural measure of capacity limitations in visual working memory. Indeed, we see this specific usage of the individual-differences approach as having the most straightforward application to cognitive-neuroscience research. In fact, there are already several neuroimaging studies that have used this approach. For example, Todd & Marois (2005) found that activation in the intraparietal sulcus increased as a function of number of items in a change-detection task. Similarly, this function reached asymptote at around 3 to 4 items and was also predictive of individual differences in visual-working-memory capacity.

USING INDIVIDUAL DIFFERENCES TO HELP DEMONSTRATE ASSOCIATIONS AMONG COGNITIVE CONSTRUCTS

The cognitive constructs of attention and working memory have historically been tightly linked. In fact, some models of working memory have gone as far as proposing that they are essentially the same construct, defining working memory as the active representations in memory that are within the focus of attention (Cowan, 2001). These links have been further strengthened by the results of numerous neuroimaging studies that have shown substantial overlap in the cortical areas active during attention and working-memory tasks (e.g., Awh & Jonides, 2001). However, the demonstration of a coarse anatomical overlap is generally not sufficient for establishing a functional relationship between two constructs. A common

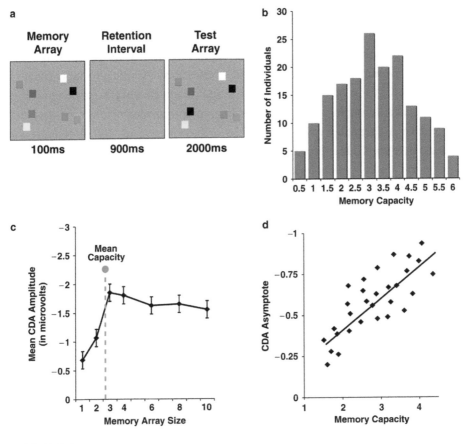

FIGURE 9.1

Measuring visual-working-memory capacity. Panel a shows change-detection stimuli and procedure, in which subjects must attempt to remember colors from the memory array and then, after a brief interval, detect any color changes in the test array. Panel b shows distribution of visual-working-memory capacity estimates from 170 healthy undergraduates, with a mean of 2.88 items and a standard deviation of 1.04 (unpublished data from E.K. Vogel). Panel c shows mean amplitude of contralateral delay activity (CDA; a measure of electrical brain activity) as a function of the number of items in a memory array. Panel d shows correlation of the asymptotic limit of the CDA (derived as the difference in amplitude from 2 items to 4 items) and individual memory capacity. Panel a adapted from Luck & Vogel (1997); panels c and d adapted from Vogel & Machizawa (2004).

alternative approach to establishing whether two constructs are either functionally isomorphic or at least tightly associated is to measure whether they strongly covary. The examination of individual differences in performance is particularly useful for establishing such relationships because it allows for tests of a given association along the entire range of values of performance. That is, if two constructs are tightly related, then an individual's performance on a task that is primarily limited by one construct should be predictive of his or her performance on a task limited by the related construct.

This general approach has been used successfully many times within the working-memory domain, with individual differences in working-memory capacity being shown to be highly predictive of several relatively distal constructs such as intelligence, reasoning ability, and reading comprehension (Cowan et al., 2005; Daneman & Carpenter, 1980; Miyake, Just, & Carpenter, 1994). Moreover, Kane and Engle have used this approach to measure the more proximal associations between memory capacity (operation span) and an individual's performance on various kinds of attention tasks. For example, their work has demonstrated that individuals with a high memory span tend to perform much better on antisaccade tasks, in which they must look away from the location of an object that just appeared, and Stroop tasks, in which they must report the color of a word while ignoring the conflicting meaning of the word (e.g., the word "black" drawn in red), than low-memory-span individuals do (Kane, Bleckley, Conway, & Engle, 2001; Kane & Engle, 2003). This is particularly impressive because most of these tests appear on the surface to have fairly negligible memory requirements, yet individual differences in performance can be predicted by working-memory ability, so it is clear that some common factor underlies both constructs.

Beyond simply demonstrating an association between the two constructs, Kane and Engle's work has provided new insights into the nature of the limits on working-memory capacity. Specifically, their results suggest that memory capacity may have more to do with how well an individual can selectively attend to information than with how much information he or she can hold at a given time. Following this general logic, Vogel, McCollough, & Machizawa (2005) tested whether an individual's memory capacity predicted how efficiently he or she could control what information was stored in visual working memory. To do this, they measured the amplitude of the CDA component of the ERP while subjects voluntarily attempted to store subsets of items from a memory array. For example, in one experiment, subjects were asked to remember only the red items in a display consisting of a mix of red and blue oriented bars. They found that high-capacity individuals were highly efficient at storing only the relevant items and disregarding the irrelevant items. By contrast, the low-capacity subjects were found to be highly inefficient at excluding the irrelevant items, unnecessarily storing all items in the array into visual working memory. These results are somewhat counterintuitive, because they indicate that the low-capacity subjects often store more information in memory than high-capacity subjects do. However, this extra information is often irrelevant to the current task and hinders access to the relevant information. Thus, the pattern of individual differences in this study reveals more than a general association between attention and memory. These data show that the ability to control what information is stored in memory may be the primary limiting factor in measures of memory ability.

USING INDIVIDUAL DIFFERENCES TO DEMONSTRATE DISSOCIATIONS BETWEEN SIMILAR CONSTRUCTS

While it is common to use individual differences in performance as a means of demonstrating associations between constructs, a powerful but underutilized approach is to use this variability as a way of demonstrating that two similar constructs can be dissociated. This general idea was proposed by Underwood (1975); he argued that if a theory proposes that two variations of a given task are determined by the same underlying construct, then an individual's performance on task A should predict his or her performance on task B. If the two measures of performance do not correlate at all—assuming they are both reliable measures—the theory relating the two tasks should be dropped. We have recently used this general approach as a way of teasing apart the constructs of number and resolution as separate factors that underlie visual-working-memory capacity.

First, a little background information will be helpful. In 2004, Alvarez and Cavanagh were interested in measuring how object complexity influenced how many items could be held in visual working memory (Alvarez & Cavanagh, 2004). To do this, they used a change-detection task in which the to-be-remembered items in a given array were drawn from several categories of visual objects that ranged in complexity or "information load." They found a strong inverse relationship between working- memory performance and complexity. When the objects were simple items such as colored squares, participants could remember on average about 4 of them. However, when the memory items were more complex—such as Chinese characters or 3-D shaded cubes—memory-capacity estimates were in the range of 1 to 1.5 objects. From these results, the researchers concluded that memory capacity is not determined only by the number of objects but also by the total amount of information contained within the objects. Thus, number and resolution were proposed to be intimately intertwined: The higher the resolution, the fewer the number of items that can be held in memory, and vice versa.

A further wrinkle in the complexity issue was provided in a neuroimaging study by Xu and Chun (2006), in which three primary cortical areas were found to show load-sensitive activation in a change-detection task. Of these three, two (the lateral occipital complex and the superior intraparietal sulcus) were highly sensitive to object complexity, reaching asymptotic activation for smaller numbers of complex items than of simple items. By contrast, a third region (the inferior intraparietal sulcus) was completely insensitive to the complexity of the objects, always reaching asymptotic activation at approximately 4 items. These neuroimaging results

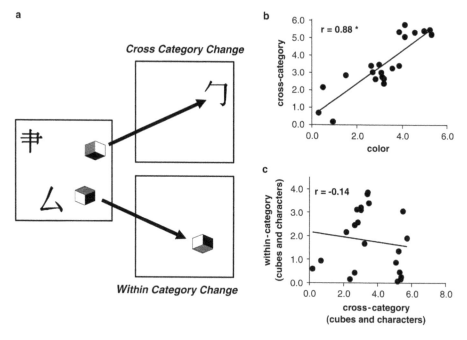

FIGURE 9.2

Change detection and working-memory capacity. Panel a shows cross- and within-category change-detection stimuli (Chinese characters and 3-D cubes) and procedure used in Awh, Barton, and Vogel (2007). Panel b shows correlation between working-memory capacity estimates for colors and for complex items in which the changed item was from a different category. Panel c shows correlation between working-memory capacity estimates for a complex item in which there was a cross-category change or a within-category change. Panel c adapted from Awh, Barton, & Vogel (2007).

constrained the existing models of memory capacity by suggesting that both complexity and number of items determine working-memory performance. Further, they provided initial evidence that these constructs might be somewhat distinct factors, because separate cortical areas are sensitive to each.

Following this general line of logic, we (Awh, Barton, & Vogel, 2007) reasoned that poor performance for complex objects might not be the consequence of an inability to maintain multiple objects in memory but, rather, might be due to limitations in discriminating whether the object had changed or not. That is, as the complexity of a given object category increases, the subjective similarity among members of the category also increases. Thus, poorer working-memory performance might be due to more errors in comparing an object in memory with the highly similar object it changed into. To test this hypothesis, we presented observers with memory arrays that were a mix of two categories of complex objects (Chinese characters and 3-D cubes) and manipulated what type of change occurred on a given trial: either a within-category change (i.e., cube to cube or character to character; see Figure 9.2a) or a between-category change (i.e., cube to character or character to cube). On the within-category change trials (when sample–test similarity was high), working-memory performance was quite poor, and the results replicated Alvarez & Cavanagh (2004). By contrast, on the between-category trials (when sample–test similarity was low), working memory for these complex items was very good and was equivalent to performance for remembering simple objects (i.e., colored squares). These data suggested that errors in change detection with complex objects were not caused by a failure to represent the items in memory but by the fact that the representations did not have sufficient resolution for the detection of very small changes.

Our (Awh et al., 2007) data suggested that performance in the between-category change trials was limited by the total number of items that could be maintained in working memory whereas performance in the within-category condition was instead limited by the resolution of those representations. In this case, the consideration of individual differences became a powerful means by which we could test two critical hypotheses. First, was performance in the between-category change condition limited by the same ability as that which limits the maintenance of simple colored squares? We tested for this expected association and found a strong positive correlation between an individual's memory capacity for colored squares and his or her capacity for complex items that changed across categories ($r = .88$; see Figure 9.2b). Second, was performance on the between-category change trials limited by a different construct from that which limits performance on the within-category change trials? We tested for this expected dissociation and found no significant correlation of performance between these two types of trials ($r = .14$; see Figure 9.2c), despite the fact that both performance measures were from the same task, blocks of trials, and objects. Moreover, within-category change performance was shown to be a reliable measure because character-to-character performance strongly correlated with cube-to-cube performance ($r = .66$). Thus, while the data showed a clear association between two measures of the "number of items" that could be maintained and two measures of "mnemonic resolution," number and resolution appear to represent distinct aspects of individual memory ability. Of course, these results don't discount the important observation that complexity plays an important role in working-memory capacity, but they do argue against models that propose that number and resolution are the same intertwined construct. If a single shared resource determined both the number and resolution of representations in working memory, then there should have been a strong correlation between these two ability measures. Indeed, these results, when coupled with Xu & Chun's (2006) neuroimaging data, predict that there should be neural measures that are predicted by an individual's mnemonic resolution but that are not related to the number of items that they can hold in memory. Hopefully, future studies exploiting this powerful individual-differences approach will be able to test this prediction.

CONCLUSIONS

The consideration of individual differences in performance can provide a powerful addition to many standard cognitive-neuroscience studies because it can help further constrain existing cognitive theories. We have outlined three general benefits of this approach and discussed how we have utilized these techniques to address specific issues within research on visual working memory. However, these techniques should be applicable to any domain within cognitive neuroscience, so long as the performance measure to be used is a reliable measure of the construct of interest and there is not much restriction of the range of observed values (e.g., ceiling or floor effects). It is our hope that many others will begin to exploit this wealth of systematic diversity across individuals to further specify the cognitive constructs and mechanisms that we all share.

RECOMMENDED READING

Awh, E., Barton, B., & Vogel, E.K. (2007). (See References). A study that used an individual-differences approach to determine whether the "resolution" of items in memory determines the "number of items" that can be held in working memory.
Cowan, N., Elliott, E.M., Saults, J.S., Morey, C.C., Mattox, S., Hismjatullina, A., et al. (2005). (See References). A study that examined the within-subject correlations between many measures of attention, working memory, and intelligence.
Cronbach, L.J. (1957). (See References). A classic article describing the virtues of combining the individual-differences and standard experimental approaches.
Vogel, E.K., & Machizawa, M.G. (2004). (See References). A study showing that an electrical brain wave is highly sensitive to an individual's specific working-memory capacity.
Vogel, E.K., McCollough, A.W., & Machizawa, M.G. (2005). (See References). A study providing evidence that low-capacity individuals are much poorer at controlling what is stored in memory than are high-capacity individuals.
Acknowledgments—The research reported here was supported by grants from the National Science Foundation to EKV and the National Institute of Mental Health to EA.

REFERENCES

Alvarez, G.A., & Cavanagh, P. (2004). The capacity of visual short-term memory is set both by visual information load and by number of objects. *Psychological Science, 15*, 106–111.
Awh, E., Barton, B., & Vogel, E.K. (2007). Visual working memory represents a fixed number of items regardless of complexity. *Psychological Science, 18*, 622–628.
Awh, E., & Jonides, J. (2001). Overlapping mechanisms of attention and working memory. *Trends in Cognitive Sciences, 5*, 119–126.

Cowan, N. (2001). The magical number 4 in short-term memory: A reconsideration of mental storage capacity. *Behavioral and Brain Sciences*, 24, 87–185.

Cowan, N., Elliott, E.M., Saults, J.S., Morey, C.C., Mattox, S., Hismjatullina, A., et al. (2005). On the capacity of attention: Its estimation and its role in working memory and cognitive aptitudes. *Cognitive Psychology*, 51, 42–100.

Cronbach, L.J. (1957). The two disciplines of scientific psychology. *American Psychologist*, 12, 671–684.

Daneman, M., & Carpenter, P.A. (1980). Individual differences in working memory and reading. *Journal of Verbal Learning and Verbal Behavior*, 19, 450–466.

Kane, M.J., Bleckley, M.K., Conway, A.R.A., & Engle, R.W. (2001). A controlled attention view of working memory capacity. *Journal of Experimental Psychology: General*, 130, 169–183.

Kane, M.J., & Engle, R.W. (2003). Working memory capacity and the control of attention: The contributions of goal neglect, response competition, and task set to Stroop interference. *Journal of Experimental Psychology: General*, 132, 47–70.

Kirchoff, B.A., & Buckner, R.L. (2006). Functional-anatomic correlates of individual differences in memory. *Neuron*, 51, 263–274.

Luck, S.J., & Vogel, E.K. (1997). The capacity of visual working memory for features and conjunctions. *Nature*, 390, 279–281.

Miyake, A., Just, M.A., & Carpenter, P.A. (1994). Working memory constraints on the resolution of lexical ambiguity: Maintaining multiple interpretations in neutral contexts. *Journal of Memory & Language*, 33, 175–202.

Thompson-Schill, S.L., Braver, T.S., & Jonides, J. (2005). Individual differences. *Cognitive, Affective and Behavioral Neuroscience*, 5, 115–116.

Todd, J., & Marois, R. (2005). Posterior parietal cortex activity predicts individual differences in short-term memory capacity. *Cognitive, Affective and Behavioral Neuroscience*, 5, 144–155.

Underwood, B.J. (1975). Individual differences as a crucible in theory construction. *American Psychologist*, 30, 128–134.

Vogel, E.K., & Machizawa, M.G. (2004). Neural activity predicts individual differences in visual working memory capacity. *Nature*, 428, 748–751.

Vogel, E.K., McCollough, A.W., & Machizawa, M.G. (2005). Neural measures reveal individual differences in controlling access to working memory. *Nature*, 438, 500–503.

Wilmer, J.B., & Nakayama, K. (2007). Two distinct visual motion mechanisms for smooth pursuit: Evidence from individual differences. *Neuron*, 54, 987–1000.

Xu, Y., & Chun, M. (2006). Dissociable neural mechanisms supporting visual short-term memory for objects. *Nature*, 440, 91–95.

Yovel, G., & Kanwisher, N. (2005). The neural basis of the behavioral face-inversion effect. *Current Biology*, 15, 2256–2262.

Name:_____

READING COMPREHENSION QUESTIONS

Refer to the information you have just read to find the answers to these questions. Be sure that you do not simply copy what is already written in the article. Think about your answer and write it in your own words.

1. Write any words that you had to look up here, along with their definitions. If you did not need to look up any words, list and define several of the words you think the average college student may have found difficult. All students should have at least three words and definitions for this question.

2. Write the full reference for this article in APA style. For advice on APA style, consult www.apastyle.org.

3. Explain what is novel about this study that made it publishable. Be sure to describe exactly what previous studies lacked that this study offers. Simply describing this study, or simply describing previous studies, is insufficient.

Name:_____

4. Generally describe the methods used in the paper.

- How many subjects were there? If there was more than one experiment, list the number of subjects in each experiment.

- Who were the subjects (e.g., older adults, schizophrenic patients, college students)?

- What was it like to be a subject (i.e., what were the subjects required to do)? Provide enough detail that the reader can truly imagine what it was like to be a subject.

5. What were the main findings of this paper?

Name:_____

COMPREHENSION CHECK QUESTIONS

Refer to the information you have just read to find the answers to these questions. Be sure that you do not simply copy what is already written in the article. Think about your answer and write it in your own words.

1. Experiment Proposal

Pretend that you are an author on this paper and are tasked with determining future directions. Taking into account what has already been done in the field (i.e., the information presented in the Introduction) and the present study, what is a novel next step in this research? If you were one of the authors of this study, what would you do next and why? Be sure to explain why you would perform this next step. For example, proposing to replicate the study sampling from a different subject population is not sufficient, unless you explain why it is a reasonable next step.

Name:_____

2. Writing Critique

Pretend that you are a reviewer on this paper and are required to make a substantial suggestion on how to improve the writing. For example, you could offer an alternative explanation of how to describe the importance of the work, explain why the real-world application is insufficient, or suggest how the authors could describe their work in a more interesting way. If you were a reviewer, what would you say to improve the writing (not the methods) of this paper? Be sure to provide concrete suggestions. For example, do not simply say that an aspect of the paper was confusing. Demonstrate that you took the time to understand the material and offer a better way to explain the portion you found confusing.

Name:_____

3. Application Question

Think about how the work in this paper applies to the real world. Describe a scenario (either real or imagined) under which this work applies to your life. Do not use the real-world application mentioned in the paper. Rather, consider how this work is relevant to you (again, it could be imagined). Be sure to demonstrate that you understand the results of the paper through your real-world application.

Name:_____

TRUE OR FALSE STATEMENTS

Write three *true* statements here, noting the page number where the answer can be located.

1. _____
   _____
   _____
   _____
   _____

   • Page number where answer can be located: _____

2. _____
   _____
   _____
   _____
   _____

   • Page number where answer can be located: _____

3. _____
   _____
   _____
   _____
   _____

   • Page number where answer can be located: _____

Name:_____

Write three *false* statements here, noting the page number where the answer can be located. Then rewrite each statement to make it true.

1. _____
   _____
   _____

   • Rewritten to be true:
   _____
   _____

   • Page number where answer can be located: _____

2. _____
   _____
   _____

   • Rewritten to be true:
   _____
   _____

   • Page number where answer can be located: _____

3. _____
   _____
   _____

   • Rewritten to be true:
   _____
   _____

   • Page number where answer can be located: _____

CPSIA information can be obtained
at www.ICGtesting.com
Printed in the USA
LVHW060007270522
719862LV00001B/6